Sport Studies

Active Learning in Sport – titles in the series

Coaching Science	ISBN 978 1 84445 165 4
Personal Training	ISBN 978 1 84445 163 0
Sport Sociology	ISBN 978 1 84445 166 1
Sport and Exercise Science	ISBN 978 1 84445 187 6
Sport Management	ISBN 978 1 84445 263 7
Sport Studies	ISBN 978 1 84445 186 9

To order, please contact our distributor: BEBC Distribution, Albion Close, Parkstone, Poole, BH12 3LL. Telephone: 0845 230 9000, email: **learningmatters@bebc.co.uk**. You can also find more information on each of these titles and our other learning resources at **www.learningmatters.co.uk**

Sport Studies

Barbara Bell

First published in 2009 by Learning Matters Ltd

British Library Cataloguing in Publication Data
A CIP record for this book is available from the British Library

ISBN: 978 1 84445 1869

Cover design by Toucan Design
Text design by Code 5 Design Associates Ltd
Project Management by Swales & Willis Ltd, Exeter, Devon
Typeset by Kelly Gray
Printed and bound in Great Britain by TJ International Ltd, Padstow, Cornwall

Learning Matters Ltd
33 Southernhay East
Exeter EX1 1NX
Tel: 01392 215560
E-mail: info@learningmatters.co.uk
www.learningmatters.co.uk

FSC
Mixed Sources
Product group from well-managed
forests and other controlled sources
Cert no. SGS-COC-2482
www.fsc.org
© 1996 Forest Stewardship Council

Contents

Acknowledgements

This book is a culmination of many years of teaching and study, across various departments and institutions, with a number of close and supportive colleagues. My particular thanks must go to those who have provided inspiration, ideas or more directly, suggestions and material for inclusion, or feedback on drafts.

My thanks to former colleagues, now at University of Chester, for their encouragement and support, when I began working in Sport Studies at University College Warrington. Colleagues at Edge Hill University, particularly Mike Hartill and Leon Culbertson, provided ideas for resources and advice about social, historical and philosophical aspects of sport, while working together on the Sport Studies programme, which also provided the inspiration for the book. I've also benefited from advice, guidance and support from many others, including in my current departmental colleagues at Manchester Metropolitan University, Department of Exercise and Sport Science and many others across various institutions I have had the pleasure of meeting at various conferences and events or in my examiner role. I hope the book will provide those teaching and studying Sport Studies some helpful ideas and information. Thanks also to various students on whom I've 'tested' some of these activities and ideas, in seminars and workshops across the years.

I have attempted to credit all the specific sources used, and have used with permission, data from Deloitte Sport Business Group, and Youth Sport Trust in case studies and tables. I hope all other material has been credited or acknowledged within the text where appropriate.

Introduction: on the blocks and ready to go?

This book is an introductory text for those studying sport at degree level. I assume no prior knowledge or study of sport, or of the disciplines that contribute to sport studies programmes. In fact, that is what the book has been devised to do – introduce you to sport studies, which I hope you will find as interesting and engrossing as I do. The aim of this book is to help prepare you to tackle some of the excellent, but more specialised, texts available for degree level study, and provide a good overview of relevant subjects and disciplines that contribute to sport studies. We have designed it to be user-friendly, and to provide you with some of the essential underpinning knowledge, skills and understanding for your degree in sport studies.

What is 'sport studies'?

I have focused here on the social science-based study of sport. The term 'sport studies' has come to describe a range of sport-based courses, which in turn evolved from programmes in physical education, recreation management and leisure studies programmes over the past 30 or so years. The term 'sport studies' implies a greater breadth of disciplines contributing to the analysis of sport than a purely scientific or performance orientation. Programmes in sport studies adopt a multidisciplinary approach to the study of sport, physical activity, exercise and recreation in all its forms. As a subject at university undergraduate level, sport studies has a fairly recent history compared to the disciplines, for example sociology or history, that it draws upon. In order to formally recognise the characteristics of sport studies, academics have come together to set out benchmark statements that describe what a sport studies programme will usually be concerned with, and what you might expect within any course that has sport studies in its title.

Sport currently sits within the subject benchmarking statements for Hospitality, Leisure, Sport and Tourism, or Unit 25 of the Quality Assurance Agency (QAA) for Higher Education in England, revised in 2008.

Sport studies programmes

According to the QAA benchmark statements, those degrees incorporating the term 'sport studies' will normally be expected to embrace two or more of the five study areas considered under the broad heading of sport (QAA 2008). These study areas include the performance of sport, human responses and adaptations to sport and exercise and health-related and disease management aspects of exercise and physical activity, which are usually related to sport science programmes. Other books in the *Active Sport* series deal with these different aspect of sport; however, in this book I concentrate upon the following benchmark statement:

6.20 The study of the historical, social, political, economic and cultural diffusion, distribution and impact of sport, including:

- displaying a critical insight into the organisations and structures responsible for sport, and the political ramifications arising from these
- employing social, economic and political theory to explain the development and differentiation of sport throughout society
- demonstrating the application of the social and cultural meanings attached to sport and their impact on participation and regulation.

(QAA 2008: 13)

As it is possible to draw from such a broad spectrum of knowledge, the curriculum content of sport studies programmes this book is designed to support includes: sociology and cultural study of sport, philosophy and ethics, sport history, sport business and economics, and sport policy. This book also provides some essential underpinning knowledge relating to the final benchmarking statement relating to the policy, planning, management and delivery of sporting opportunities, by looking at the governance or running of sport, sport policy and provision across various sectors.

The sector to which sport and the other subjects in this unit (leisure, hospitality and tourism) belong is the service sector/experience economy (QAA 2008). This is recognised as one of the most dynamic and increasingly important sectors of the global economy. We cannot get very far from some aspect of sport in our daily lives, even if we are not sport students or fans. A steady stream of sport-related media – newspapers, national televised news bulletins, internet articles – provides reminders of how significant sport is in modern society. We engage in some form of sport in increasing numbers and a small but significant minority of people invest their time and great effort, involving huge personal sacrifice, into becoming top-level sports performers. Others display fanatical support for teams or individuals, travelling great distances or spending large amounts of money, buying merchandise, tickets or equipment to emulate their sporting heroes. A great many people engage in some form of sport or activity on a daily basis, and even more engage less frequently – simply for fun or for personal fulfilment. Sport can inspire great passion and emotion, interest and enthusiasm – and arguments about whether sport is really important or just a trivial pursuit.

Studying one of the great passions of the twentieth and early twenty-first centuries and attempting to understand the complex and dynamic contemporary sporting landscape has also clearly engaged and enthused a great many scholars. A great deal has been written about sport, from many different perspectives. Such interest and enthusiasm has fuelled a great increase in the number and range of courses in sport studies, investigating this hugely important cultural and social phenomenon and its impacts on society.

The study of sport from this social science perspective is also about equipping students with the essential knowledge and skills to develop more critical and analytical approaches and informed practice. Students of 'sport studies' would therefore be expected to employ relevant theory, from social, historical or economic perspectives, to explain the development of sport, or its significance, addressing questions such as:

- Why do we have more men than women playing or watching certain types of sport?
- Why do we have particular forms of sport in contemporary society?
- Who decides which sports should get public funds?

Sport studies also involves the application of relevant theory to understand and develop better practice in understanding consumption patterns or the provision of sporting opportunities. How can we provide better sport opportunities that are inclusive and accessible to all?

As well as providing essential knowledge about sport, courses in sport studies are also expected to equip students to enter the world of work – whether in sport or another field. Courses usually include some vocational elements; hence the final part of this book deals with both skills and employability – in and out of sport.

As sport is expected to be delivered within a suitable ethical environment, the study of sport is also expected to incorporate a moral and ethical framework for possible professional applications or careers. The issues of equity and diversity are key to understanding how and why 'best practice' in sport is delivered; hence sport studies is expected to incorporate understanding of the ethical and moral aspects of the sector.

Though there is great diversity in specific modules and topics under the broad 'sport studies' banner, they tend to share some common characteristics, as they will have been developed to be consistent with the QAA benchmark statements referred to above.

How can this book help me?

This book can help you by providing a useful introduction and framework for your studies. I want to help make the subject more accessible, so have included many activities and ideas for further study, or sources of advice and guidance. We hope you take a very 'active' role in your learning about sport, as you probably (hopefully?) do in being active in sport.

Structure and format of the book

The book is divided into three parts. Part 1 deals with introductions to the historical, social and philosophical aspects of sport. Each chapter takes one particular theoretical perspective and examines important concepts and theories about how sport has developed and its social impacts and meanings.

Part 2 introduces the political and economic aspects of sport, including sport policy, sporting structures and sport business. The chapters in this section look at how sport in the UK is organised and by whom, and recent developments in sport policy in the UK. It goes on to introduce the economic and business aspects of sport, highlighting the role of the media and global markets.

Part 3 focuses on your personal development, in both academic and vocational skills, and introduces careers in sport. Chapters concentrate upon academic skills, vocational skills and employability, within a personal development framework.

An expectation of the subject group is that students are expected to develop multidisciplinary approaches to addressing the same phenomenon. Using this book, for example, you could look at the forthcoming London 2012 Olympic Games from historical, political and sociological perspectives.

Within each chapter I have tried to provide you with some introductory information, key concepts and theories, with examples and ideas to take your learning further. Throughout the book there are examples or case studies drawn from a range of possible areas of sport, and activities to encourage you to use a variety of methods to explore topics and concepts.

The intellectual skills expected of a sport studies graduate are incorporated into each chapter. These include being able to research and assess specific facts and theories or concepts, evaluate evidence and interpret data. Activities are designed to make you think, read or apply knowledge to particular problems or issues.

Boxes will develop specific cases or add detail on particular issues. Some activities are simple 'time outs' – to give you space to think about something and reflect on what you've read or consider your personal experiences.

An important skill the book is designed to help you develop is the ability to manage your own learning and continuing development. You are encouraged therefore to move between the chapters and make your own links and examples in order to build your own understanding of this fascinating subject. I hope you enjoy the book and find it useful!

PART 1

Core theories and essential perspectives in the study of sport

Chapter 1

A historical perspective of sport

Introduction

This chapter is not going to attempt to provide a potted history of sport in 20 pages. As attractive as that might be to you, a hard-pressed student, it would be a rather pointless exercise to attempt! This chapter is essentially about why you might study sport from a historical perspective and how you might go about it. We are also going to identify some important trends and periods in the history of sport, key authors, and highlight some of the important changes in sport, particularly in the UK. Through examples and case studies, the chapter will introduce students to the study of sport history and provide links to develop their knowledge and understanding of this very important aspect of sport studies. As the QAA has identified, a historical perspective is felt to be fundamental to our understanding of the forms and practices of sport in contemporary society.

Learning outcomes

After completing this chapter and the related learning activities, you will be able to:
- explain the relevance of sport history to contemporary sport practices;
- identify different approaches to the study of sport history;
- identify some of the important authors in the history of sport;
- identify further sources useful for investigating specific topics in the history of sport.

Why study the history of sport?

in the modern world sport is everywhere; it is as ubiquitous as War. E. J. Hobsbawm, the distinguished Marxist historian, once called it one of the most significant of the new practices of the late nineteenth century Europe. Today it is one of the significant practices of the world.

(Mangan 2006: 1)

Sometimes sports students, who often prefer to 'learn by doing', complain about having to read about sport history or refer back to past events or out-dated practices. They argue their interest is in the future and not in the dry and dusty past. However, the fact that most courses in sport studies include and often start with a historical perspective should alert you to the significance of history for our study of sport today.

The QAA benchmark statements for sport studies referred to in the introduction call for students to have some recognition of the historical perspective. However, this expectation can sometimes be problematic, as many students have not got a strong grounding in history, coming from a diverse range of backgrounds. So, one potential reason for a reluctance or resistance to historical study for sport students could relate to lack of confidence and knowledge of the past – history may not have been one of your subjects at GCSE, for example. As a result, when students are asked to discuss or read about sport in the broader context of social history, from even relatively modern periods, they may lack the wider knowledge that their (usually older) tutors sometimes take for granted.

However, the study of history, it is argued, brings with it a sense of perspective, and the development of analytical, research and judgemental skills. Students will need to weigh up various accounts, from a range of sources, testing and probing for explanations and interpretations. So, despite the initial reluctance of some, the study of sport history provides some fascinating subject and topics, and provides students with an opportunity to engage in interesting and useful study.

According to Polley (2007), advice on 'doing' sport history is rather neglected, and he has produced a useful guide that has provided some of the ideas for further activities used in this chapter. Another important resource guide has been produced by Martin Johnes (2003), which provides an extensive annotated bibliography of potential sources on a wide range of sport history topics.

Students come to the subject of sport studies with diverse interests, experiences and academic backgrounds. The main purpose of any introductory sport history course would be to enable students to gain a better understanding of the development and emergence of contemporary sporting practices, forms or institutions and be able to identify key historical processes and events.

Analysing the history of sport: history and histiography

Sport history involves the investigation, analysis and interpretation of sporting practices, traditions, organisations and individuals. Histiography is concerned with *how* historians work and *why* they work in particular ways. It is also concerned with how other academic disciplines or perspectives, such as sociology, cultural theory or philosophy, can influence the historian's interpretation and understanding of the past.

A review of the recent papers published in the *International Journal of the History of Sport*, in Table 1.1 shows the diversity of topics, periods and questions addressed, even within a single issue of a journal.

Table 1.1: Recent journal articles in sport history

Topic	Period	Main sources
1954 British Empire and Commonwealth Games	Middle twentieth century	Official documents, newspaper reports and internal communications
C. L. R. James' view of the aesthetics of cricket	1930s	*Glasgow Herald* cricket articles, 1937–38
Doping scandal at Nordic World Ski Championships in Lahti, Finland 2001	2000s	Finnish and international Press and media reports

Source: *International Journal of Sport History*, 23(1).

Social history and sport

Most sport historians would tend to agree that it is difficult, if not impossible, to consider sport as some sort of 'separate' part of culture and society. According to Polley, sport: 'is a cultural product linked to all kinds of contexts and traditions, and carrying both positive and negative values relative to those settings' (2007: x).

Therefore, we have to accept that sport can be viewed in many different ways and that, over time and across different cultures, values and beliefs about sport may change. The task of the historian is to shed some light on these changes and continuities, and provide better understanding of them. When looking at the history of sport, we must also consider broader events, traditions and other cultural practices.

Nancy Struna (2000) noted that evidence of sport history goes back to 'pre-historic' times, through the pictographs of sporting practices recorded in caves dating back thousands of years. Later societies, in Ancient Greece, Rome and China, provide many examples of sport being recorded in different forms, including written records, art and poetry. In more modern times, popular culture and mass media forms have recorded sporting activities and events, telling 'stories' against a background of wider social contexts and circumstances. Struna (p. 187) points out that such 'stories, located and understood in the context of their time and place' are important parts of social historians' work. One such example is the film, *Chariots of Fire* (1981), recently voted one of the best all time films about the Olympics.

Sport history on film

Though the film *Chariots of Fire* (Director: Hugh Hudson, Screenwriter: Colin Welland, 1981) is a dramatised version of events, it provides an interesting perspective of social class, religious beliefs and cultural identity in sport and the Olympic movement in the 1920s. It tells the story of Eric Liddell and Harold Abraham, athletes in the British Olympic team for the Paris Olympics in 1924. Forms of dress, speech, competition values and traditions are all represented in such a way as to bring the subject to life, which is why it may be used by tutors to prompt discussion of various topics, such as social class in sport or the changing role of the sport coach in this period.

This popular cultural form, film, showing a reproduction of sporting and social history, enhances an understanding of the dominance of Olympic sport by the establishment of the time, based in Oxbridge and the aristocracy. It is also interesting to consider the different portrayals of the American and British teams, and indeed other nations, at the games. The stadium shown in the film was actually Bebbington Oval in Cheshire, as this provided a close resemblance to the Paris stadium. Film-makers were able to reproduce fairly accurately the appearance of the Paris games, due to the existence of extensive newsreels and photographs of the time.

Many social historians and sport historians in particular recognise that any good history of a sporting activity, event or pursuit is about more than sport. Social historians see sporting practices as part of a 'bigger picture' of a particular time or context. How and why particular sport came to prominence, for example, are the sort of questions asked by social historians. These may ask questions such as, 'Why did professional sport begin to emerge in the North of England?' They also seek to examine the meanings attached to sporting practice and events and their cultural significance. Examining changes over time, historians look for patterns of continuity and change or struggles for power or dominance by particular groups, individuals or ideologies. The story of rugby, for example, provides a fascinating case of how sport has been a site for class struggle and disputes over domination since the mid-nineteenth century.

Rugby's 'great split'

Read this short summary of the 'great split' in rugby, which established the game of Rugby League.

The so-called 'great split' between the two codes of rugby is usually dated as 1895. According to Collins (1998), the seeds were sown, however, some years earlier, when the Yorkshire committee adopted the MCC's regulations on amateurism in 1879, whereby 'gentlemen' were allowed to claim out of pocket expenses. The gradual incursion of player payments into the amateur sport brought inevitable conflicts between clubs. Those who relied more heavily on players taking time off work to play and train, which were often based in the North, clashed with those who recruited from the professional classes, and who preferred to keep their sport true to its amateur ethos, in the Rugby Football Union (RFU).

Collins' account describes how eventually, when in 1895 RFU laws were amended to prevent any professionalism, the situation was brought to an inevitable climax. In July 1895, a group of 12 Yorkshire-based teams formed the Northern Union, and were joined some months later by senior clubs from Lancashire in the Northern Rugby Football Union, in direct conflict with the RFU.

Though still an amateur body, they allowed 'broken time payments.' These 22 clubs formed the basis of the teams we now know as the Rugby Football League (RFL). Rule changes followed and continued throughout the next 100 years, so that the games became quite distinct, and quite separate – a very acrimonious split, which had significant consequences for both sides.

Clearly, this was more than a split based on geography, or a North–South divide. Issues of class, control and culture were apparent. Though with public school-educated administrators on both sides, who were fiercely protective of the amateur ethos, RL always retained a mixture of amateurs alongside semi- or fully-professional players. Union never accepted professionalism, and players were not permitted to cross from the professional into the amateur game. After 100 years of bitter separation, finally, when faced with increasing economic pressure from leading clubs and the taint of 'shamateurism', the International Rugby Board finally agreed to accept professionalism in 1995. In accepting professionalism, the RFU had come full circle.

Sources: Collins (1998), Rugby Football League (2008), Rugby Football History (2007).

Questions
Identify the different social groups involved in a 'struggle for control' in this period. Discuss the relevance of the debate about amateurs and professionals encapsulated in this case to modern sporting institutions and practices.

Further sources: See Horne et al. (1999) for more on this topic and issues regarding amateurism–professionalism in other sports, such as cricket and athletics. Collins (1998) is recognised as an excellent text on this issue and period, though there are others; see Further study for details.

Trends in sport history writing

Early sport historians tended to reconstruct sporting events, the origins of particular sports or careers of individuals. Though this remains a common approach today, accounts are now more likely to be a critical or interpretive account of a historical period or figure. Such early histories are often detailed descriptive accounts, which have helped to build a body of knowledge about our collective sporting past. Struna (2000) asserted that early, largely uncritical work provided only limited interpretation of the relevant period and the social world of the time, as there tended to be little depth to the wider social interpretations. Nevertheless, this scholarship has provided the basis for many historical accounts of sports in early recorded history.

Sport may also have featured as part of a wider review of a period. For example, the nineteenth-century saw the emergence of many of the popular forms of sport practised today, so accounts of the public schools or figures such as philanthropists or social reformers, included accounts of sporting or recreational activities or events in order to provide evidence of social change or a commentary of the time.

Later work in sport history emerged, which was more critical and multidisciplinary in nature – drawing on social or critical theory, for example, or political science to help explain and examine in more depth, the relative position of sport in the period. Social theories (which we examine in more depth in the next chapter) were recognised to a much greater extent in the study of sport generally and particularly in historical analyses. Tomlinson (2007), citing the sociologist C. Wright Mills, has emphasised the need to have a sound understanding of the historical context for any serious study of social change. History and social theory therefore share interests, methods and concerns. See Table 1.2.

Some key authors in sport history at this time were: Malcomson – (*Popular Recreations in English Society, 1700–1850* (1973), Walvin – *The People's Game* (1975) and Mason – *Association Football and English Society* (1980). According to Struna (2000), Malcomson in particular 'challenged' concepts of linear change and demonstrated the social power of sport in local experiences and social relations and on institutions and individuals. Malcomson provided extensive evidence of the changes happening to British society and, in particular, the impact of the move to urban and industrialised centres on the largely rural and agriculturally-based pastimes of the eighteenth and nineteenth centuries. His view has remained influential for subsequent sport historians. At this time, rural life and 'popular sports' were strongly linked, and, even though some of the activities were not what would be recognised as 'sports' now (such as bull baiting, cock fighting), playing 'foot-ball' was criticised for its violence and vulgarity by the middle classes, so perhaps 'sports' were not so different after all!

Throughout this period of tremendous social upheaval and change, there was a tolerance of sport, largely on its 'tranquiliser' effect for the masses, and the assumption of its value in the development of 'manly discipline' and martial (fighting) qualities. Sport was recognised as a training ground for courage, perseverance, physical strength and group loyalty, beliefs and themes that have persisted to the present day. Cunningham (1980) suggested that the provision of 'recreation', was clearly a 'proper concern of the government' by the late nineteenth century; though this had not been led by popular demand but by a concern of the paternalistic elite to control and improve the working classes – this has direct consequences for modern day recreation provision, as we can see in Chapter 4. Therefore an examination of the nineteenth century provides a rich background within which to examine current attitudes and values enshrined in sport.

Table 1.2: Genres of sport history writing (based on Struna 2000)

Deep, internal histories of sport	'No stone unturned' accounts of specific sports, games, ideologies and attitudes, often examining issues of control and power.
'Classic' social histories of sport	A perspective of sport in society, telling the story of a broader picture of the nature and meaning of sport, embedded in a particular context or period.
Sport in popular culture	Primarily studies framing sport within studies of popular culture or leisure

Another significant author, Richard Holt, in *Sport and the British* (1989), examined the patterns of persistence and change in the wider context of social structures and experiences of British life. He looked in detail at the transformations happening in the late nineteenth and early twentieth centuries, which were so critical to the emergence of contemporary sporting forms in the latter part of the twentieth century – industrialisation, urbanisation, economic change, political upheaval and the regulation of popular pursuits. His main theme was the survival and adaptation of sporting forms in this period. Legislation was passed to outlaw some of the activities deemed 'cruel', such as dog-fighting, while others persisted and survived, such as pigeon and greyhound racing. Football and other team sports became more codified, regulated and organised and moved to national rather than local competitive structures. It was in this period that we saw the emergence of the governing bodies for sport, so again, a period that has enormous significance to modern sporting structures. How and why some sports survived, albeit in small enclaves or in adapted forms, is of interest to us today, when we consider what it is that makes a sport popular or lose its appeal.

More recently, Polley (1990) has focused on British sport in the twentieth century. His work has shed light on the repercussions of the social changes seen in wider society on the structures and forms of sport in the twentieth century. For example, the persistence of the North–South divide in some sports; the amateur–professional distinction, which persisted in many sports until well into the latter part of the twentieth century; the conflicts in sports established by Victorian ideals when attempting to adapt to more modern social attitudes; the emergence of greater ethnic diversity in British sport; and greater recognition of gender equality in sport. All of these themes, and the social changes they represent and reflect, maintain a relevance to modern sport.

Dig deeper

- **Find an article or book on sport history and place it in one of the above categories.**
- Identify the type of data or sources of information the study is based on.
- How does this study enhance our understanding of modern sport?

Learning from history

What we might learn from sport history is very significant. Looking at past forms or practices and undertaking deeper investigations of social and historical facts or data, current scholars attempt to draw out lessons and interpretations which might inform or illuminate current practices and debates. The issue of violence in sport, for example, though topical is not new. Though it may have had very different interpretations in earlier societies, the regulation of violence in sport has been a feature of the development of many societies in the past. Studies of violence in the past may help improve our understanding of why such behaviours persist and can be found across societies. Comparative approaches can also help improve our understanding of contemporary sport and also help shape the sort of sport we might experience in the future. (This and similar topics are also the subject of a later section on philosophy and ethics.)

Sport historians can help to address the questions we need to consider when we look at the future, such as:

- What form of sport will persist in the twenty-first century?
- Why do many forms of sport seem to be disappearing, as some sports seem to dominate?
- Who will have the power to organise sport in the future?

By looking more deeply at our past experiences, we can help come to a better understanding of present and future sport.

Time out

Identify some of the current problems in modern sport. Try to examine whether or not there is a historical precedent or example in the past. What parallels can we draw between modern sport and the past?

Methods in sport history

Methods and sources

Polley (2007) suggests the main methods available to the modern sport historian are:

- oral history
- documentary archive
- artefacts and ephemera
- commemoration

We can examine the history of sport in a number of ways. Even today, there are traces of the past in the forms of sport we enjoy and our experiences of them. Polley identifies the following, to which I have added some examples and questions you may consider.

Laws, rules and regulations

The dates of inceptions of rules and regulations provide interesting evidence of change. You might trace the dates of important changes and examine why such changes were brought about. For example, when did hockey introduce the push back in place of the famous 'bully off' and why?

Names

Events and stadia, or even famous moves or techniques (the *Cruyff* Turn, the *Fosbury* Flop) often commemorate significant individuals in a particular sport, city or club. Such individuals can provide an interesting subject for a sport history project, and will usually have a legacy of biographical or other archive material for further study.

Language

The jargon and specific vocabulary of sport can be like another language – completely alien to the outsider (see 'bully off' above!). How has this language emerged – why does it persist? How and when did the terms used enter into the discourse of the sport? Have they entered wider discourse – how?

Places

There are some places that have a keen historical significance – for tragic or heroic reasons. For example, the name *Hillsborough* has very tragic connotations for Liverpool F. C. supporters but very different associations for Sheffield Wednesday supporters because it is their home ground. Again, taking a Liverpool theme, why is the 'Kop' so called?

Access and etiquette

At a recent visit to Marlow in Buckinghamshire during Regatta week, the issue of access and etiquette was brought to life. Never having had the privilege to attend Ascot or Henley Royal Regatta, watching from afar the cut glass champagne glasses emerging from picnic hampers reinforced my lack of social status! Events such as Henley, Ascot and even to an extent Wimbledon have traditionally restricted access by a combination of expense, exclusion and scarcity. In recent years there has been some attention to the changing social make-up of events as crowds have increased and tickets have become accessible to wider sections of society. Access to 'Royal enclosures' or similar at events such as Ascot continues to be restricted, however. The regulation of dress and behaviour code also continues to cause some controversy – why do we expect people to dress in elaborate (and often expensive) clothing to attend a horse race? How and why have certain sports restricted access to their events in the past and what evidence of this persists today?

Records

Perhaps the most obvious of the historical evidence provided through sport is the record kept of results, the statistics and 'roll of honour' of past champions. Though somewhat 'dry', nevertheless the examination of these records can often provide illumination for evidence of social change and/or trends in sports. For example, who (and where) were the first clubs to win the F. A. cup? How many of them survive today and where are they now?

Activity

Working in groups, provide some more examples and investigate at least one in each of the above categories. Produce a short presentation of your findings to the rest of the group.

Primary evidence in sport history

Looking at forms of evidence from the past is where the history scholar uses their independence and judgement in the selection, analysis and interpretation of the material. The first task is to identify what sources may be available and to go about finding them. This is not always as easy as it sounds and there may be some problems in getting access to materials that are rare, fragile or even in private hands. Not all of the records of the past have survived, and some of them you might begin with, such as databases of materials kept by libraries or archives, are complete or categorised for searching under your chosen topic. Searching for primary evidence may at times be frustrating or problematic. A good starting point would be the records kept by the British Society for Sport History (see Further study).

Sources for the sports historians include:

- records of organisations and individuals: minutes, reports, letters and papers;
- digital archives – increasing amounts of historical material are being archived digitally, making it possible for historians to do searches and analysis from their own desks. One excellent example is the American Amateur Athletic Federation, which has archived extensive resources relating to the Olympic movement, American and Australian athletics and other sport organisations (see Further study for the LA84 website);
- museums and collections (Lausanne, International Olympic Committee collections, national or more local museums and county archives);
- oral history (often digital records) – e.g. sound collection interviews and transcripts, such as those held by the BBC or local history societies;
- media sources;
- newspaper CD-ROMs;
- film and TV archives – e.g. NW Film Archive and BBC archives
- photograph collections – e.g. Humphrey Spender's Worktown studies in Bolton, which include photographic records of sport and leisure in Bolton in the 1930s, maintained by Bolton Museums.

Newpapers and magazines feature in the examples of recent studies shown in Table 1.1. These include press reports, periodicals and magazines of the time. The historian would have to be aware of the validity and representativeness of the data provided and sensitive to the language and style of the journalism of the time.

Sport has long been associated with the popular press and printed media; their development has been 'hand in hand' since the late nineteenth century (Boyle and Haynes 2000). Materials include text reports, photographs, feature articles, witness accounts, interviews, letters and editorial comments. While digital media and television may have eclipsed press coverage of sport in more recent times, for the historian, the press provides rich and varied sources of evidence and comment on the events of the time; searching archives has also become more accessible with the digitisation of many source materials. Newspapers are also relatively free to access (under academic licences) and so are ideal starting points for many topics.

Film and broadcast media has also been made more accessible recently, and the vast resources of organisations such as the BBC and newsreel companies provide a rich archive of 'first-hand' records of important events and individuals, as well as the more day to day experiences of communities and societies. The MMU-based NW Film Archive has been used by the FA to provide material to show women playing football in the early twentieth century, as part of the promotional material for the Euro 2005 Women's Football Championships held in England. Again, however, we must be sensitive to how such material has been produced and who by, in order to fully appreciate its significance. Editing and careful camera work can provide a particular or selective perspective of events. We should also consider how such recordings can be used, and their original purpose.

Government records

The government creates large archives of its decisions, and records all of its major processes. There is a certain amount of access to this archive through the National Archives, and there is a 'Freedom of information' enshrined in law, which means that legitimate access is available on request in relation to matters of public interest. This provides a rich resource, but also a complex and extensive one; this is also a challenge for the historian to interrogate, requiring both skill and perseverance. Minutes of government committees and legislative bodies, reports and memoranda, correspondence and other papers are available. Some papers are restricted under the '30 years rule', which means they will not be available for researchers until 30 years have elapsed.

The government also produces vast quantities of official statistics and other official data, on the economy, industry and other activity. The official Census has been produced every ten years since 1841. The last Census was completed in 2001, and anonymised data is now accessible via the Office for National Statistics website. Some of the earlier census records are also available digitally, as are the records of the Ministry of Defence (for looking up service records of veterans) and other official databases and historical geographical records, such as maps. Local area statistics and records are also kept at a local level for reference, usually in the county or district library.

Activity

Undertake some research on your own favourite sport or organisation, using the following sources.

Documentary sources and archives

Look for evidence related to your own favourite sport or organisation. Has there been a published history of the club? Ask the club secretary if it is possible to have access to minute books or other archives to see what they contain. These can often be an interesting record of how the club developed and the role of some of the important figures in the club. Membership records might also give some interesting data on who belonged to the club in the past. The box below, a case study of Winnington Park, is an example of a historical study of a sports club, based on minutes and other records of the club by a local history enthusiast.

Oral history

Interview, if you can, someone who may have been a member or a fan of that club more than 40 years ago. Analyse this in relation to your own experiences and compare and contrast them. How has being a member of the club changed in this time? How has the social environment changed – what have been the big changes locally that might have influenced the club's development in the post-war years? Is the club thriving now or does it struggle to survive compared to its heyday?

Commemoration

Find examples of *commemoration* in your local area, sport or club. Has there been a famous sportsman or woman in your town in the past? (Extra credit if you find something commemorating a sports*woman* from the past!) What commemorates their sporting career? Is there a plaque, a statue, building or sport venue, or a competition named in their honour?

Artefacts and ephemera

See if there is a collection of artefacts relating to the club or organisation you belong to. This may be on display in the club house or a facility. If there is not an existing display, perhaps you could contact older members and begin to collect such material relating to the way in which the club might have developed. Such collections are sometimes of interest around particular anniversaries – 50 years, or for some clubs, 100 years after their establishment (see the box on Winnington Park below).

Museums and exhibitions

Visit a historical display, museum or exhibition; examples include the National Football Museum in Preston (located at Deepdale, the home of Preston North End Football Club). Many modern stadia have museums, though there is often a charge, and will usually be of interest to fans of that particular club or sport.

Your nearest city museum may also have sporting exhibitions or artefacts. Liverpool has an excellent museum celebrating Liverpool life, and this includes many interesting artefacts and material about sport – perhaps not surprisingly, this tends to be about football too! In 2008–09, as part of the Capital of Culture celebrations, the UEFA Football exhibition *Only a Game?* was held in the World Museum in Liverpool.

The velodrome in Manchester has an interesting collection on display throughout the venue, with examples of early competition cycles, memorabilia and artefacts from the history of cycling and displays showing important events and successful British cyclists from the past, including Beryl Bainbridge and Reg Harris.

Winnington Park: 100 years of sporting history

The Winnington Park Recreation club is situated in one of Cheshire's chemical manufacturing areas, Northwich, within a once thriving chemical works, which at its height employed thousands of workers in the production of Soda Ash. Brunner-Mond and Company founded the chemical works in 1873. This company eventually grew to become a huge industrial chemical complex, merging with other manufacturers to form ICI Ltd in 1926, and incorporating other sites in Cheshire, the North East, London and Lancashire to form one of the most successful British companies of the mid-twentieth century.

Very early in the history of Brunner-Mond, the company took what might be described as a 'rational' and paternalistic approach to employee welfare, as they laid out the recreation ground at Winnington to complement workers' housing, shops, a school and other facilities in the area of the factory. The original sport facilities, built in 1890, included a modest changing pavilion, bowling greens, and grounds for cricket and football, surrounded by a cinder track for cycling or running. All this was provided with a £500 grant from Brunner-Mond, and the club was partly financed from subscriptions paid by workers. Tennis courts were subsequently added during the 1890s.

The original object of the club was:

> the cultivation of cricket, football, athletics, cycling, tennis, bowls and other such games as the club, in general meeting should decide.
>
> (from Lavelle 1990: 9)

In 1901, a much grander pavilion was built, at the cost of £5,000 – complete with concert halls, a very grand billiard hall and social rooms, and extensive and well-equipped changing rooms overlooking the cricket pitch – with a resulting increase in social membership, including to non-employees of the company. A library was also added to the site. Hockey began to be played on the cricket outfield when more extensive football and rugby grounds were set out on land owned by the company at nearby Moss Farm, along with other sports such as archery (the original changing hut became an equipment store and eventually the women's hockey changing facility). Rugby and football sections of the club have, over the years, now become independent, and Moss Farm is now owned by Cheshire County Council. At its heyday, in the 1930s, the club boasted 5,000 members.

From its origins in employer paternalism, the club is now independent of its former host: ICI has since been broken up, and sold its interests in the Winnington works, though the club still provides important recreational opportunities to the local population, some of whom still work for the Australian-owned chemical company based there. The club has largely shrunk back to the original 1890 grounds, though it uses other local facilities for some sections and club activities, for example hockey, which is now played on an astroturf pitch at a local school.

Typical of many similarly voluntary amateur sports clubs, today the club depends on the 'social' side to subsidise its sport. Brewery sponsorship, facility hire and alcohol sales continue to make important contributions to club funds and support the upkeep of the building. The pavilion was originally teetotal due to the rather puritanical views of the founders, but in 1895 the club management had recognised employee demands to sell (cheap) beer on the premises as a means to maintain the recreational and social basis of the club and keep subscriptions down.

The club was always male dominated, in both activities and governance, but wives of employees or female employees were admitted as members from 1890. Only in the 1940 constitution were they officially recognised, but as 'second-class citizens' with associate rather than full membership. For example, even until the late 1970s the billiard hall was out of bounds to female members, until sex equality legislation finally forced the club to accept that female members had to have equal rights of access to all club services.

Today, the club proudly boasts of its more than 100 years of history – for example, men's and women's hockey celebrated their centenaries in 2005 and 2006, respectively. Archery, bowls and cricket are also still sections of the club, though its offerings also include Arabic dancing, fitness classes and tumble-tots, alongside the more traditional 'club' activities of snooker and dominoes.

I was a club member in the 1970s, when it was my nearest hockey club (still a 30-minute bus ride from home). At that time hockey club members included senior ICI managers and workers from all parts of the company, as well as local businessmen, teachers and other professionals – all playing alongside labourers, clerical workers or skilled workers from ICI or other local companies. This was a real social and sporting mix, including junior sections and veterans; some players were at national standards, while many played purely for recreation. This social mix was certainly unusual for hockey at the time, but certainly replicated in many of the ICI or other employer-based sports clubs across the country. This is the club where I, along with many others, met my future partner (still the present Mr Bell). My children subsequently had their first taste of club hockey at the same club, but by this time the game had been moved to the astroturf pitch of a local school.

Throughout all the changes of the twentieth and twenty-first centuries, club organization has remained similar – a hierarchical structure that reflects society in the nineteenth century, with the original club officials taken mainly from the management of the company. Today, in a more democratic and voluntary-based structure that would be familiar to many multi-sports clubs across the country, the club depends on the support of a dedicated band of volunteers and officials, who give up their time and efforts to maintain the club as an active and vibrant provider in the local sporting scene.

Source: Lavell, P. (1990) *100 years of recreation with Brunner-Mond, ICI & Soda Ash Products: Winnington Park recreation Club Centenary 1890–1990*. Winnington Park Recreation Club

Some questions to think about:

- Compare the dates of this club to others provided in your area.
- Were major employers like ICI providers of sporting and recreational facilities locally?
- What sports were part of the club when it was founded? Why do you think some of these sports survive in the modern sports club and others have not?

Golden ages and the role of sport in modern society

> We are currently living in a golden age of sport. Never, since ancient times, has sport occupied as important a place in society as it does today.
>
> (J A Samaranch, cited in Chappelet and Bayle 2005: vIii)

As indicated by Juan Samaranch, many people consider that the early twenty-first century represents a 'golden age' for sport. Others may hark back to previous periods and suggest sport long ago had its 'golden age', and despite its importance, modern sport has lost its core values. Historians could argue that their role would be to examine and illuminate this debate.

A particular sport or organisation may have its own 'golden age', what Polley (2007) refers to as a peak or 'pinnacle' of development and performance, without any of the negative connotations of 'progress', such as drug abuse, cheating and corruption. A 'rose-tinted' view of the past would overlook such occurrences in past sporting eras, and would not appreciate the advances made in modern sport performances in athleticism or technique (due to more advanced training and better technical preparation). Indeed, such is the nature of sport, that one person's 'golden age' may well be someone else's 'annus horriblis'. Colin Shindler's book *Manchester United Ruined My Life* (1998) provides an amusing example of this, describing his life as a young Jewish boy growing up in Manchester in the 1960s, supporting Manchester City.

The sport historian therefore has an important role in critically analysing the constituent parts of such 'golden ages' and unravelling fact from fiction and myth from informed comment and analysis.

Sport in history – important trends and concepts in the UK's sporting history

Historians have long debated the role of sport in British history. Mangan (2006) asserts that sport demands the attention of historians due to the significance of sporting practices, the emotional, political and economic impacts and influences as the new 'opiate of the masses'. Such a role having previously been attributed to religion, it is perhaps not surprising that Sunday observance legislation meant that until fairly recently it was impossible to see professional sport or even be charged to attend amateur sport events on a Sunday in the UK. The emergence of different views about the role and significance of sport in British society is shown briefly in Table 1.3.

Table 1.3: Themes and periods in sport history

Key theme	Period	Sport's role and purpose?
Folks games and pastimes	Pre-nineteenth century	Folk traditions and skills, seasonal celebrations, rural pursuits based in village, town or district, country fairs and exhibitions. Sports often violent contests, with only limited resemblance to activities of the modern day.
Rational recreation	Late eighteenth and nineteenth centuries	The promotion of healthy bodies for hygiene and for preparation for militarism, sport or recreation provided through philanthropy by social reformers, sport played for a purpose was more acceptable – hence rational.
Athleticism	Nineteenth century, Victorian	Physical and moral development, especially in public schools (Eton, Rugby, etc.) and particularly through team sports; manly, combative pursuits, emphasising loyalty, deference to authority, individual sacrifice, anti-intellectualism.
Amateurism	Nineteenth century to mid-twentieth century (in some sports still persists)	Sport for its own sake, played by amateurs or 'gentlemen', i.e. for no monetary reward. Distinctions emerged when professionalism began in nineteenth century. 'Players' were professionals and were strictly regulated; they were even prohibited from competing in some sports.
Muscular Christianity	Mid- to late-nineteenth century	Sport was seen to exert a healthy or wholesome influence, away from the pub or other less desirable uses of time. Such religious influence seen in many clubs and sports: the cultivation of 'healthy bodies and healthy minds' was the duty of every Christian. Many clubs and facilities provided by churches.
Commodification	Later twentieth century	Passive sport consumption becomes significant, increasingly commercial role for sport, sporting goods and services, growth of professional and international sport, global influences and organisations, player migration as result of global spread of sporting practices.
Celebrity	Late twentieth and early twenty-first centuries	The emergence of the sporting celebrity, epitomised by David Beckham; sporting superstars are featured across multi-media platforms or sources, often unrelated to sporting performance or where sporting personality is a vehicle for promoting a 'brand'.

Now, in our largely secular (non-religious) society, it may be considered slightly odd to think that sport on Sunday should be frowned upon. However, there are some differences of opinion and interpretation of how and why sport has gained and exerted such influence on wider society. Has sport simply mirrored social change or helped to shape it? For example, to what extent has the greater ethnic diversity in professional football since the 1970s helped to challenge and change attitudes to racism, both in sport and in British society more widely? This sort of question helps to reinforce why both historical and sociological perspectives can be seen as mutually dependent.

The topics referred to throughout this chapter may help to illustrate some of the areas where social change and social history can be traced in and through sport. Timelines, such as the one compiled by England Netball, show important dates in the chronology of a sport. Though timelines are a useful starting point to examine key dates in chronological order, wider social changes and events provide context and help explain and illuminate the significance of these dates and achievements. The example timeline for netball highlights key dates and events in the history of the sport. This provides us with a starting point from which to organise more evidence and contextualise these changes. However, for a more complete history of a sport like netball, issues of gender equity, as well as wider social changes, must be incorporated to help explain its relatively weak position in the sporting hierarchy; standing outside the Olympic family, for example, despite its relatively long history, popular appeal for girls and women, and international spread.

England netball: a timeline of development

1891 – Game invented in USA and called basket ball. First match recorded in America 1900.

1895 – Visit of Dr Toles, an American, to Madame Osterberg's P. T. college (became Dartford College). Basket ball taught with the use of wastepaper baskets for goals.

1897 – Game played out of doors on grass. Now called net ball, a larger ball used with rings and nets instead of baskets. The court is divided into three parts.

1900 – 250 copies of the first set of rules are revised and published by the Physical Education Association.

1926 – An inaugural meeting in London forms the All England Net Ball Association.

1932 – First inter-county tournament held, with Essex emerging as the first county champions.

1933 – First edition of the magazine Net Ball published, priced 3d.

1935 – Name changed to All England Women's Association for Net Ball and other Hand Ball games.

1939 – Middlesex, the county champions, represent England versus Scotland at Glasgow Exhibition.

1944 – Association now known as the All England Netball Association.

1949 – England wins the first international matches against Scotland and Wales (both scores 25–3).

1951 – Silver Jubilee celebrated. Netball demonstrated at Festival of Britain Exhibition.

1960 – Inaugural meeting in Ceylon of International Federation of Women's Basketball and Netball Associations. International code of rules adopted. Position names changed and matches lengthened to 60 minutes.

1963 – First World Tournament held in Eastbourne and is won by Australia. England is third, behind New Zealand.

1964 – National headquarters acquired in London with a full-time staff.

1966 – Harbourne club wins the first National Clubs Tournament.

1976 – Celebrations for the Association's Golden Jubilee held throughout the country. Canada and the Trinidad and Tobago teams visit England.

1994 – The English Schools Netball Association merges with the AENA after 25 years as a separate body.

1996 – High Five Netball, a five-a-side mini-game, is launched. AENA publishes its first Disability Development Plan, and adopts a new logo.

1997 – Lottery grant secured to support the World Class Performance Plan.

1998 – Netball is played at the Commonwealth Games for the first time.

2003 – Netball named as priority sport for Sport England funding.

2004 – First Marion Smith Championships for Players with Learning Disabilities

2005 – Netball Superleague launched, televised by Sky Sports.

2006 – England takes bronze medal at Commonwealth Games in Melbourne.

© Copyright England Netball 2007–08. Selected information from England Netball website: http://live.englandnetball.co.uk/About_Us/History_of_England_ Netball.php

When we are faced with the question, 'why does sport take this form or that?' historical analysis can help trace and investigate reasons and factors. When we consider the forms of sport that have persisted and developed, we may want to identify what it is about a sport that makes people embrace it and develop such a passion about and commitment to it – these are all interesting and relevant questions for modern society and so too for students of sport.

> Persisting expectations, relations and behaviours may also help account for visible contemporary differences in sport forms, structures and meanings across nations and social blocs.
>
> (Struna 2000: 197)

In drawing conclusions and interpretations from history we cannot really ignore the social dimension therefore. The figurational or 'process sociological' approach of Norbert Elias (1897–1990) was associated with the University of Leicester's Department of Sociology and the tradition of this approach was continued by the staff, such as Eric Dunning, and students of the former Centre for Research into Sport and Society. This approach to history was seen to be crossing boundaries between history and sociology, and included the consideration of 'figurations' – the social relations or interactions in sport as part of the quest for control 'excitement' – as part of a 'civilising process'. In this process, sporting activities and pastimes have become increasing more civilised, regulated and controlled. Figurational approaches have been used to consider the development and change in various sports, including football, rugby, cricket and baseball (Dunning et al. 2004).

Review

This chapter has attempted to map out what sport history is about, and how you might go about conducting a historical analysis of sport. A variety of methods and approaches are available, and the UK has a rich history of sport to explore. By looking more deeply at the past, we can find much to help our understanding of the current issues and debates in sport and develop better understanding of why we do what we do today. If you have specific units or modules in sport history, you should follow up reading this chapter with additional reading. Through completing some of the related activities and following recommended links, a diverse range of historical sources and topics can be explored. The selections below are suggestions for some useful starting material.

Further study

The following sources are recommended on particular periods or topics.

On social histories of some of the major sports, incorporating social and cultural aspects, social changes and social theory:
- Horne, J., Tomlinson, A. and Whannel, G. (eds) (1999) *Understanding Sport: An Introduction to the Sociological and Cultural analysis of Sport*. London: E & FN Spon/Routledge

On modern history:
- Holt, R. (1989) *Sport and the British: A Modern History*. Oxford: Oxford University Press

On post-war British sport:
- Polley, M. (1998) *Moving the Goalposts: A History of Sport and Society Since 1945*. London: Routledge

On sources:
- Cox, R. (1994) *History of Sport: A Guide to the Literature and Sources of Information*. Frodsham: Sport History Publishing (you should also look at the various texts Cox has produced listed on the website below, which he also maintains)
- British Society of Sport History: www.sporthistinfo.co.uk – includes extensive resources for the student of sport history and contains details of additional texts and sources available for historical studies of sport
- Scholarly Sports Sites (hosted by University of Calgary): www.ucalgary.ca/ lib-old/ssportsite – has many links with resources, archives, databases and

searchable bibliographies; good for topics of interest to sport historians; is international
- LA84 Foundation: www.la84foundation.org – established as part of the legacy for the 1984 Los Angeles Olympics, this site has searchable archives for Olympic resources and for periodicals from the US, Canada, Australia and the UK

LTSN Resource Guide for Sport History (authored by Martin Johnes, 2003): www.heacademy.ac.uk/assets/hlst/documents/resource_guides/sports_history.pdf – this is available as a pdf file and contains an extensive annotated bibliography of over 100 sources, categorised and organised into periods and types, as well as brief reviews of significant historical texts. An essential study aid for this subject, freely available, from one of the leading current sport historians

Journals in sport history:
- *International Journal of the History of Sport*
- *Sport in History* (formerly *The Sport Historian*)
- *Sport History Review*

Chapter 2

Sociological perspectives of sport

Introduction

This chapter is designed to introduce you to the essential tools with which to analyse sport from a sociological perspective. Sport, as we saw in Chapter 1 has long been of interest to scholars of society and social relations. Sociology was one of the more prominent disciplines in the latter part of the twentieth century, when sport studies really began to expand in UK universities.

In this chapter the main 'schools of thought' in social theory are identified and their relevance to understanding contemporary sporting structures and practices are examined. Though space prevents detailed explanation, the key topics considered within the sociological aspects of sport are identified. This chapter will provide further links and suggestions for additional reading in more specialised and advanced sources. You will also be provided with a number of activities, which hopefully will help you to bring more relevance to this subject for your own studies.

Learning outcomes

After completing this chapter and the related learning activities, you will be able to:

- identify and explain the some key sociological perspectives on sport;
- identify key authors and their contributions to theories in sociology of sport;
- provide examples of the application of social theory to sport, such as gender and media;
- identify further reading on selected topics of interest.

In the chapter a number of key topics in sociological analysis are identified, for example gender, social class and ethnicity, which continue to form the essential content of many units or modules addressing social theory in sport studies programmes.

What is sociological analysis?

As identified in the previous chapter, attempts to explain and/or understand the significance of sport in society date back to the early nineteenth century, with the emergence of sport as a form of popular recreation. Early sport historians began to provide evidence of different sporting practices across social groups and societies. Similarly, early sociologists tended to look at popular sport and recreation in terms of what people did and looked at differences in the forms of and purposes for sport in different societies.

Later, as the study of the sociology of sport became more established, issues of control and power in sport began to be of more concern, as more radical and critical ways of thinking about both sport and society emerged in the latter part of the twentieth century. Sport, with its growing commercialism and global reach, became the focus for many sociologists, particularly those interested in global trends and the impact of major corporations. Gradually the sociology of sport has grown to become one of the key disciplines in sport studies. There are many journals, conferences and publications devoted to the study of the sociology of sport, which demonstrate how significant the discipline is, both in scope and influence.

What is this discipline concerned with?

Essentially, sociological analysis attempts to explain or critique the social relations and functions of sport – its practices, institutions and forms. According to Giddens (2006), the sociological perspective means cultivating the imagination (based on the work of C. Wright Mills), in order to 'think ourselves away'; so, for example, looking at what we might think of as everyday routines or activities, and thinking again about them in terms of their social meaning and significance. Hence, 'going to the match', is no longer simply about spending some time watching a game with friends or family – it becomes full of social meaning and ritual; what match in which sport, for example, or who you attend it with; the replica shirt wearing, or scarves and flags; travelling with other supporters; pre-match drinks at a specific pub. At the match, a person may take on a new identity, that of a 'fan'. Having some half time refreshment takes on a particular ritual, as does singing or chanting. Investigating such ritual, symbols and interactions is what interests the sociologist and the sociological imagination. The game on the pitch (whatever form of game it is) is played out against a backdrop of many interactions processes and experiences.

According to C. Wright Mills, the 'sociological imagination' (1970) is a threefold exercise that involves a historical, anthropological and cultural sensitivity. Jarvie (2006) explains this as the basis for much of the value of how sport contributes to our understanding of social relations:

1. Recovering our own immediate past and understanding the basis of how historical transformation has influenced the social and cultural dimensions of life.
2. The cultivation of anthropological insight – understanding how the diversity of modes of human existence and cultures extends beyond the materialistic West, or advanced capitalist models of society.

3. By combining the above, the scholar avoids an analysis based on the 'here and now' and this involves the possibility of gaining an understanding of the social relations between societies.

Within a sociological analysis, we therefore need to look at social relations and structures, including a micro- and macro-perspective. This means that we are concerned with the individual (micro) level processes as well as the broader, macro, or social level systems and processes at work.

Social structures can represent some regularity in the way in which society is organised. These are said to reflect human diversity and the interactions between the individual and society. Giddens (2006) suggests, therefore, that our activities, such as our forms of leisure and sport, both structure and give shape to the social world around us, and at the same time are structured by that social world.

Sociologists looking at sport look particularly at the issues of choice and constraint or *agency* and *structure*. Agency or social action is concerned with the extent to which our actions or choices are freely made – or are influenced by social structures and other external influences. Just how free are you to act as you want to do? Society has gradually evolved a complex system of constraints on individual behaviours, and sporting preferences and forms certainly fit within this framework of control. At the same time, the diversity of expressions and forms of sport tell us that the individual has many potential ways in which to express their interests and enthusiasms. Webers' influence on social analysis was also to show how individuals can shape and give meaning to their experiences – hence interpretive or interactionist perspectives of the social world. The role of symbols and language in expressing meaning and shared understandings is also important in this tradition.

Chapter 1 considered how the history of sport has emphasised the way in which popular beliefs and ideas about sport can sometimes develop a mythological nature, in that some interpretations or representations of historical events can become widely held 'beliefs', or that everyone shares common beliefs about the value of sport for character building or social development. Sociological analysis therefore attempts to separate some of the 'myths' about sport from the reality and examine how sport influences both at the individual and the social level. Social theories tend to address key questions about the structure of society and the extent of 'free will' we have when we make such choices as whether or not to participate in sport, or the form that such participation may take. Jarvie (2006: 20) has suggested that:

> what sociological theory may provide is a mode of critique, a language of opposition and a promise that the potential for radical transformation actually exists.

This suggests that sport, as a particular form of cultural practice, is an interesting area for sociologists to examine social change and provides an opportunity for looking at issues of personal choice, freedom and the emergence of new social structures. According to Jarvie, one of the most important functions of theory is criticism. The sociological study of sport therefore provides the student with an opportunity not just to attack the potential for myths in sport, 'but also to ensure that the choices that are made about sport and the world in which it operates are genuinely free' (p. 21).

Brante (2001) has commented that the purpose of sociological analysis is the explanation of differences in society. In this context, then, we could argue that sociological analysis provides some insight into what we might observe in sporting forms and practices, meanings and values in sport, across and between different social groups and individuals and even countries. This analysis can then help to inform our future development of sporting participation and experiences.

Social theorists and sport

Giddens notes that the Frenchman, Auguste Compte (1798–1857), was the first to coin the term 'sociology', which he conceived as a positive or natural science. He thought it was appropriate to apply the tools of natural science (such as physics or chemistry) to study the social rather than the physical world. He was followed by a range of social theorists, who have influenced the sociological study of sport – some more significantly than others.

Table 2.1 shows the broad groupings of the 'schools of thought' in sociology, and the key authors with which they are associated.

Functionalism

Giddens (2006: 20) suggests that functionalists see society as 'a complex system whose various parts work together to produce stability and solidarity'. To investigate those parts, e.g religious beliefs and customs, or sporting practices and institutions, functionalists look at how they relate to each other and what contribution they make to society. In this approach, sport is seen as performing a stabilising role or function in society. It is possible to analyse sport in various forms across societies and cultural traditions, to determine what function it performs and how this may differ in different societies.

Sport could be seen to help to maintain individual and social balance, the opportunity for individual self-expression, or for national or cultural preferences, as shown in Table 2.2. Sport sociologists in this tradition see sport as an important social institution, which reflects the many complex relationships and interactions in wider society. Early functionalists viewed sport as a sort of 'mirror' of society. For example, sporting practices may have been used to prepare for or even replace 'warfare' or 'hunting'. In modern society, as noted in Chapter 1, certain sport activities and practices were promoted to maintain appropriate physical activity levels for health or militaristic purposes and to provide a forum for socially acceptable forms of aggressive or competitive behaviours.

Table 2.1: Theoretical approaches to society

Theoretical approaches	Associated with:
Functionalism	Durkheim (1895–1917)
Conflict theories	Marx (1918–83)
Interactionist/interpretive	Weber (1864–1920)

Table 2.2: Possible functions of sport in society

Basic functions of sport at societal level	Contributes to:
Socio-emotional	Psycho-social stability
Socialisation	Inculcation of cultural beliefs and mores (attitudes)
Integrative	Harmonious integration of disparate groups
Political	Sport being used for ideological purposes
Social mobility	Source of upward mobility for those with talent

Source: Based on Stevenson and Nixon (1972), in Loy and Booth 2000: 15.

Functionalists have also seen sport as performing an important socialising role – where social values and norms of behaviour are transmitted and maintained across generations. The modern functionalist perspective of sport can be seen when we look at the government supporting sport through policies as a means to improve social cohesion or health. Table 2.2 shows how these basic functions were identified.

Criticisms of the functionalist view of sport

It could be argued that the functionalist view does not pay sufficient attention to history and social change over time. There are also criticisms of the assumptions made about the relative stability in society and lack of attention to issues of conflict and lack of agreement, which are frequently found in our more recent past. Others have criticised functionalists for being either too scientific (in talking of variables and social structures) or not scientific enough (being unable to 'prove' their theories with observable, scientific methods). Either way, functionalism has been the subject of extensive writing and examination. Perhaps the most detailed review is by Loy and Booth (2000). However, this is quite a dense and difficult chapter, which assumes an existing knowledge of the essentials of sociology.

If sport is a mirror of society, we also need to think about some of the negative aspects that we find in sport, not just the positive. According to Eitzen (2003), sport mirrors society in profound ways, but he also examines the 'myth' that sport is a positive experience for all. He identifies racism, sexism and homophobia, as well as greed, exploitation and alienation, for example, as being persistent problems in sport.

Activity

Investigating functional views of sport – what's the game plan?

Find the 'Game Plan' (2002) document on the DCMS website and consider it in relation to the functional view of sport (see Chapters 1 and 2 in particular and the summary recommendations). What did the Blair government suggest is the value of sport to society?

Are there any aspects of sport that could be described as dysfunctional, or not being of social benefit?

Interpretive sociology

Donnelly (2000: 77) has argued that, 'interpretation is the basis of all sociology and all science'. In this context, however, 'interpretive' refers to a particular grouping of sociologists and theories which position the interpretation and understanding of human meaning and action as their central focus. Central to the interpretive sociologists is the meaning social actors (individuals) give to what they and others do. They are part of a 'social action' approach to studying society – along with what has been described as the sociology of everyday life, symbolic interactionism and hermeneutics. The interpretive approach is influenced by the work of Max Weber, who considered individual motivations and ideas should be the focus of analysis, rather than social structures. His work was rooted in the philosophy of Kant (which we look at in Chapter 3) and was aimed at achieving an interpretive understanding of human action.

Hermeneutics (after Hermes the messenger)

This term was first used by the Greeks to describe those attempting to define 'true' meanings of biblical texts. It is now more closely associated with critical media studies – and the deconstruction and analysis of the meaning of written texts or visual media for themes and messages.

Some sociologists take a relatively 'common-sense' approach to meanings. Those involved in more complex theories, such as hermeneutics, adopt more refined, sophisticated or multi-layered approaches, which look more deeply beyond the actors' own (individual) understanding of what they are doing.

Sociologists in the interpretive tradition will often use qualitative methodologies, such as ethnography and in-depth interviews, in order to arrive at their analyses. In the sociology of sport, such an approach emerged from the so-called 'Chicago School' of sociology in the 1930s.

A number of studies in boxing and other 'sub-cultures' in sport emerged using ethnographic methods such as participant observation. Other work has included critiques of media representation of female athletes (see 'Women, the media and sport' below).

Interpretive approaches have therefore made contributions to the methods used in sociological analysis, including the use of biographies and 'insider accounts' to study sport. This has shown a greater *reflexivity* – in that the use of hermeneutics, particularly in gender, sport and media studies, has added depth and a greater richness to understanding the complex interactions and influences at play, and thus deeper insight into what sport means to the individual in modern society. These relationships and influences are briefly examined below.

Criticisms of the interpretive sociology of sport

The criticisms of interpretive approaches address both methods and theories. Critics suggest that it is not possible to interpret and provide standard explanations of meanings as, even if such interpretation was valid, how could it be possible to ensure it was appropriate or accurate? Those who believe in stable social systems, such as functionalists, also point to the issue of cultural relativism – this refers to when our understanding is limited by our own cultural beliefs and experiences. The constraints we may suffer on our freedom to act are also difficult to measure or observe.

Critics of interpretive sociology consider the data collected by ethnography and similar approaches too subjective and insufficiently rigorous compared to the data collected using the 'scientific' approach or positivist tradition.

The problem of replication means that fieldwork is often criticised for being 'unreliable' or unrepeatable. Others argue that there is too little distinction between investigative journalism and hermeneutic sociology. However, when you think about investigations of particular sub-cultures or possibly even potentially 'deviant' behaviours (for example, drug use amongst body builders), such 'journalistic' methods may be the most appropriate to get 'inside' a subject or group.

Women, the media and sport

Kay (2003) has clearly described the history of exclusion in women's sport. In sport, gender analysis is also concerned with how gender is reflected, reproduced or even resisted in males as well as females. But the experience of women is often missing from earlier analyses of sport – as if sport has always been a male domain. However, this has been challenged by some more recent studies, which show that, though there have been clear differences and distinctions between men and women and despite male domination of many sport forms and practices, women have a rich history of sport. One of the problems has been the male-oriented media reporting and recording of this history, which has tended to continue a stereotypical view of women in sport. Bernstein (2002) reported that, despite the enormous strides made by female sport performers, there was still some way to go to find any level of gender equality in the media treatment of sport. Studies in this aspect of sport tend to focus on the quantity of coverage of female sport and the media portrayal of female athletes.

In terms of coverage, there is little debate that male sport gets more coverage in any media. What is of interest is the pattern of this coverage and how it has changed over time or differs between countries. Women remain under-represented and as a result have been 'symbolically annihilated' from media coverage. This has been shown in many studies, with some slight distinctions around major events, such as the Olympics and Wimbledon (Bernstein 2002).

Qualitative differences are also clear in the way in which females are represented when they do appear in various media. While men's performances are often described using war-like metaphors (going into battle, fighting for their life) or terms that emphasise their 'macho' or masculine qualities, females are more likely to be infantilised (the girls play. . .), or have their appearance noted (she looks   ) This approach is said to trivialise women's sport and emphasise so-called 'feminine' sports, which emphasise grace and aesthetics over skill and athleticism.

Questions

- Analyse the content of the media coverage of female sport performers in any popular media form in one week. You could measure how much (column centimetres or time) and where in the paper or channel this is shown/printed. Compare this with the equivalent male performers in the same sport.
- How can any differences be explained? Is there any difference in how this performance is reported? (e.g. in language, images, style of presentation)?
- Consider the impacts of this media treatment of women, and the levels and types of participation in sport and physical activity by women. For example, examine the results of the Women's Sport and Fitness Foundation survey results on women's attitudes to sport and activity (see Further study for website details). As a group, you could discuss the extent to which these results reflect the experiences and attitudes of your fellow sport students (male and female).

Socialisation in and through sport

Coakley and White's (1992) study provided greater insight into the interpretive contribution to understanding of the socialising process in and through sport. In this study, the qualitative data from interviews with young people was used to explore how they were socialised into sport, grounded in an interactionist approach. They found that young men and women shared concerns about their transition to adulthood – but there were significant differences between males and females. Gender differences were found in the ways in which sporting experiences and opportunities were perceived and interpreted; particularly for girls, the constraints were to do with money, parents and boyfriends, as well as negative experiences with PE in school. When playing sport, young people also had different views of how they perceived themselves – young women were less likely to consider themselves to be 'sportswomen' and tended to count themselves out of sport, even if it was something they enjoyed. Sport was something they were socialised into thinking was not for them. This was particularly acute in girls who considered themselves to be 'working class'.

Socialisation *through* sport has been widely referred to within the social psychology of sport as a site for teaching fundamental concepts of rules and expectations of society or social learning (Bandura 1997). Unfortunately this can, as shown above, be both positive and negative – for girls, for example, socialisation might be said to teach them that sport is a masculine preoccupation, from which they are often excluded. Some of the claims for sport socialisation regarding the positive social values and behaviours inculcated through sport participation have therefore been questioned, as there is some lack of specific research evidence that has proved conclusively that sport can achieve these outcomes.

Conflict theories: Marxist and neo-Marxist approaches to sport

Though it is clearly beyond the scope of this type of textbook to do justice to the work of Marx, this section is a summary of how Marxist approaches have influenced the study of sport, under the broad heading of conflict theories.

Marxism and sport

Marx's theories provided a coherent model of society, a critique of political economy and a multidisciplinary and complex philosophical argument, which incorporated anthropology, economics, history and sociology (Rigauer 2000). Marxist theory is based on the impact of economic activities and relations (the base) on the other social institutions of politics and culture (the superstructure). Central to a struggle for control is the mode of production and the way individuals are involved in the production process. Although it was not clear in his writing what his view of sport was, many have subsequently applied his theories to sport, particularly in relation to 'valorisation' or class-based struggle. Marxist theory was essentially about the struggles for power between the aristocracy, the newly emerging bourgeoisie and the working class. Marx could therefore have seen sport as part of the larger 'superstructure' of society, helping to stabilise the means of production and reproducing ideologies and behaviours which maintain the ruling elite under capitalism. His theories have been used to examine the capitalist model of sport in the US and the Soviet bloc in Europe.

Under Soviet influence, after the Second World War, the communist states of the USSR and the Eastern bloc countries of Europe developed their own sporting structures and systems. Communism was adopted in China (under Mao Zedong), Cuba (under Castro), North Korea and Vietnam, and still operates in these countries, albeit in very different forms. Rigaur (2000) suggests that the 'utopia of a fully operational communist society' as envisioned by Marx has arguably not been realised. In all of these states, however, sport was seen as an important domain for state intervention and the promotion of communist ideals. Sport became, for some time, a potential battleground for alternative ideologies and political systems, particularly in international sport, a situation that arguably persists today.

Questions
- What are the main characteristics of the Marxist/communist sporting systems in the countries noted above?
- What might be Marxist criticisms of the modern capitalist and commodified sporting world?

In the latter part of the twentieth century, some Marxist interpretations of the sociology of sport gained recognition, largely as a reaction to the perceived excesses of the capitalist, commercialised and increasingly globalised influences of the major sport organisations and sporting goods manufacturers. Paul Hoch wrote *Rip Off the Big Game* (1973) as a scathing attack on the capitalist and exploitative American sport system. This was set against a wider anti-establishment counter-culture in the US from the mid-1960s.

Various academics have developed Marx's earlier work and subsequently developed their own theories; these are so-called 'neo-marxist theory', critical theory, hegemony theory and feminist theory. Critical theory emerged originally during the inter-war years (1918–33) in what was called the Frankfurt School. This approach applied to the study of sport essentially looks at the systems of power and control in sport and seeks to analyse power relations and the commodification of sport.

Other related theories and approaches: cultural studies and Gramsci

Cultural studies is concerned with the social significance and systematic analysis of cultural practices, experiences, and institutions. Its particular characteristic is to direct attention to and analyse critically the 'everyday world of lived reality'.

(Hargreaves and MacDonald 2000: 48)

Sport, as it is clearly enjoyed by millions in many societies across the world as part of their 'lived reality', is of interest to cultural studies scholars. Cultural studies also includes many different disciplines, such as communication studies, film or media studies, history, literary criticism, politics and philosophy. Perhaps the best known of the theorists in cultural studies is the Marxist, Antonio Gramsci (1891–1937).

The term 'culture' is often taken as being what might be called 'high culture', such as the opera or exhibitions of old masters' paintings or the ballet. However, culture has a much more broad definition, relating to beliefs, practices and activities. Culture can be about what you might consider to be traditional values and ideas about everyday things, such as sport. For example, sport is often said to be an important part of British culture, reflecting our concerns for fair play, teamwork and our national identity. Australia is however regarded by many (not least the Australians themselves) as a country which sees sport as their most important aspect of national culture and identity, associated with athleticism and the active, outdoor life.

American sport also said to reflect American culture, characterised by commercialism, capitalist approaches and competitiveness. These are seen as being essential American values, which transfer quite naturally to sports that have been developed and devised in the US, baseball for example. Such sports can be said to have grown because they reflect, celebrate and so develop such values.

Sport in the City of Culture 2008

Not surprisingly, in a city where Bill Shankly is reputed to have said: 'football, it's not a matter of life and death . . . it's much more serious than that', football is seen as a key ingredient to Liverpudlian culture. As such, several sporting activities and institutions were involved in the Capital of Culture celebrations. This included the UEFA Football exhibition at the World Museum and the hosting of the BBC Sports Personality of the Year show in December 2008.

Gramsci looked particularly at the relationships between culture and power. He argued that power was maintained not by physical force or coercion but through ideological control – through everyday activities and interactions in civil society. For example, trades unions, families, schools, the church and other cultural processes including sport practices and sporting institutions. Gramsci used the concept of *hegemony* to explain how a dominant group or class established and maintained power, control and leadership, using a complex series of cultural practices, to bind society together (Hargreaves 1994).

Hegemony can therefore help to explain why at certain times particular ideas or practices gain more importance, even though minorities may be formed and suffer as a consequence. Gramsci saw hegemony as part of a complex process, a sort of 'battle for ideas', which would eventually see one particular group gain dominance.

Clarke and Critcher (1985) made an important contribution to the cultural studies tradition with their analysis of British leisure and sporting cultural practices. Whannel (1992) has also applied this approach to the cultural and economic relationships between sport and television, in both shaping and challenging stereotypes.

Feminism and feminist analysis of sport

Hargreaves (1994) saw this hegemonic process working at the 'everyday' level in sport, which meant it was a male-dominated activity – organised by and largely for men. She has argued that the *feminist* tradition in sociology has helped to redress some of the imbalance by focusing more on the neglected stories of female sport. The work of Hargreaves, Kay and also Scraton in this area has been very significant. Though male hegemony of sport has been shown to be largely dominant, they have also shown this to be a complex and changing relationship.

Feminist analyses of sport emerged from feminist theory in the late 1970s. This was when a more critical approach was developing across the sociology of sport. Because of the continuing imbalances in sport noted above, feminists continue to find sport a fruitful area of analysis. Sport is seen as an important site for the reproduction of the hegemonic ideology of male domination and the institutions that continue to underpin masculine hegemony in wider society.

Feminist theory is grounded in the analysis of experience and there are many sub-groups and specialisms under this broad heading. While earlier studies focused on pointing out imbalances and inequity, more recent efforts tend to focus on achieving change and implementing more proactive policy; for example, the Title IX legislation in the US, which introduced gender equality in state-funded sports in colleges and schools. A good overview of this area is provided by Hargreaves and MacDonald (2000).

Sport at the movies

Popular culture can provide some interesting examples and cases for sociological analysis, for example:

- *Bend it like Beckham* (directed by G. Chada, 2002) – this film illustrates the challenges faced by females in a male-dominated sport – football. As the heroine is from a British-Indian family based in West London, it also includes aspects of racism or discrimination, stereotypes, family and gender relations, ethnic minorities and the assimilation of cultures. Due to its popular appeal, this film has arguably helped to change perceptions about women's football, and young South Asian women growing up in Britain. It is certainly worth watching and discussing on this basis.

Other films with similar potential for discussion and debate from a sociological perspective are:

- *This Sporting Life* (set in a 1960's Northern town, a story of a rugby league player)
- *Million Dollar Baby* (about a female boxer in contemporary America)
- The *Rocky* series (East v. West, capitalist v. communist, hard work v. science – a film series to examine the American Dream and issues of corruption, violence and exploitation in sport and the triumph of the underdog in society)
- *Chariots of Fire* (Olympics, class and nationalism in the 1920s)
- *Chak De India* (Indian film about the women's national hockey team)
- *One Day in September* and *Munich* (contrast the story of the Munich hostage crisis from documentary and fictional perspectives)

You could identify other films where social and cultural aspects of sport are portrayed in either fictional or documentary style – i.e. depicting real life or fictional characters or events.

Figurational sociology

In this tradition, based on the work of Elias (1887–1990), as noted in Chapter 1, history and social analysis are seen as part of a broad developmental process of change, in a historical approach to sociology. Dunning and Elias (1986) and, later, colleagues in Leicester University carried out studies in the figurational sociology of sport. These have focused on the motivations, contexts and desires expressed through leisure and sport activities. These sporting behaviours need to be analysed, they argue, through their total context, at both individual level and in their wider social settings.

Sporting activities demonstrate both a civilising process and the human 'quest for excitement'. This approach tends to reject the agency–structure distinctions noted above. Figurational interpretations suggest that aggression, violence or even excitement have been regulated by society or confined to acceptable sporting forms. Games and sports have become increasingly more regulated, and also less violent or risky in the process of civilising. Studies in figurational sociology have looked at hooliganism in football, and at the development of particular sports, such as football or rugby (Dunning et al. 2004).

> **Time out**
>
> - How has your favourite sport changed since it was first recognised? Was it more violent or risky in the past?
> - Have rule changes, technology or other changes made it safer?
> - What examples could you provide of a civilising process at work in this sport?

Sport and social divisions

Sporting engagement and interests have been shown to be shaped by various social differences. Broadly, these are:

- social class
- ethnicity
- gender
- disability

We can see the impact of these when we look at the results of sport participation surveys or the make-up of groups of those who watch or administer sports. You will find extensive sources on each of these particular topics, and they could each justify a chapter in a specialist sociology of sport text – as they usually do. Arguably, therefore, I cannot do each of these subjects justice in this short chapter. It is important to note, however, that each of these distinctions and divisions can be considered separately or as part of a larger, integrated analysis – our social circumstances can affect either positively or negatively our attitudes towards and chances of participating in sport, and the form that such participation may take.

Those in different social classes may have more material resources, but can choose to spend these in quite different ways. The work of Pierre Bourdieu has been quite important in this respect, considering the expressions of taste and attempting to gain social status through sporting preferences. He has identified that certain activities in the use of the body have appealed to different groups.

In the UK, social class has long been a fascination of social scientists, and sport participation in the UK is demonstrably strongly linked to social class, based on occupation and attitudes to sport. Lower levels of sport participation in those in the lower social classes (unskilled manual workers) have been found in repeated surveys, compared to the professional, middle classes. Some argue that this is a matter of economics and resources; that it is poverty not social class that is to blame for lower participation, as people just don't have the money to join clubs and pay for expensive sport equipment, even if they were interested.

Whether or not poverty, social class, gender or ethnicity can explain differences in specific levels of sport participation, persistent differences in participation rates across these divisions in society mean that social scientists will continue to be interested in investigating them. Despite the advances made through equality legislation, and increased investment through lottery and other funding, surveys have reported that the number of people participating in sport on a regular basis has remained stubbornly static and continues to reflect the distinctions of gender, class and ethnicity in society. Though there may be slight gains in general activity levels, the notion of 'sport for all' remains an aspiration rather than a reality.

The value of sociological analysis of sport for future sport

The different sociological approaches outlined above have given rise to a range of different methods, tackling a diverse and changing phenomenon – sport. Sociologists therefore ask different questions about sport, depending on their interests and beliefs about how sport 'works' and its role for and significance to a particular group or individual.

Examining social divisions, for example, can take on many forms. For example, when looking at a sport event (a game of football or athletic event), various questions might arise from different perspectives:

- An *interactionist* may be interested in what is going on between different sectors of the crowd, or between the players and the crowd – looking at the communications, symbols and language, or media coverage. They might look at social class or gender distinctions within the crowd or the between players/athletes.
- A *Marxist* (or conflict theory approach) might be concerned with the economic and power relations between the players and their 'owners'.
- A *feminist* may also be asking why there are so few women at the event, or whether the females there are cheerleaders and not on the field of play.

Such sociological analysis involves both 'factual investigations' and more interpretive or qualitative considerations of the nature and meaning of activities and processes. Therefore, both quantitative and qualitative approaches are found in sociological research. Using or applying this sort of theory and analysis can help those involved in providing sport to make it more inclusive and positive for those taking part.

The emergence of sport as a key cultural and social phenomenon of the twenty-first century also emphasises the need to be aware of the potential for sport to challenge and change social attitudes and beliefs. Sport matters to many people and therefore has great reach and influence in modern society. Using a sociological perspective, research is helping to underpin modern policy and practice in sport, as well as criticise its impacts. Though there are many who also criticise the speed of change, nevertheless it is hard to ignore the changes in modern sport, or its growth.

Some reflections on feminist critiques of sport

As a professional woman, a mother, academic, former sport performer and parent, I am somewhat surprised at the extent to which the issue of gender in sport continues to be a challenge. As an undergraduate I felt we were at the cusp of major changes, in the 1970s, as our university (and others) saw a huge rise in female undergraduates and professionals working in sport. However, despite the clear gains made and some key positions in sport being filled by very capable women, sport in the UK remains largely male-oriented and male dominated professionally. Women can still be made to feel like second-class citizens when playing, watching or even talking about sport – let alone work in the sector. For students of sport, this creates a challenge and a 'mission' – to make our subject and the work we do more inclusive of female or feminist perspectives and to challenge the stereotypes and traditions which persist in creating barriers for women to progress in sport, not just in participation but in administration, management, physical education, coaching and sport science.

The recent *Handbook of Sport Studies* (Coakley and Dunning 2000) points out that almost one-third of the contributors were women, a huge improvement since an earlier edition. However, this proportion of academic contributions still arguably reflects a gender imbalance in sport studies more generally.

In over 15 years of teaching sport in higher education, I have never taught a year group that even approached a 50:50 balance between men and women. Our sport courses still appear to be rather dominated by the male perspective of sport. Consequently, in academic life, female academics and sport sociologists can struggle for wider recognition and are often pigeon-holed into feminist studies or gender studies work. Some excellent work has continued to be produced however, using a critical perspective and diverse range of methods and approaches. Work by Kay, Scraton, Cauldwell and Hargreaves, amongst others, continues to be at the forefront of critical policy and feminist work. A good source for material in this area is the reader by Scraton and Flintoff (2002).

Because of the ongoing 'battle for ideas' in sport, the area of gender continues to be a fruitful one for sport scholars. But this is not just about women's sport, as increasingly attention is drawn to issues of the hegemony of a masculinity based on 'macho' sporting behaviours and masculine ideologies which may alienate both young males and females in their everyday experiences of sport. Feminist analysis of sport seeks not only to analyse these processes but also to challenge them – and eventually bring about change. Unfortunately change is a slow process – and there is still plenty for up and coming sport students to do!

There are some important females operating at the very highest levels of sport in the UK. Sue Campbell CBE, for example, has recently been appointed to the House of Lords and is the Chair of UK Sport. She has been described as one of the most influential people in sport and, as President of the Youth Sport Trust and a former advisor to both DCMS and DFES on school sport, she has been involved in many high profile policies. She is also a former head of the

National Coaching Foundation and has worked as a top-level coach, a regional development officer for the Sports Council, a teacher in secondary schools and a lecturer at Loughborough University (where she taught me!). Her vast experience in the male-dominated sporting world has meant that she continues to be a major force in the development of sport at all levels in the UK. Sue Campbell is recognised as an inspirational speaker and has also led an important programme to increase the number of female leaders in the sector.

In the academic world other inspirational and influential women include Professor Sheila Scraton, Professor Celia Brackenridge and Dr Tess Kay, who have all influenced and helped encourage my own work, as they have for many other academics, male and female. So, while many female scholars (like myself) would not label themselves as 'feminist' writers, nevertheless, as females working in this world, it is clear that a feminist perspective is an important antidote to the male-oriented and dominated view of sport that many women and girls experience on a daily basis. This approach helps to make sure that we continue to challenge stereotype and generalisation in sport studies and provide a more balanced view of the potential for sport for all sectors of society.

Discussion topics in the sociological analysis of sport

The following questions are examples of investigations in sport from a sociological perspective:

Gender
- Are there differences in preferences in activities?
- Is sport in the twenty-first century still a male domain?
- Discuss how and why males could be more likely to take part in some activities rather than others.
- Is it appropriate in the twenty-first century to consider some sports to be either male or female? Why do such ideas persist?
- Find out about Title IX legislation in the US. In your group, discuss whether or not similar legislation could work in the UK. What would be the implication for student sport in the UK?

Social class
- Does the notion of social class have any relevance in a modern society?
- What evidence shows persistence in the differences between social groups?
- What interventions has the government initiated to reduce social class divisions in sport, and how successful have they been?

Ethnicity and racism
Examine the different rates of participation by different ethnic groups in the UK in the Sport Equity Index from Sport England (this should be available from the website).

- Why does sport participation not match population diversity?
- What are the barriers to participation experienced by those from ethnic minorities?
- Identify a programme or initiative designed to combat racism in sport.

Review

This chapter has identified the key social theories and approaches in the sociological analysis of sport. Throughout, various authors and their contributions to the subject have been noted and the section below offers sources of more reading or further investigation of their work. The sociological perspective illuminates issues of freedom and constraint and choice and opportunity. Sport can be examined at various levels – the micro or individual, as well as the middle range theories, which seek to explain the differences in engagement or practice.

The chapter has been designed to make you think about how sport can be analysed from a sociological perspective and what the implications are for current and future practice. For example, by having a greater appreciation of issues such as gender and how they can impact on sport participation, sport studies can contribute to improving practice and challenging the stereotypes and myths that surround sport.

There are various perspectives on or approaches to sociological analysis, and for each there are some criticisms to be aware of. While social divisions persist in sport, sociological analysis can help us both understand these divisions and devise more inclusive and positive sport experiences in the future.

Further study

On essential social theory:
- Giddens, A. (2006) *Sociology* (5th edition). Cambridge: Policy Press – this book is recommended for an introduction to social theory and for many of the broad social topics: media, social class, ethnicity and others.

On sport and gender:
- Scraton, S. and Flintoff, A. (eds) (2002) *Gender and Sport: A Reader*. London: Routledge – this book also has readings on historical developments, feminism, media, ethnicity and race, masculinity, sexuality and the body, policy and politics.
- Coakley, J. and Dunning, E. (eds.) (2000) *Handbook of Sport Studies*. London: Sage – the edited collection on Sport Studies has additional chapters on key topics, including focus on research in other countries.

Journals:
- *Cultural Studies*
- *International Review for the Sociology of Sports*
- Leisure Studies
- *Recreation*
- *Sociology of Sport Journal*

- *Sociology of Sport Online (SOSOL)*
- *Sport, Education and Society*
- *Sport in Society* (prior to 2004, was *Culture, Sport and Society*)

Online sources:
- A good annotated bibliography and resource guide is provided on the LTSN website – Velija, P. (2008) Resource guide to sport and sociological theory: www.heacademy.ac.uk/assets/hlst/documents/resource_guides/sport_sociologcial_theory.pdf
- Centre for Research into Sport and Society (Chester University): www.chester.ac.uk/ccrss
- Women's Sport and Fitness Foundation (WSFF) surveys and other useful information and sources or links: www.wsf.org.uk
- British Sociological Association (BSA) has a study group for sport, as well as Leisure and recreation: www.britsoc.co.uk/specialisms/Sport.htm; www.britsoc.co.uk/specialisms/Leisure.htm
- Leisure Studies Association: www.leisure-studies-association.info – this site includes details of events and publications; membership includes many of the sociological researchers in sport and leisure noted above

Chapter 3

Philosophy and ethics in sport

Introduction

This chapter focuses on a discussion of the philosophical aspects of sport and the ethics of sporting practices and processes. A commonly used phrase aptly sums this up, 'It's not what you do; it's the way that you do it . . .' Throughout the chapter we are reminded of the duality of sport: one the one hand, considered a relatively trivial thing, but on the other, a significant social phenomenon, with great reach and influence in modern society: 'sport, a seemingly trivial pursuit, is important' (Eitzen 1999: 2).

Also paradoxical about sport is its 'nature' – and how it is valued as a positive experience, summed up in the concept of 'sport for all'. For example, most people reading this book probably think sport is a 'good' thing. However, in wider society, sport can be yet another area of social life where many feel disadvantaged or excluded, with few positive memories, or have experienced physical or emotional abuse or harm.

As pointed out by Eitzen (1999), if sport is a mirror of society, why do we expect people to have different or higher moral values in sport than we might expect in other spheres of life? As our newspapers and TV screens show us on a regular basis, sporting events, celebrities and issues are often the source of some quite fierce debates, often around philosophical or ethical conduct, or behaviour, not all of which are about the sport.

This chapter is therefore designed to examine the philosophical and ethical perspective of sport. Our focus is on the problems and issues which continue to attract major debate amongst students and practitioners in sport – particularly given the value attached to sport in modern society and the claims made for it. These issues include the value and purpose of sport, the role of competition, the issue of 'fair play' and why people cheat at sport. The chapter also considers those ethical issues which shape the experiences of many involved in a great variety of sporting practices and forms, such as discrimination and exclusion, cheating and ethical codes of practice.

You should consider your own philosophy for what makes ethical sporting practice and how well you understand the codes of conduct or ethics that apply to a range of potential careers in sport. How these are implemented and why such ethical guidelines are needed are examined through various case studies and examples in the chapter. Sources for further study are provided, as well as ideas for debates and discussions in class and for personal reflection.

Learning outcomes

After completing this chapter and the related learning activities, you will be able to:
- identify essential concepts, theories and principles in the philosophy of sport;
- outline the important contributions to philosophic enquiry in sport;
- examine some of the relevant codes of ethics for sport professionals;
- apply philosophical and ethical approaches to debates in contemporary sport.

Theories and approaches in the philosophy of sport

Essentials of philosophical enquiry in sport

According to McNamee, the philosophy of sport is concerned with 'the conceptual analysis and interrogation of ideas and issues of sports and related practices' (2005: 1). Therefore, sport philosophers are concerned with outlining the nature and purposes of sport and incorporating philosophical insights into the work of sport institutions and their practices, and the experiences of sport participants. This is a dynamic area, where views and ideas are constantly emerging and being challenged in turn. Concepts, questions and theories are examined across a number of sub-disciplines or branches of philosophical thought in their application to sport.

For example, a philosopher of sport would look at questions like these:

- *Aesthetics* – are sports a form of art? What constitutes a 'good performance'?
- *Ethics* – is sport good for the development of character?
- *Morals* – in education, does sport act as a 'moral laboratory'? The high moral expectations of sport are deeply rooted in our views, values and beliefs about it. These are widely held and, as indicated in the preceding chapters, have historical, cultural and social dimensions.

Defining sport

The definition of sport used by the European Commission is based on the European Sport Charter (1992):

> sport means all forms of physical activity which, through casual or organised participation, aim at expressing or improving physical fitness and mental well-being, forming social relationships or obtaining results in competition at all levels.

The *Sport For All Charter* was launched in 1975 by the European Sport Ministers and subsequently adapted and updated across Europe. The values enshrined in this original charter were then important in underpinning most sport policy in European member states to date, including the UK. The Sport Charter provides a framework for sport in these countries, and ensures that the work in sport helps contribute to the wider objectives of the European Community. This is based on the principle that:

> ethical considerations leading to fair play are integral, and not optional elements, of all sports activity, sports policy and management, and apply to all levels of ability and commitment, including recreational as well as competitive sport.

The ethical consideration and the principle of fair play are therefore enshrined in European sport policy, underpinned by a code of sport ethics, shown below.

Council of Europe Code of Sport Ethics
Sport must be:

- Accessible to everyone
- Available for children and young people in particular
- Healthy and safe, fair and tolerant, building on high ethical values
- Capable of fostering personal self-fulfillment at all levels
- Respectful of the environment
- Protective of human dignity
- Against any kind of exploitation of those engaged in sport

Source: Council of Europe (2008): www.coe.int/t/dg4/sport/sportineurope/charter_en.asp

The Council of Europe definition reinforces the view that ethical considerations and fair play are essential elements of sport practice and require all institutions, organisations and individuals to be aware of their moral and ethical responsibilities.

Why sport matters

> [S]ports are precisely the sort of things we moderns care about, and care about passionately.
>
> (Morgan 2007: 8)

Sport is therefore not a trivial thing and so has deserved its attention from modern philosophers. Morgan has also confirmed that, as sport matters to many people globally, it is something that should be firmly seen as an end in itself, not as a means to an end, which is a common approach in modern sport policy and politics, for example.

It is possible to distinguish between types of sport, for example:

- *Aesthetic* (gymnastics or ice-skating) – where we may be scoring the 'performance'.
- *Purposive* (football, tennis) – the outcome is specified independently of the performance (goals scored, points won).
- *Team or individual, or according to the skill sets required* – striking and fielding, or invasion games for example.

The diversity in sport and the relative importance of skill in relation to sporting success provides many possibilities and great variation in potential experiences and outcomes. What sport means to any individual is quite unique. However, many agree, it is not always the 'best' player that wins, and the uncertainty of sporting outcomes means that sporting contests retain a great fascination, not just for those who play, but also those who watch or follow sport with great passion.

Despite only very few making it to the top or elite end of sport, it remains a passion for many to simply 'take part'; and if this is not possible, many seek pleasure in watching the contests between others as fans or spectators, or in nurturing the performance of others in coaching or volunteering. Sport can also therefore be about altruism as well as individualism. This is when individuals give up time and invest in helping provide sport to give benefits to others – we can see how important this is when we look at the scale and importance of volunteers in sport and their enormous significance, particularly in Europe, to the practise of sport.

Meaning and sport

Gaffney (2007) points out that a philosophical approach to sport attempts to explain it from the inside. So many people take part in or are engaged by sport because it is full of meaning to them. But this often takes many forms. He identified three concepts of meaning ascribed to sport:

- Sport possesses a value, such as signifying 'the good life' (sport becomes central to a person's life and they eat, sleep and 'live' football, for example).
- Sport provides some deeper almost spiritual meaning; sport becomes like a religion, so deep are the rituals and behaviours associated with it.
- Sport can replace warfare or conflict in a more socially acceptable expression of conflicting beliefs.

Time out

As an individual you might want to reflect on the relative 'meaning' and value *you* place on sport. How has this come about? From where (or who) have you been influenced? As a group, you might compare your experiences of sport and consider how sport values and beliefs are developed and transmitted.

The emergence of a philosophy of sport

Various authors in this area appear to agree that the birthplace of the philosophy of sport as an academic sub-discipline was the US from the mid-1960s to around 1972. As noted in Chapter 2, this was a period of intellectual and social 'revolt' and challenge to established academic disciplines of the time. The British Philosophy of Sport Association was only formed in 2002, very much influenced by the US approach of 'analytical philosophy', with European traditions looking at concepts of play, games and sport, to embracing ethics, logic and moral development through sport. Arguably, as philosophers from Plato to the modern day have addressed issues related to sport, the discipline has a long history, beyond a narrow emphasis on academic journals or professional recognition.

According to Morgan (2000), two particular developments that emerged in the 1970s were crucial to the growth of interest in the philosophical aspects of sport:

- the emergence of 'sport studies' from the more established field of Physical Education, displacing the dominant scientific approach;
- the new attention given to sport by mainstream philosophers, who previously dismissed sport as marginal or trivial.

Morgan (2000) also identified that 1972 marked the establishment of the Philosophic Society for the Study of Sport (PSSS) and 1974 saw the publication of the first issue of the *Journal of the Philosophy of Sport*.

Branches of philosophy and their essential features

Many authors agree that philosophers essentially consider three main questions:

- What is reality? (metaphysics)
- What is knowledge? (epistemology)
- What is value? (axiology)

While the sport sociologist would also examine sporting practices, like a game, they would tend to consider the social relations involved, so might look at the differences in engagement between social groups and/or the extent of personal choice and equality of opportunity. Sport psychologists might look at issues of personal motivation or the effect of activities on emotional level – what people enjoy or find exciting during the game. Sport philosophers, on the other hand, consider questions of the nature of the activity being undertaken, and the meaning or value of this to the individual, or indeed to the wider society. They are also concerned with issues of ethics and morals – about how the game is played, as well as the results.

What is a philosophical perspective of sport concerned with?

Ethic and morals are of central interest to sport studies students. Any week's news in the broadsheets can reveal an issue or problem that involves some philosophical debate. At the time of writing, such news included the question of whether it was ethical for someone to claim a wicket in a closely fought international match, when the batsman had been impeded by colliding with one of the fielders. According to the report in *The Times* (Hobson 2008: 74), the England cricket captain, Collingwood, was 'messing with the spirit of the game' in making an appeal, upheld by the umpire, for the New Zealand wicket. Collingwood later apologised and, when England lost the match, cricket commentator Mike Atherton (2008) stated that, 'the gods got it right in the end', implying that ultimately England did not win because of their unjust methods in attempting to gain advantage. It may have been within the 'letter of the law, to appeal, but it 'just wasn't cricket'.

Also reported extensively in the media on the same day was the government decision not to allow the Zimbabwe cricket team to tour England in 2009 (25 June 2008). The Department for Culture, Media and Sport (DCMS) had taken the unprecedented step of writing to the England and Wales Cricket Board (ECB), which led to the ECB severing ties with the Zimbabwean cricket authorities. This was reported as the government taking a 'moral lead', though it was also noted as helping to avoid any financial penalties for the ECB, as had happened with their refusal to play against Zimbabwe in the 2003 World Cup. Atherton, writing in *The Times*, appeared to criticise the ECB, despite their stand, as he noted:

> [O]nly now, after years of human rights abuses, has the ECB found the courage to speak. It appears that it is fine to be moral as long as it does not cost you money.
>
> (2008: 74)

This, then, reveals some interesting and deeply held views about cricket and about sport. These are clearly philosophical, in that they deal with issues regarding 'the spirit' or nature of sport, and also what is 'good' or bad in sport.

Key authors in philosophy

There are many philosophers who have influenced sport studies, even if they may not have written directly on sport at the time. Principal amongst these are the German philosopher, Kant (1724–1804), who proposed some important principles for moral philosophy, regarding duty and universally applied moral codes. Essentially, this could be summed up in the so-called 'golden rule': 'treat others as you wish to be treated yourself'. This essential moral philosophy has been particularly important in framing modern views about the fairness, rules and social justice in sport.

There is some value for sports studies students in examining in more detail some of the essentials of philosophy, as some of the sources and specialist texts in the philosophy of sport tend to be quite difficult and sometimes assume some prior knowledge. A recommended source text is Gensler (1998), which has an accompanying website. This chapter can only look closely at the application of philosophical ideas and approaches to sport so I have selected those which seem most appropriate for the sport studies student to focus upon.

Approaches in the philosophy of sport

A metaphysical approach looks at the activity and attempts to explain what it is that makes it 'sport' – and so distinguishes it from a game, play, dance or merely physical exercise. This approach looks at the distinctions to be drawn between sport and other forms of human movement or social practice. Some may argue that such distinctions are largely useless. They consider culture and history mark such changes in the perception of sport so that such intellectual activity is a rather wasted effort. Houlihan (1991) has argued that all such attempts are simply 'grey areas' and McFee (2004) has similarly dismissed this sort of debate as largely futile. Nevertheless, classifying sport forms has occupied many sport philosophers, and has been a key part of the US influence in this area.

What is the difference between 'games' and 'sports'? Is this merely a linguistic distinction or one of real difference in nature and purpose?

This sort of debate occupies a lot of space in books and journals in the philosophy of sport. Morgan (2007) includes useful reviews and chapters by many of the leading western authors in this area, though it is heavily biased towards the US writers. In his book, Suits (2007) describes the necessary and sufficient conditions for an activity to qualify as a sport: it is a game, with rules, which includes skill and the use of the body. It must also have achieved institutional stability (that is, recognition as an organisation).

Time out

How would you group or classify sports? Is it possible (or even worthwhile) to attempt to consider whether we consider horse racing alongside athletics as a sport? Look at what is included in the 'sport' section of the newspaper. What does this tell us about contemporary views of sport, games or play?

Sport for its own sake?

Philosophers have also considered how the issue of motivation, for example, can make an activity play-like or work-like. Sport can be either intrinsically or extrinsically rewarded. The intrinsic rewards of enjoyment and personal satisfaction are, according to Butcher and Schneider (2007), central to sport being played 'for its own sake'. Extrinsic rewards, such as medals or financial gain, can also be motivating, but they also mean that an activity becomes, for some, more like work than play, and so the relationship between fair play and ethics can sometimes become rather complicated.

This definition represents sport as a continuum between work and play, dependent upon the motivation of the individual participating. This helps in understanding the moral and ethical distinction between sport 'for its own sake' and professional or commercial sport; that is, the paradoxical or two-sided nature of sport – on the one hand, it is a very serious and important undertaking, signified by its economic importance, but on the other, it is meant to be enjoyed and is a meaningless pursuit. Many people consider golf 'a good walk ruined' and watching football, merely 22 grown men 'chasing a bag of wind around a field', or 'cheap pictures for TV'. However, this also gives us a clue as to why it is important to look at *how* the 'game' is played. We are constantly reminded that, in sport, taking part is important, not just winning. Every competition must have at least two sides, and will result in only one winner, with potentially many 'losers'.

For any sport, however, we would expect to see rules play a central part in defining what the sport is about and how it should be played. If, for every sport, we must also have some form of 'rule', this leads to an inevitable concern with what happens when rules get broken, either deliberately or unintentionally.

Despite its apparent futility, many see having a definition of sport as essential, so we can at least have some shared understanding of what it is we are discussing. There are also some more practical considerations; for example, if something is not recognised as a sport, how will it be eligible for government funding or support? Therefore, using the Council of Europe definition of sport above is useful, both for clarity, to foster shared understanding, and for pragmatic or practical reasons of organisation.

A good sport?

The central philosophical question regarding value in philosophy is concerned with axiology – or the judgement of good and bad or right and wrong. This is at the heart of ethics: how people ought to treat each other, or behave for the common good – so-called social ethics. Many believe this should be a prescriptive effort – rather than just describing *how* people treat each other, ethics should be about setting out appropriate behaviours or norms about how we *ought* to behave. As we have seen above, such ideas about appropriate behaviour are central to our views on sport.

Values are also to do with our views on the 'worth' of things. The notion of 'value' also considers the qualities of things. So, in aesthetics, we are concerned with judgements of what qualifies something as 'a work of art', or as sport, or how we can judge performance or expression.

An ethical or value-based enquiry of sport often seeks to address one of two questions:

- How should athletes treat each other in a sport setting?
- What forms of conduct and/or aids to performance are compatible with 'good practice' in sport?

This is broken down into two main groups, according to Morgan (2000). The first concerns sportsmanship, competition, cheating, equity issues and the treatment of animals in sport. The second concerns the use of performance-enhancing drugs, ethical performance enhancement, rules and ergogenic aids. We examine selected ethical issues below.

Cheating is also something that most sport participants would have either an opinion on or direct experience of. Not surprisingly, therefore, a great deal of current work in sport philosophy is about cheating in all its various forms – what is cheating, how is this defined and what does it tell us about sport (and sport performers?).

One of the features of modern sport is that it is widely accepted that sport should be more accessible to all sections of society, as identified in the European Charter above. Therefore a concern for equity, or equality of opportunity, is central to sport values, and has underpinned much sport policy, particularly the development of more inclusive sport and the promotion of equality standards, in relation to ethnicity, gender and disability in particular.

Finally, concerns about performance enhancement and technical advancement are very much at the forefront of sport, in the drive for continually increasing standards of performance – the implications for performers and professionals in all aspects of sport practice are therefore at the heart of ethical codes of practice. These codes reinforce the need for all students of sport, especially scientists involved with testing or research into sport performance, or anyone coming into contact with young people in sport, to have an understanding and awareness of the ethical and moral debates in this area.

Ethical issues, debates and concerns in sport

A so-called normative approach sets out how people should behave, in this case in sporting contexts. This section addresses ethical issues that are often raised in sport studies courses, such as:

- What is 'fair play' and why is it so important in sport?
- Is competition a 'good thing'?
- What is ethical sport practice?
- What is so 'good' about sport?
- What happens when things go wrong?
- How far can we push the rules to get advantage over our opponents?
- What is the value of sport?

Our understanding of what is 'normal' behaviour depends on our expectations and beliefs about what is right, or preferable, in any situation. There are concerns about 'relativism' – that the norm may vary according to our 'opinion' about something or the values related to it. For example, in our society, violence towards someone is proscribed /prohibited by the law, yet boxing is allowed (albeit carefully regulated) and the goal of this sport is to harm the opponent. Behaviour that would be unlawful on the street is acceptable in the boxing ring.

What is 'right' and 'good' in the sporting context is often set out in both written and unwritten 'rules of the game'. For example, one such expectation is that you should treat your opponent with respect. We often prefer a good loser to a bad winner – for many, doing the right thing or playing in the right way is more important than the outcome of the contest. This might be because, as social beings, humans often have to work cooperatively as well as in competition, so having some basic and agreed standards or expectations of behaviour is to everyone's benefit.

Some argue that the attitudes toward sport are indicative of wider social values and are shaped by ideas of national identity and the particular values of that society at any given time in history. Hence, argued Morgan (2006: 2), at the turn of the twentieth century sport became a key vehicle for more progressive American values, in a 'highly fractured, ecocentrically riven society', polarised between rich and poor, and inequitable distribution of resources. Fair play and team spirit became a sort of 'moral antidote' to cure a fragmented and commercialised society. Morgan argues that modern day US society is largely ambivalent regarding these inequalities, responding to them 'with nothing stronger than a yawn'. He sees sport as playing a role in lowering social moral expectations in a modern US society based on consumerism, xenophobia and narcissism – and so as less likely to provide a moral vehicle for any higher purpose. This more critical view of sport is part of what he sees as a 'leftist' tradition (echoed by Eitzen 1999), which questions some of the assumed values and benefits of sport.

Morgan identifies two main groups of critics of modern sport:

- Those who argue that money is at the root of sport's ills.
- Those who argue that sport encourages 'sadism' or the humiliation of minority groups; that sport is contributing to the continuation of stereotypes and the abuse of women, homosexuals and ethnic minorities.

Morgan's moral case against sport is largely targeted towards the contemporary sport markets and commercial sport in the US, but can also be seen to some extent in Olympic or collegiate sport, due to increased commercialism. We will return to this argument in Chapter 5, on the business of sport, when we look at developments in the economics of sport.

Morgan further examines the relationship of sport and cultural values in national identity, by looking at its 'social imaginary', that is:

> [T]he way people imagine their social existence, how they fit with others, how things go on between them and their fellows, the expectations that are met, and the deeper normative notions and images that underlie these expectations.
> (Taylor, cited in Morgan, 2006: 167)

He provides the examples of baseball and American football as sports that are more revealing of the 'social imaginary' of America than others. Those sports that have been developed in the US have incorporated the concepts of personal freedom and equality that are enshrined in the constitution; even if such freedoms became widely available only more recently.

While the cooperative character of sport softens its more competitive tendencies, it also, Morgan argues, moralises them, as the concept of fairness is so central to sport. Though everyone should be treated equally in opportunity and conditions, they cannot be equally in results – there has to be a distinction based on performance, each must also have a fair chance to succeed. Sport is therefore the ultimate meritocracy and so fits well with the notion of the 'American Dream'.

We can make similar claims for sport and national identity in the UK, as many of the world sports emerged in Britain, and the concept of fair play became enshrined in our national culture.

The concept of 'fair play'

Fair play can be described as respect for the rules of the game and one's opponent, firmly based within a tradition of the philosophy of moral rules espoused by Kant. The origins of the concept of fair play can be traced to the public schools of nineteenth-century England and the 'Muscular Christianity' movement, which had its origins in Greek philosophy, referred to in Chapter 2.

According to Butcher and Schneider (2007), sport, as a preserve of the elite at that time, needed little explanation to aristocratic youth, destined for careers as leaders in the empire or commerce. However, with the growth of sport and eventual codification came the setting of 'rules' and penalties for misconduct or foul play, seen by many at the time as an insult as it would be unnecessary to penalise a 'real' gentleman who would never deliberately trip or hinder an opponent.

The democratisation of sport widened the social catchments for sport. This inclusion of 'working class' players, meant that previously taken for granted assumptions about conduct on the field of play by 'gentlemen' had to be agreed, codified and regulated. Subsequently, we have come to recognise 'fair play' as the way in which sport should be played, and to teach social values. The language of fair play – having a 'level playing field', being a 'team-player' – has thus become part of everyday language to represent these ideals.

Moral social values associated with and thus reinforced in sport include:

- compassion (to one's injured opponent, for example)
- fairness
- sportsmanship
- integrity/honesty

We might also expect justice (in the case of a referee making a decision) and responsibility and deference to, or respect for, officials, referees or judges. These sort of moral values are found across various societies and are recurring principles in some of the major religions that provide ethical guides to behaviour (such as the Bible and the Koran) (Butcher and Schneider, 2007). Based on their almost universal acceptance, we could conclude that honesty, respect and fairness are the underlying moral values in sport. However, not all sport is conducted in complete compliance with these expected standards, as we have already identified.

Time out

For a sport with which you are familiar, try to identify the unwritten rules that could be said to encapsulate the 'spirit of the game'. How important are these in learning how to play? Where and from whom do you learn these behaviours?

Sportsmanship and cheating

Please note that I use the term 'sportsmanship' in a non-gender specific way – it applies to both female and male performers! Sportsmanship is widely regarded as being essential to 'good sport' and an indicator of high personal moral standing or virtue, which are highly valued socially. However, sportsmanship is not always well defined and arguably is culturally determined.

Some behaviours that indicate a respect for your opponent are: 'walking' in cricket, before being given out by the umpire; acknowledging or apologising for a frame shot in tennis that results in winning a point; or applauding a good move or shot by an opponent.

On the other hand, we are also quite often aware of 'unsporting behaviour' or 'gamesmanship'. These are practices that show a lack of respect for the opponent, such as sledging, time wasting or distracting the attention of opponents in order to deceive. Unfortunately in sport, the most sportsmanlike are not always the most successful.

Much attention is given to the incidence of cheating and deception in sport. In some instances, however, sending your opponent the wrong way or practising a 'deception' may be considered a skill. A recent example, described below, indicates the various points of view on this – it may be skilful, but is it sporting?

Pietersen and the left-handed stance

This story was debated in the press after a game between England and South Africa in June 2008. Kevin Pietersen, a right-hander, changed his stance when the bowler approached, and swept the ball away into an open field, scoring four runs. Was it cheating or genius for Peiterson to change his stance and hit 'left-handed'? In cricket, the field is set and re-set if a left-handed batsman replaces a right-handed one. His critics argued that this move was against the 'spirit of the game'. Pietersen's fans would say this was highly skilled and innovative to gain advantage over his opponents. What do *you* think?

Whether we agree or not on the above, cheating to gain advantage over opponents has long been unacceptable in sport. There are many examples of cheats, both on the winning and losing side. There have been cases of ball tampering and match- fixing in cricket; similar cases occurred in World Series baseball in the 1930s, and English football experienced cases of match fixing in the 1960s and 1980s.

Unfortunately, much of the discussion of professional sport is about unsporting and unacceptable behaviour. So problematic is the situation that, in some cases, official recognition and/or support for sport or sport performers from commercial sponsors and the public has come under threat. In Australia, the Sweeney report has recently indicated a potential withdrawal of sponsorship funding to some Australian sports associated with poor off-field behaviour of high profile sporting stars. The Tour de France cycling race has seen sponsors withdraw rather than be associated with a sport so tainted by drug scandals.

The so-called 'logical incompatibility thesis' suggests that you cannot win if you cheat – but, as we know, in practical terms this does not deter some from trying. Some sports also retain in their disciplinary codes the notion of 'bringing the game into disrepute', or 'ungentlemanly conduct', which, you could argue, is a throwback to a long-gone moral code, which means sports participants should have the highest possible personal morals, in both private and public life (at least, if they fall short in the moral department, they should not be found out).

The activity below should encourage an examination of the 'ethos' of sportsmanship.

How relevant is the concept of 'fair play' in modern sport?

In his foreword to *Young People, Sport and Ethics*, the head of research for Sport England, Nick Rowe, noted that:

> Fair play is not an optional facet of sport; it is the very essence of sport. Without fair play – abiding by the rules and spirit of the game and respecting opponents and officials – sport becomes a perverse caricature of itself and serves to degrade rather than uplift the human spirit.
>
> (Rowe, cited in Lee 1998: i)

Perhaps most heartening in their research, was the finding that the notion of 'winning at all costs' was rejected by young people – more of them rated 'personal achievement' as more important. This research reinforced the responsibility of those in positions of influence and authority to maintain the right environment for young people to thrive and enjoy their sport. It also made clear that young people enter sport with positive moral values, and so the challenge for sport practitioners and professionals is to keep them thinking and behaving in this way.

This research also identified that young people felt that their coaches and clubs, teachers and schools, and friends or peers influenced their sporting values. For those performers on performance pathways, parents remained more influential, perhaps reflecting the extended influence and support in these environments.

Of some concern was that the research also identified that the use of banned substances, violence and aggression, and even professional misconduct (taking bribes, time-wasting, sledging), had been experienced in youth sports. Furthermore, though moral development has often been associated with team activities (traditional games), Lee's research found that 'socio-moral' values were more important to participants in individual sports than those in team sports. They also found girls attached less importance to winning than boys, though their 'values' tended to be similar. As children engaged more with clubs outside of school, the influence of teachers and even parents was reduced.

This research firmly undermined the notion that there was some form of 'moral crisis' in youth sport, as young athletes clearly believed in 'fair play' and rejected a 'win at all costs' approach. It also reinforced the notion that a sporting environment that was likely to retain the interest and enthusiasm of young people was a 'fair' and ethical one. As bullying, exploitation and an emphasis on winning were a 'turn off' for young people, it was also counter-productive to expect such behaviour to engage young people or to achieve success. Below, we will examine how such behaviour is prohibited by the various codes of conduct governing the work of coaches, development officers and scientists working in sport. However, it is clear that understanding ethics and fair play is an essential prerequisite for anyone considering a career working in sport. Whether or not this is so important for success in sport performance is another issue, however, and we consider the implications for professional sport later.

Activity

- Observe the activities at a junior sporting event or game. Consider the extent to which values of sportsmanship and respect for others are upheld on and off the pitch, by coaches, parents and players. Compare this to the behaviours in any comparable televised sport event.
- As a group, compare and contrast sporting and unsporting behaviour in various sports you have seen. Try to identify what indicates 'fair play' and the values your sports events or activities attempt to promote. Are the elite players in these sports more or less likely to illustrate 'sporting behaviour'?

Competition in sport

The issue of competition in youth sport, particularly in the status of competitive sport in physical education, has been quite a widely debated one in the UK, US and other western education systems since the 1970s. During the late 1980s and 1990s, sporting competition in British physical education and school sport largely declined due to the emergence of a more individual and inclusive approach to physical education. More recently, the notion of inter- and intra-school competition has enjoyed a resurgence, as the government has funded a new role in school sport, that of the competition manager, to coordinate this work across school sport partnerships in every county. The debate has at times been quite heated, and there remain some opponents to this move in schools among the PE profession.

For some, competitive activity, whether self-referent (beating your own performance/time) or against others, provides for the human need to be challenged, and offers a potential for risk, stimulation and uncertainty, missing in everyday life. Sport can provide the space and a safe environment for striving for personal improvement and the opportunity to meet and compete against others, providing fun and enjoyment in the trying as well as the succeeding. The research referred to above has shown how important this is for many young people.

For many, such competition can provide thrills and emotions – both high and low – they are unable or unlikely to achieve in 'normal life'. The so-called extreme sports can provide the more obvious examples of this adrenaline boost, but there are also more gentle challenges, in a game of golf for example, with great problem-solving potential. Which club to use? From what direction is the wind blowing? How far to the pin? The potential challenges in sports like golf are almost inexhaustible, given the courses, weather conditions and opponents you may face on each occasion.

The pursuit of excellence, in constantly striving to improve personal performance, is another feature of competition that means sport remains an important practice for achieving human satisfaction. The determination to win at any cost, however, may be said to exceed other important values in sport, such as playing by the rules; the over-emphasis on competition, is for some, thus inappropriate or potentially harmful. We need to remember that, as noted, sport has, because of its nature, more losers than winners. The challenge is to play the game 'right' (i.e. fairly) in competition, in order that everyone who competes at least gains something, even if it isn't possible for everyone to win.

Cheating and sport

Given the centrality of the notion of fair play and adherence to 'rules' in sport, a topical concern at any time is with the issue of cheating – either not playing by the rules or seeking an unfair advantage over opponents. Check out the news whenever you study this topic, and sport will undoubtedly throw up some useful examples and case studies for debate. The history of sport is littered with examples of cheats and villains as well as sporting heroes:

- Boris Uneshenko – USSR, Olympic modern pentathlete
- Ben Johnson – Canadian sprinter
- Hansie Cronje – South African cricket

Activity

Research the background and ethical issues relating to one of the above 'cheats'. Report back in a group discussion. You might discuss what appears to drive people towards cheating and what harm it does – to the individuals concerned, or their sport, or sport more generally

---

Drugs and anti-doping issues

Drugs in sport could be termed a 'hot topic' – in recent history, there seems always to be a current story in the news. At the time of writing, this included the jailing of Marion Jones, the American athlete, for her drug use and the on-going saga of Dwain Chambers the British athlete, who, after serving a two-year ban for taking banned substances, went on to challenge the British Olympic Association's life ban on competing in the Olympics (which he subsequently lost). The annual Tour de France means that at least once a year, sport pages across the globe will include a story about the apparently endemic use of drugs in professional cycling.

There are many arguments around the issue of drug use and abuse in sport. These include:

- cheating and unfairness
- harm
- perversion of sport

There are some interesting debates around these points, which could take up another chapter on their own; however, using the philosophical perspective, it could be possible to conduct a review of anti-doping as the 'default' position in sport, using some of the resources listed below. Drug use has been around a long time and, some would argue, is unlikely ever to be eradicated; whilst the rewards for sporting success make winning at all costs override the perceived harm or ethics of cheating.

The fair play argument about drugs is based on the fact that, as drugs are banned because seeking to gain advantage through using drugs is unfair, they are taken to increase (unfairly) the chance of winning. Critics of this argument suggest lots of advantages – good genetics, wealthy parents or the best equipment can also be 'unfair' in that not everyone has them, but this does not constitute cheating.

The harm that drugs do, to those taking them and to the sport, is also given as a reason for banning them. Again, the counter-argument might be that this would be down to personal choice rather than the control of sporting authorities. However, this is far from clear-cut, particularly with young athletes, and the disputed nature of some of the long-term consequences of drug use. Another argument is the perversion of sport: that drug taking is against the spirit of the sport or is 'unnatural'.

Whatever the argument, or your views of it, anti-doping activities occupy many sport scientists; those working in doping control, trying to find cheats, and those who attempt to find out more about their impacts and effects on performance.

Activity

- Go to the UK Sport website and investigate the substances that are banned and the system for monitoring and testing athletes in the UK.
- Identify the main types of banned substances.
- Give two examples of banned substances and their effects on performance.

Some questions to consider:

- Is the use of performance-enhancing drugs increasing or are we simply getting better at catching the cheats?
- How confident can we be in testing procedures? Identify some of the potential problems in the system.
- Which body regulates international anti-doping policy and maintains the 'banned list' of substances?

Discrimination and exclusion in sport

Arguably all sport is a case of discrimination, as in a more literal sense we are attempting to identify who is the best – by distinguishing one performer or team compared with others. However, in sport we have rules to 'even up' a contest to make sure it is a fair test of ability or performance. Examples of levelling the playing field include:

- a weight handicap in horse racing
- restrictions on the technology allowed in Formula 1 racing
- the handicap system in golf

Unfortunately, not all groups have equal access to sport, and there remain significant barriers to some, which undermine the positive benefits of sport; these problems include racism, sexism and homophobia, as well as the problems of those with varying disabilities. Such problems are underpinned by prejudice and stereotyping, and have led to sport being criticised as helping to reinforce inequality rather than combating it.

In the UK, we have campaigns that seek to 'Kick Racism out of Football' and an Equality Charter for sport, in order to respond to these problems, but these are relatively recent developments. Ending exclusion in sport remains an aspiration, while even the perception of discrimination continues to make sport unattractive to many minority groups.

A topic for debate: what is an unfair advantage?

In the case of the Paralympics and the participation of those with a disability in inclusive sport, there remain many issues and problems to resolve. For example, when does having some prosthetic or technological device give an athlete an advantage over their fellow competitors?

While it has long been accepted that sport should be inclusive, it is also accepted that this may not always mean competition between people with different disabilities, or the non-disabled playing alongside those with some disability. Hence we have Paralympic divisions according to the nature and extent of different (dis)abilities: wheelchair, non-wheelchair, amputees or cerebral palsy athletes all compete in divisions, even if they race or swim or ride together. In this way, the competition is made more 'fair' and those competing are given the appropriate aids to complete their event/performance.

Many competitors look to technology to help them improve their performance. In the Beijing Olympics, some swimmers had the advantage of a new form of all-in-one suit, made from a fabric designed to make them move more quickly through the water. This led to calls for the suit to be banned because it gave an unfair advantage to those who could afford this technological advance. This gives rise to the question, what types of advantage are 'fair'?

Why does Oscar Pretorious want to run in the mainstream rather than Paralympic Games? His attempt to be allowed to compete in the Beijing Olympics was unsuccessful, as the International Olympic Committee deemed his prosthetic limbs gave him an unfair advantage over athletes with 'normal' legs.

If it is later confirmed that Oscar Pretorius has no 'unfair advantage' in his prosthetic limbs, to what extent does this give some incentive for scientists to come up with artificial limbs that would make a 'super-athlete'. Could the 'super-athlete' be achieved through genetic engineering?

> The limits to human performance may soon be reached, given the amount of science now applied to training and preparation for competition. The desire to go that bit further to achieve success means that bio-engineering and genetic manipulation may be considered both possible and acceptable in the future. The sort of debates we now have about anti-doping may well be extended into the field of genetic 'doping'.

Philosophy in action: a personal philosophy of sport

Debates about advantage, fairness and ethics mean that any practical work that complements sport studies needs to reinforce the need for 'informed consent' and respect for persons. For example, in sport science, study participants are expected to give informed consent and should expect to be protected from any potential harm resulting from an experiment or test. In many sport studies programmes, looking at philosophical and ethical aspects of sport includes the use of scenarios for ethical debates, such as issues in coaching young people, child protection or exploitation. Anyone working in sport, whether professionally or as a volunteer, also needs to comply with their legal obligations in anti-discriminatory practices and child protection.

Laws and the legislative framework in sport

Background checks on those involved with working with children are needed for both sport volunteers and professionals. The Criminal Records Bureau (CRB) has been operating since 2002 and provides prospective employers with background checks on the suitability of applicants. Governing bodies are also strongly advised to do similar checks on volunteers, particularly where unsupervised access to young people is involved. The Children Act (2004) and *Working Together to Safeguard Children* (2006) are important documents for sport and leisure agencies to be aware of, as they set out the important role such agencies play in safeguarding children. The NSPCC is also interested in child protection in sport and has published guides and resources to help support professionals in protecting themselves and their young athletes from harmful practices (see Further study for website details).

Ethical codes in sport

Ethical codes you may need to be aware of in sport relate to professional specialism, or bodies regulating the activity of specialists in a particular field. Sport coaches and others working in sport need to adhere to these over and above any specific technical or sporting qualifications they have. These ethical codes include:

- Associate for Physical Education (AfPE, formerly PEAUK)
- Sport coaching (sportscoachUK),
- Sport science (BASES)
- Sport development and management of sport (ISPAL)

For other careers in sport, more details of ethical guidelines are available from Skills Active, the industry body responsible for vocational qualifications and training. (See the Further study section for links to the relevant ethical codes for the specialist areas.)

What these codes all have in common is that they set out the prescribed or expected standards of behaviour for professionals practising in sport. Often such professionals have what is termed a 'duty of care' to their athletes, performers or clients. They need to act in a manner that is non-exploitative, non-discriminatory and non-harming. As with other professionals, coaches and sport scientists are expected to adhere to rules of confidentiality, integrity and respect. Some codes refer to behaviour that is unacceptable or prohibited due to the position of power or authority the professional may be in, and have specific requirements regarding young people. There is also usually some note of the limits to the authority of the professional and guidance on when they must refer to higher authority in relation to particular issues or concerns.

A code of ethics might include additional guidelines for 'good practice' that professionals may be expected to adhere to. In many cases, there will be reference to disciplinary or monitoring procedures in the event that any complaints are made. It is clear, therefore, that if aiming for a career in sport, either as a professional coach, administrator or performer, it will be essential to acknowledge and respect a relevant moral and ethical framework.

Particularly when financed with public funds, the practices of all sport organisations are subject to external scrutiny; ethical professional practices thus extend to all aspects of the work of sport, not just the 'face to face' dealings between individuals or on the sport field, but also in how sport is organised and managed.

Sometimes the conflict between aiming for better or higher performance and the interests of individuals or teams can lead to some dilemmas for the coach, teacher or sport scientist. They sometimes have to decide not just what is best, but what is 'right' in a particular set of circumstances. Such guides and codes are therefore essential in setting out the expectations of the sport or the profession, even if they cannot cover every eventuality.

Activity

From the Further study section below, choose an organisation from the online sources, read their code and note the key concerns it is designed to address.

Based on your own experience of sport, and perhaps following a discussion with your fellow students, identify some of the moral dilemmas a professional (coach, teacher, sport scientist, development officer) may have to face. You may want to bring in some examples of experiences you have had or examples of behaviour you have seen on or off the field of play, and discuss their ethical or moral dimensions with your group.

Review

Sport is important from an ethical and moral standpoint, precisely because so many care so deeply about it and it is so significant in contemporary society. By examining the work of philosophers over many centuries, there are many relevant perspectives on the nature, meanings and purpose of sport in modern society. It is clearly more than a 'mere diversion' and a far from trivial pursuit.

Sport provides the opportunity for many ethical debates and throws up many examples and situations where we need to consider moral questions of what is right or appropriate behaviour. For those working in or studying sport, various codes of behaviour are relevant and help guide ethical practices.

This chapter has set out an introduction to some of the essential aspects of philosophy and ethics in sport. There are numerous examples of both good and poor practice in sport happening every day, and personal experience can add to our understanding of the implications of these actions and activities. As any professional in sport is expected to adhere to an ethical code of practice, it is important to be able to recognise the basis of such codes and understand their purpose. Having a personal philosophy of sport will be important if you aim to work in sport, but is also important to students of sport who seek to understand the deeper meanings and interactions of sport from a philosophical perspective.

Further study

On issues of sexual exploitation:
- Brackenridge, C.H. (2001) *Spoilsports: Understanding and Preventing Sexual Exploitation in Sport*. London: Routledge

For specific chapters on the ethics of sport, including contributions on fair play, ethics in PE and coaching, violence and cheating, with mainly British authors:
- McNamee, M.J. and Parry, S.J. (eds) (1998) *Ethics and Sport*. London: Routledge
- Morgan, W.J. (ed.) (2000) *Ethics in Sport* (2nd edition). Champaign, IL: Human Kinetics – this book covers a very good range of ethical issues, with up to date examples and applications, though with a mainly US focus or context. Leading authors offer chapters on doping, performance sport and genetic engineering, gender equality, and violence and other topical issues in sport ethics.

For an exploration of the philosophy of performance or elite sport, see:
- Culbertson, L. (2005) The paradox of bad faith and elite competitive sport, *Journal of Philosophy of Sport*, 32(1): 65–86

For an interesting book on the potential of genetics and biomedical advances in sport, see:
- Miah, A. (2004) *Genetically Modified Athletes: Biomedical Ethics, Gene Doping and Sport*. London: Routledge

Online sources:
- A fully annotated bibliography and resource guide is available from the LTSN: www.heacademy.ac.uk/assets/hlst/documents/resources/philosophy_ethics_sport.pdf
- Organisations with relevant codes of conduct or ethical guidelines include:
  o Sportscoachuk, for advice on codes of practice and ethical guidance for coaches, particularly on equity in coaching: www.sportscoachuk.org.

    o Association for Physical Education (afPE): www.afpe.org.uk.
    o BASES – Code of Conduct for Sport Scientists: www.bases.org.uk/pdf/Code%20of%20Conduct%20MASTER.pdf
    o NSPCC child protection in sport: http://www.thecpsu.org.uk/Scripts/content/Default.asp
    o Skills Active: www.skillsactive.com
- Philosophy:
    o Gensler's philosphy pages: www.jcu.edu/philosophy/gensler/exercise.htm – provide some self-test questions to check your understanding of the basics of philosophy. The companion book (see References below) is recommended for additional background reading on the essentials of philosophy.

Journals:
- *Journal of the Philosophy of Sport*
- *Journal of Sport and Social Issues*
- *Sport, Ethics and Philosophy*

Additional resources and guides.
- Drugs in sport – visit the web for audio-visual resources. There are occasionally special media programmes on the subject of drugs or cheating in sport. For example, Radio 4's The Long View current affairs programme did an edition on 'Cheating and Drugs in Sport' which was originally broadcast in 2003 but still available to listen to in 2008. You can check the BBC archives for other or more recent examples or other programmes: www.bbc.co.uk/radio4/history/longview/longview_20031014.shtml.
- For an interesting view on the ethics of drug use in sport, including video presentations from the Oxford University Centre for Practical Ethics, see: www.practicalethics.ox.ac.uk/Resources/Enhancement_Sport/drugsinsport_resources.htm.
- For coverage of ethical issues in the media, see: www.bbc.co.uk/religion/ethics/sport/bibliography.shtml – this site has various resources, including video clips, academic papers and newspaper articles.
- UK Sport: www.uksport.gov.uk/generic_template.asp?id=12170 – this site has more about the rules and regulations of anti-doping. The latest programme on education is called *100% ME*.
- British Association for the Philosophy of Sport – www.philosophyofsport.org.uk/journal.htm.

Contemporary sport: the significance of sport in the UK and key players in the sector

Chapter 4

Who runs sport? The political and legal framework for sport in the UK

Introduction

In earlier chapters, the early organisation and governance of sport has been both historically and sociologically examined. We have also considered the nature of sport, and the ethics that influence the way in which sport is managed and delivered today. How sport is managed and delivered within contemporary sporting structures and political systems of today is the concern of this chapter.

We look firstly at the roles and responsibilities of central and local government and how government currently influences and supports sport participation and provision. There are also sections that look at the commercial and voluntary sector and key organisations in the UK, including governing bodies of sport. It is important to be able to identify the features of governing bodies in order to see both the range of and the limits to their influence, particularly how they interact with other agencies and organisations.

Sport is a complex and multi-layered social phenomenon, often criticised for being fragmented and lacking cohesion in policy. As we have already seen in previous chapters, the current sporting structures in the UK have emerged in a rather haphazard way over more than 100 years. After reading this chapter, you should be in a better position to understand the fragmented nature of the UK structure for sport and the complexity of the inter-organisational relations.

Organisations in sport are often competing with each other for resources, participants or funds and yet a great deal is achieved through partnerships between different organisations with different but complementary interests. It is important also to recognise that much informal sport and physical activity also goes on outside of these organisations but is nevertheless influenced by the policies and regulations that affect the sector.

Sport is a fascinating area in which to see policies and programmes from a range of organisations working together (or not). Houlihan (1997) has described sport as a policy community, with many overlapping and sometimes competing interest groups, linked together by resources and common concerns, working in a sometimes 'crowded' policy space. Sport, because of its activities and influences in society and individuals, reaches into many other spheres of life, and there are bodies, outside of sport organisations, with strong influences on how sport is experienced and enjoyed. Trying to determine 'who runs sport?' is not an easy task!

Central and local government

As we saw in Chapter 2, it is only in more recent times that the UK government has become directly concerned with sport. In the latter part of the twentieth century, as sport became more organised, commercial and international, successive governments increasingly sought to regulate, direct or influence what was happening in sport organisations. Indeed, the support of government for sport has become increasingly expected, as the status and prowess of the nation at sporting events has been often equated with success and power on the world stage. This has been well illustrated by the extent of government support in the preparation of the bid for the London 2012 Olympics and the subsequent investment to enable the Games to go ahead. The increasing politicisation of sport has been a trend seen internationally – many governments recognise the political value of sport because it matters so much to so many people and has been found to be a useful vehicle for achieving other political objectives.

Government and sport interact at many levels and through various agencies. To gain an understanding of how sport is organised, we first need to appreciate the way in which government is organised and the relatively complex central, regional and local arrangements that have a bearing on how sport is delivered and managed.

Political structures in the UK

In the UK, which comprises England, Scotland, Wales and Northern Ireland, central government is represented by the Parliamentary system. Members of Parliament (MPs) are elected to the House of Commons, and there is a second, unelected body in the House of Lords. The elected government, with various departments to carry out policies, has an executive based on the Cabinet – senior ministers, usually MPs, who are selected by the Prime Minister. There is also 'devolved government' in Scotland, Wales and Northern Ireland. This means there are specific powers devolved to vary the legislation or policies from Parliament based in Westminster. This further complicates any chapter attempting to cover the political and legal framework for sport in the UK. To investigate the specific regulation of sport in Scotland, Northern Ireland or Wales, you must also consider the specific regulation or policy from the respective assembly or parliament of the home country. Where possible, some key distinctions are noted below.

How does the UK government influence sport?

The government can directly influence sport through legislation, policy guidelines, funding (direct or indirect), permissive powers, taxation and subsidy, or promotion of policies. The government has set a series of targets for its various departments, some of which directly relate to sport; others are related to wider issues such as access and inclusion, or health and wellbeing, to which sport is expected to contribute.

The government department with direct responsibility for sport-related policy is the Department for Culture, Media and Sport (DCMS). As well as being the home department for the Minister of Sport, the DCMS also regulates the media, which includes the power to protect sports events deemed to be important to the public from being shown exclusively on subscription channels.

Other departments and their influences

- Department of Health (DOH) – responsible for promotion of health and physical activity, anti-obesity strategies
- Department for Children, Schools and the Family (DCSF), the former Department for Education and Skills (DfES) – responsible for physical education in schools, school sport, qualifications in sport coaching
- The Department of Innovation, Universities and Skills (DIUS) – responsible for industry lead bodies for vocational aspects of sport, including Skills Active, university qualifications in sport
- Department of Transport and the Regions (DTR) – responsible for planning policy guidelines on the use of open spaces and the use of playing fields
- Department of Communities and Local Government (DCLG) (formerly Office of the Deputy Prime Minister (ODPM) – responsible for local authority sport, inspections of local authority sport and recreation provision through the Audit Commission
- Department of Environment, Food and Rural Affairs (DEFRA) – responsible for sport taking place in rural areas, outdoor activities regulation
- HM Revenue and Customs – responsible for VAT and tax on organisations in sport, particularly in the commercial sector, but also private member sports clubs
- Home Office – responsible for Criminal Records Bureau vetting of those who work with children in sport, supporting sport and anti-crime programmes, such as Positive Futures

The DCMS funds agencies that are classified as non-departmental public bodies (NDPBs), with responsibility for aspects of sport policy:

- Sport England
- UK Sport
- Lottery Sport Fund

They also fund the Football Foundation (through links with gambling and licensing) and London 2012, through the Olympic Delivery Authority.

As noted above, the Minister for Sport, who in 2009 was Gerry Sutcliffe, is based in the DCMS reporting to the Secretary of State for Culture, Media and Sport, Andy Burnham. The UK only appointed its first Minister for Sport in the 1960s. The 'home' of sport has since moved from various departments, from the Department for the Environment, to the Department of Education and Science, to the Department of National Heritage in the 1990s. This perhaps indicates that, for many governments, sport has not occupied a very central role in their policies.

Government funding for sport

- *Exchequer funding* – goes direct to Sport England and UK Sport via the DCMS and to other home country Sports Councils via the Welsh or Northern Irish Assembly or Scottish parliament.
- *Lottery funding* – this is much larger, as more than a billion pounds of funding went into sport projects between 1995 and 2002, though amounts to Scotland, Ireland and Wales are smaller, based on population, and distributed via the National Lottery Distribution Fund.

In 1999/2000, total government investment in sport was £2.2 billion (excluding DoH spending on physical activity). Over £1 billion of the funding was through the block grant given to local authorities, for environmental and cultural services and for use in school sport. Similar amounts have been provided throughout the years since, with the current level of investment standing at about £1.8 billion per year (Carter 2005), though this does not include additional investment into the preparations for the London 2102 Games. The government has set aside a budget of £9.4 billion to deliver the Games in 2012.

Though it's not all that clear whether or not government should be involved in sport, investment into sport, particularly in recent years, has become very significant. There is no doubt that in the current political climate, sport is recognised as important for health, education and social cohesion.

Though sport can be enjoyed for its own sake, governments tend to get involved where it can bring national prestige and substantial economic activity or could contribute to achieving some other social objectives. Despite the figures listed above, the amounts provided to sport have been significantly less than those provided to the Arts, the Arts Council and to provide libraries, museums and galleries. As political choices and priorities change, so governments need to ensure the spending they do is actually achieving their objectives.

The Blair Labour Government published their policy for sport, *Sporting Future for All*, in 2000. This had two priorities:

- more people of all ages and social groups taking part in sport;
- more successes for top competitors and teams in international competition.

In 2001, the Labour party's election manifesto identified a third:

- the successful hosting of major sporting events.

There were three main strands to this policy:

- Sport in education
- Sport in the community
- World class programmes

However, the government was concerned that, despite having a policy for sport, the ability to deliver the outcomes and coordinate the work of various bodies, inside and outside of government, was hampered by a lack of strategic planning and decision making.

As a result of concern over their support for sport, a major review of government involvement in sport took place in 2002. The Cabinet Office and Policy Innovation Unit, in conjunction with the DCMS, conducted a major study and their report, *Game Plan*, was published in December 2002. Having taken evidence from a range of sources, and considering all the ways in which the government supported sport, both directly and indirectly, this report had a very significant effect on the way in which sport has been supported by government since. Despite the claims in *The Times* (2008) that the report had been 'secret', it no doubt shaped the emphasis on sport and physical activity in subsequent Sport England policy. The news that this was considered a secret report no doubt came as a great surprise to the many sport studies students who had been reading and analysing the report ever since it was published (and made available via the DCMS website). Even though this report was so significant, the government did appear to disregard the limited evidence of benefits to sport participation through major games, when it subsequently supported the London 2102 bid.

There was also a review of the work of Sport England in 2001, which resulted in some reorganisation and, once *Game Plan* was published, a new emphasis on sports participation. This trend has continued in the more recent review (2008) of Sport England's strategy. The extent of government influence on the policies of Sport England is perhaps not surprising, as they fund the agency to carry out their policy, but there is some criticism that this is at the expense of the 'arm's length' principle, under which the original GB Sports Council's Royal Charter was established.

Why did the UK government recognise that sport was important?

Although sport is an enjoyable pastime and a passion for many, some governments would consider that such activity is a private concern and not something they should interfere with. However, sport was recognised as having the potential to contribute to a number of beneficial social outcomes by UK government:

- *Health and education* – participation in sport can benefit health and well-being, and bring educational advantages.
- *Social cohesion* – sport participation can bring different social groups together and revitalise disadvantaged communities.

- *Employment* – sport can bring jobs, tourism and spending to areas, e.g. on construction, retail goods for sport and equipment, event spectators.
- *Image and national pride* – sporting success can provide a source for positive images of the country abroad and boost national pride.
- *Social interaction* – major events can provide significant social experiences (The Ashes in 2005 and the Manchester Commonwealth Games in 2002 provide good examples of this).

Game Plan looked carefully at the evidence for these potential contributions in order to see if they justified continued government intervention and spending. The Strategy Unit also looked at whether local government, which we examine below, was better placed to deliver local objectives.

Activity

Many people argue that the state should stay out of sport – if people want to play or take part in something it should be up to them and at their expense.

- What are the arguments for providing support for sport out of public money?
- What are the arguments against state support for sport?

You could debate these different views in a group situation.

What was the Game Plan?

The *Game Plan* report found that, in active participation, the UK clearly lagged behind her European neighbours, with a clear decline with age and in some social groups. For example, only 32 per cent of adults reported taking 30 minutes of 'moderate exercise' five times a week, compared with 70 per cent of Finns taking three hours per week of exercise or physical activity.

However, the UK was found to be performing reasonably well in international sport, if not always in the most popular sports. In a ranking exercise that looked at success in international events in 60 sports, the UK came third, behind the US and Australia. The report also found that mega or major events had not always been successful, but the positive impacts of the Manchester Commonwealth Games in the summer of 2002 was seen as pivotal in demonstrating the potential benefits of such events for national prestige and regeneration of local areas.

Overall the plan recommended a 'twin track' approach that involved:

- developing participation;
- developing success internationally.

Recommendations were made in four areas:

- *Grass roots participation*: where a wide range of initiatives were needed, with a focus on disadvantaged groups, in order to tackle barriers such as cost, information and motivation.
- *High performance sport*: with a need for better prioritising of which sports would be supported and improvements to delivery of services to top athletes.
- *Mega sporting events*: a more cautious approach to hosting events, with clearer assessments of benefits.
- *Delivery*: organisational reforms were needed before more government funding could be offered, and more cooperation across sectors.

The aim was to mirror the Australian success at high performance sport, whilst at the same time achieving the sort of participation figures enjoyed by Finland, where 70 per cent of adults were taking part in regular sport or exercise. Of course, this was not without its critics; as Collins (2003) pointed out, the targets set were both ambitious and arguably unrealistic, given the existing UK sporting base.

Similar reviews took place in Wales and Scotland, as their home country sports councils, parliaments and elected assemblies were in a position to consider some alternative priorities. An example of such specific decisions was that the Welsh Assembly decided to offer free swimming for children under 16 in holiday periods across the country.

One of the key developments in government policy after *Game Plan* was the *Physical Education, School Sport and Club Links* (PESSCL) strategy, which received additional funding and more significant help through the Lottery-funded New Opportunities Fund. The strategy was also important in bringing additional resources into sport via School Sport Partnerships, supported by the Youth Sport Trust and the DfES, later the DfCSF.

Once the London 2012 Olympic Games were awarded in 2005, additional funding and support was also provided by government through the Olympic and Paralympic Games Act 2006. The levels of funding for the Games have come under increasing scrutiny as the costs associated with hosting them have risen to over £9 billion – not all of this is about sport, but about regeneration, infrastructure and security.

The DCMS plays a key role in the delivery of a range of government Public Service Agreement (PSA) targets and leads on one: PSA 22 – Olympics and PE and School Sport. The aim of this PSA is to:

Deliver a successful Olympic Games and Paralympic Games with a sustainable legacy and get more children and young people taking part in high quality PE and sport.

(DCMS 2008)

The DCMS is also involved in supporting the achievement of PSA 21 – 'to build more cohesive, empowered and active communities' – through supporting Sport England and the local authorities to increase the percentage of people who participate in culture or sport.

In Wales, Scotland and Northern Ireland, the specific targets related to their national priorities have been set in additional plans and strategies, which mirror the approach taken in England, so, though the levels of funding are lower, there are similar schemes and initiatives in place.

Activity

As information in textbooks like this can quickly go out of date, for example if there is a general election or cabinet reshuffle, information about government policies and even the names of the departments can be changed. Go to the website of the DCMS (www.dcms.gov.uk) and identify the latest government reports on progress towards participation targets or how the plans for the 2012 Olympics are going along.

Local government and sport

Local government is essentially about delivering local services to communities, whereby elected representatives decide on local policies, and an executive – employed by the local authority – carries them out. The system of local government in the UK is relatively stable, though some important changes having taken place since the 1970s, which have impacted quite considerably on the provision of sport and recreation. For example, the introduction of Compulsory Competitive Tendering (CCT), in 1988, introduced private contractors into the operation of publicly provided sport and leisure facilities.

The essential basis of the services provided locally was established by various acts from the late nineteenth and early twentieth centuries:

- Bath and Wash Houses Act 1875
- Public Health Acts 1875, 1936
- Physical Training and Recreation Act 1937

These Acts saw sport and recreation firmly placed within the social concerns relating to public health, hygiene and fitness. They gave 'permissive powers' to locally elected councils to provide facilities and services from local taxes, including sport and recreation.

In the 1960s and 1970s there was a growing call for 'sport for all', based on the European Sports Charter, outlined in Chapter 3, which meant that government grants (via the GB Sports Council) could be used to help fund the provision of sports facilities by local councils. These facilities were often subsidised by local councils who were seeking to maintain sport as part of their social welfare policies.

In the late 1980s, the Conservative Government introduced CCT as part of their reforms of local government finances. This meant that the management of public services provided in sport, recreation and leisure had to be offered to commercial companies if they were successful in submitting a tender for the contract. This has had the impact of more local authority facilities being operated by commercial contractors and non-profit-making trusts. More recently, the *Best Value* regulations of the Labour government have seen local authorities assessed on the effectiveness of their services and the potential for improvement of their management of sport and recreation provision. In Comprehensive Performance Assessments (CPAs) local councils now have to demonstrate how well their services meet local needs. Sport and recreation, however it's provided, is part of this assessment. Overall, the government has set PSA targets in adult sport participation, and access to services to which local authorities are expected to contribute.

The amount of money invested by local authorities into sport, particularly into facilities, has far outstripped that given to sport by central government via grants of the GB Sports Council throughout the 1970s and 1980s. By the late 1990s, though funding was under severe pressure, local councils were investing about £1 billion per year into sport in the UK. This level of funding has remained fairly consistent ever since.

The provision of sport by local authorities, borough or metropolitan borough councils is by 'permissive powers' given to local government by Parliament. Sport and recreation were identified as contributing to social welfare, and so local government was empowered to spend on sport provision for their local communities, from the income they collected locally – from charges or rates (now called the community charge) and from their block grant from central government. However, government does not specify how much of the block grant the local authority receives is to be spent on sport and recreation provision. Councils also have discretion over pricing for services and how they are provided, for example by contractors or 'in-house'. So, while the local authority has the discretion to devote resources to providing sport, it is not required to do so in any particular way, or to spend a specific amount of money. Therefore, sport is a 'discretionary' service, rather than a statutory one, such as housing or education, where the government sets out much clearer national standards.

As a result of this discretion, the services offered in local authorities differ a great deal, even between relatively close neighbours. Local authorities vary in how much they spend on providing sport, the way in which services are delivered, pricing, range and quality of provision, and development work. Areas can differ in the sports and activities provided or supported locally. Local authorities are given some performance targets relating to culture and sport, but these are quite limited. The efficiency and effectiveness of the services provided are monitored by the Audit Commission as a part of the *Best Value* approach. For example, councils are expected to monitor the proportion of young people who can swim 25 metres in their Best Value inspections. However, their CPA will look at the number of sports pitches per 1000 of population as the only performance indicator of their overall performance as a council. Arguably, again, this shows that sport occupies a relatively low level of priority for local as well as national government.

Figure 4.1 compares the prices charged for swimming in different cities in the UK. Though the differences are relatively small, it shows that different local authorities charge quite different rates for essentially the same activity. This basic price is also subject to many different concessions and each city council has its own approach to membership or discounted prices.

Generally, the local authority will focus on increasing participation in sport, and in making sport more accessible. In some of the larger authorities, some work is devoted to excellence – through provision of more enhanced competition or training facilities for particular sports. For example, Manchester City Council, following the Commonwealth Games in 2002, established regional centres of excellence for athletics, squash, swimming and hockey in the facilities built for the games. This was made possible by

Figure 4.1: Comparison of selected prices for adult swim in local authority pools
Source: author's own research into city council prices for standard adult swim, December 2008.

Adult Swim Price

governing bodies, Sport England, the English Institute of Sport and the City Council working together in partnership. The facilities provide for community and elite athletes as well as development work in local schools. This work is funded by income from the City of Manchester Stadium, through a unique 'waterfall' fund, paid for by the lease of the stadium to Manchester City Football Club.

What's the score? The current position of local authority sport

A recent Audit Commission report (2006) found various contributions made by councils to their local sport and recreation provision and government targets. They pointed out that, though the Local Government Act 2000 permits councils to spend their funds on providing sport as it seen as part of the local remit to 'secure the economic, social and environmental well-being of their residents', not all councils were performing well. The Audit Commission compared the provision by councils who operated their own facilities with those operated by private contractors or trusts. They found that the quality and accessibility of public sports and recreation facilities were in danger of failing to support and match the aspirations of the government in raising participation:

> Sports and recreation have a key role in health improvement, social inclusion, regeneration, community safety and educational achievement. How councils choose the level and range of public sports and recreation provision and how well they work in partnership with others will be significant in determining how effectively councils are exercising this power.
>
> (Audit Commission 2006: 9)

There has been an increasing trend for local authorities to consider setting up trusts to run their facilities because of the potential benefits for increased funding and tax or other efficiency savings. Many councils also have a specific plan or strategy for the development of sport, but not all. Some councils have a specific sports development unit to focus on issues of accessibility and non-facility-based work in communities.

However, as the Audit Commission makes clear, the general stock of sports centres has deteriorated in quality. In England, 65 per cent of council facilities are over 20 years old and capital public expenditure on sports and recreation has not kept pace with the deteriorating condition of facilities. Over the last ten years, council expenditure on sport and recreation has not increased significantly, accounting for only 1.4 per cent of the net current expenditure of councils. Over £0.5 billion investment was estimated to be necessary to keep the stock of facilities in working order. This was double, in real terms, the estimated required investment in 1995. The relatively stable level of funding is shown in Figure 4.2.

Therefore, the government of the day can set out policies for the local authorities to follow, but will sometimes only have limited powers to see they are carried out, unless they make such polices subject to strict legislation, specific guidance or conditional funding. The way in which sport operates, through such diverse funding and operational arrangements, makes any coherent delivery plan for sport very difficult for the government to manage.

The government agency involved in the provision of sport, Sport England, can work with local authorities to provide facilities and services, through the provision of grants

Figure 4.2: Capital and revenue expenditure on sport and recreation
Source: Audit Commission 2006

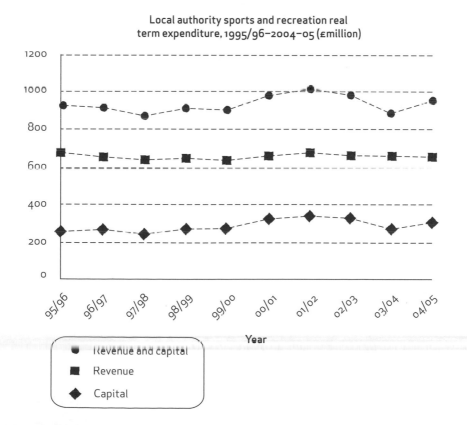

Local authority sports and recreation real
term expenditure, 1995/96–2004–05 (£million)

● Revenue and capital
■ Revenue
◆ Capital

or Lottery funding. They can also provide advocacy and information to councils or other bodies seeking to promote sport participation in certain areas; to help local councils achieve more effective local sport delivery, for example, by supporting local club developments. Also local authorities may go into partnerships or other arrangements with governing bodies or commercial organisations in order to provide services they want to offer in their local area. The next section looks at more of these types of organisation operating in sport in the UK.

Activity

- Draw up a list of the sort of facilities and services provided by your local authority. Compare these to those of other members of your group.
- Compile a table detailing the facilities provided by *all* authorities and those provided by only a few. Compare prices for activities such as swimming, or hiring a sports hall or a football pitch.
- Discuss why and how these differences exist and what the consequences may be in terms of opportunity and participation in the different areas.

Agencies and organisations in sport

A range of organisation types exist in sport, across three main sectors – public, voluntary/charitable and commercial/private. To add to the complication, there are local, regional and national structures for many of these organisations. *Game Plan* shows a notoriously complex diagram of organisations involved in sport in the UK. It is useful therefore to identify the key differences between organisations in terms of their legal status and methods of organisation. The key features of each type are listed in Table 4.1 (some organisations are in more than one category!).

Some of the key organisations in sport are examined in more detail below. Though it has been common to look at sport organisations by sector – commercial, voluntary or public – it is increasingly difficult to do so, as organisations in sport increasingly become involved in a complex range of activities, often cutting across traditional 'sector' boundaries. For example, many voluntary sector organisations get involved with commercial activities and employ professional officers to help them run more efficiently. There are also public sector organisations operating health and fitness or similar facilities on a more profit-oriented basis, in order to cross-subsidise other activities.

NGOs and the governing bodies of sport

Non-governmental organisations (NGOs) fulfil many different roles in UK sport – a situation that contributes to the complexity of how sport operates. One such organisation is the Central Council for Physical Recreation (CCPR), featured in the case study below. Other NGOs include the British Olympic Association (BOA) and the National Playing Fields Association (NPFA).

Table 4.1: Types of organisation in sport

Organisation	Main features	Examples
Non-departmental public bodies (NDPBs)	Quasi-independent from government. Run by council of representatives, some ministerial appointments	Sport England
Non-governmental organisations (NGOs)	Independent organisations with articles of association	CCPR
Public Limited Companies (PLCs)	Shareholders own stake in the organisation, run by a board of directors. Shares listed – available to buy	Commercial fitness clubs, some football clubs
Companies limited by guarantee (Co Ltd)	The liability of directors is limited. Must file accounts annually	Some governing bodies (England Hockey) or commercial sports clubs
Trusts	Not for profit distribution organisation, may or may not be registered charity, run by board of trustees	Youth Sport Trust
Private clubs and associations	Membership-based organisations – have their own constitution	Bowdon (Anytown) hockey, cricket and squash club
Professional bodies	Membership of specific professional grouping, representative or qualifications basis, often run by council of elected representatives	Institute of Sport, Parks and Leisure (ISPAL), Professional Footballers Association (PFA)
Charities	Not for profit organisations in education or other area, overseen by Charities Commission	Fairbridge (outdoor activity organisation)

CASE STUDY 1: THE CCPR

The CCPR started out as the CCPRT in 1935, an independent body representing the interests of the governing bodies of sport; it was renamed the CCPR in 1965. The CCPR originally owned and operated the National Sports Centres, such as Bisham Abbey, Lilleshall and Holme Pierrepont, but these assets were transferred to the GB Sports Council in 1972. In return, their activities have since been supported by grants from the government. The CCPR (www.ccpr.org.uk) currently represents 270 governing bodies of sport, in turn responsible for about 150,000 clubs, providing for 13 million regular sports participants – in activities ranging from country dancing to karate.

The CCPR actively campaigns for sporting organisations. Their mission is to 'promote, protect and provide resources for sport in Britain'. They act as a voice for the sport organisations they represent, and monitor government and other (for example, European Parliament) influences on how sport is delivered. Recently they have published various reports and documents presenting the case for greater support for sport from the government and they have successfully lobbied for changes to the rule for VAT for sports clubs.

- *Board /decision-making body* – Board, President HRH Duke of Edinburgh, a mixture of elected and executive directors. The General Council acts as policy and oversight body. Chief executive heads a small team of directors.
- *Key areas of work* – protection of the interests of sport bodies, campaigns to promote the work of governing bodies, services to support the work of governing bodies.

National governing bodies are those organisations that oversee the activities in a particular sport. They often have a national, regional and even county structure. Each sport has at least one governing body – unfortunately there are sometimes more than one organisation, particularly with newer or minority sports, running a sport. Boxing, for example, has five bodies concerned with governing the sport. It is useful to identify some essential features of a governing body, such as its membership and constitution, funding and policies. This helps to explain what it is able to do, and what limits there are to its powers and so its ability to contribute to targets or objectives, such as those set by government. The case study below sets out a typical body: England Hockey.

CASE STUDY 2: ENGLAND HOCKEY

England Hockey (www.englandhockey.co.uk) is the governing body for Hockey in England, affiliated to the European Hockey Association (EHA) and the International Hockey Federation (FIH).

Though hockey was an organised sport early in the twentieth century, a single governing body for the sport was only formed in 1996, when the bodies representing the men's, women's and mixed hockey games came together to form

CASE STUDY 2: CONTINUED

the England Hockey Association (EHA). This organisation got into financial difficulties in 2002 and so the new EH was formed, as a company limited by guarantee.

- *Board /decision-making body* – the Board is made up of the chairperson, with executive (employed by EH) and non-executive directors (elected), with some appointed/non-voting members, for example a Sport England representative.
- *Key areas of work*: international performance, youth and grass roots development, coaching and officiating, competitions and club services'
- Funding – income comes from affiliation fees, grants from UK Sport (for performance/elite work) and Sport England (grass roots and youth work) and some sponsorship. EH will receive some income relating to competitions, e.g. European Hockey Championships in 2007. In 2006/07, income from SE and UK Sport was about £3.6 million. In the 2008 allocation, hockey was to receive over £14 million for elite and performance plans from 2009–2013, to support their preparation for the London 2012 Olympics.

England Hockey's objectives are:

- attract more young people into the sport
- facilitate a thriving club infrastructure:
  - o more, better qualified coaches/umpires
  - o appropriate/accessible national facilities network
  - o excellent systems and support for volunteers
  - o challenging competition structure
  - o efficient administration tools
- international success at the highest level
- enhanced marketing and communications
- a broader income base
- effective and efficient operations

About 23,000 young people under 16 belong to a hockey club in England. There are 1050 affiliated clubs and about 85,000 members (Annual Report 2006). EH employs about 40 people, in various administrative, management, coaching, technical and development roles, in the national headquarters in Milton Keynes and in development centres in regions. An extensive network of volunteers in clubs, counties and regions supports this work.

One of the main purposes of a governing body is to regulate the sport, including overseeing the rules and competitions, such as leagues or championships. They may also run representative teams and work within the wider regulation of international organisations. For example, the Football Association works within the rules of both European (UEFA) and world football organisations (FIFA). However, in football there are also bodies which run the professional leagues – the English or Scottish Premier League, the Football League and the professional clubs themselves, which are independent businesses, some privately owned, some owned by their supporters, and even clubs listed on the stock exchange as public limited companies (plcs). This makes the question 'who runs football?' an interesting one.

Similar complexities also trouble rugby union and cricket, where there is considerable private ownership and investment into the professional game. Some of the boards or councils that operate the governing body have representation from the various sectors that make up their membership. Organisations differ in the make-up or constitution of the decision-making bodies and a 'modernising' process involving some of the larger governing bodies has been one of the key activities of CCPR and Sport England. Many governing bodies now have significant numbers of paid and professional staff, as their operations have become increasingly complex, commercial and specialised.

Some governing bodies benefit from their own very successful competitions, such as the Lawn Tennis Association (LTA), which receives a large proportion of its funds via the All England Club's profits from Wimbledon every year. Sport England recognises about 112 organised sports, and 420 governing bodies in the UK. The major sports governing bodies are all essentially competing for participants, members, government funding and recognition, as well as competing in their respective sporting arenas. Though much excellent work may go on in so-called 'minority sports', they tend to suffer from lack of support and recognition, as efforts tend to be concentrated on sports which already have significant support. This may mean relying on volunteers or non-professional staff. With London 2012 on the horizon, some lesser known in the UK but high profile Olympic sports, such as volleyball or handball, have received a recent boost, as the BOA and UK Sport have recognised the potential for the Olympics to grow and showcase them. However, due to the pressure on funding, not all of these sports get the level of funding they need to increase their performance standards.

So called 'grass roots' sport is represented by the clubs that provide nationally for the non-elite players or recreational players. Such clubs may affiliate or pay fees to their governing body, in order that they can be recognised and take part in organised competitions. The governing body may be able to stipulate conditions on the club, in order to admit them to membership or grade their provision. Clubs, through their fees and membership base, can therefore determine the relative strength of a governing body, but not all clubs will necessarily conform to standards laid down by the governing body. Not all clubs are affiliated to a governing body and some are affiliated to more than one; also not everyone playing a sport will belong to a club. Therefore it's difficult to estimate the true extent of grass roots sport, as some clubs or players are not affiliated to their respective governing body.

Sport England, in the Carter Review (2005), estimated there were about 106,000 clubs, though the CCPR puts this figure at 150,000 for the UK. In Scotland, Sport Scotland estimated about 13,000 clubs, while the Sports Council for Wales estimate there are 4600 in Wales. There is a lack of accurate, recent data on this figure therefore. The CCPR estimate that about 6.5 million people are members of sports clubs, with about 5.9 million people contributing voluntary work to sport in the UK. Though this sounds a lot, it still represents a relatively small proportion of the population. Membership of sports clubs by young people under 16 has remained fairly static, at about 46 per cent (Sport England 2003). All of the home countries in the UK recognise that increasing the proportion of young people involved in sports clubs is a priority.

Activity

- Complete a short case study on a selected sports club in your local area. Identify the main sources of income, what relationship it has to the governing body, who the members are and what benefits they receive. You should be able to get hold of the last set of accounts from the club treasurer.
- Interview one of the committee members to find out what sort of problems they face on a day-to-day basis.
- Try to identify the benefits the club brings to the local community.

Charities and charitable trusts

Broadly speaking, charities and charitable trusts often perform an important role where government or other public bodies may not be involved. In order to be a charity, organisations must be recognised by the Charities Commission and be registered as meeting important criteria, they must not benefit individuals and they must be 'not for profit' organisations. Once registered, the Commission then monitors their work to ensure they continue to operate appropriately. As a charity, an organisation may be exempt from certain charges, such as corporation tax, but it must reinvest all of its income back into its charitable work as it should be non-profit-making. The case study below explains the work of the Youth Sport Trust, now a significant partner in the delivery of governmental objectives in sport. Though the organisation is independent of the government, it nevertheless receives millions of pounds of funding in order to carry out its programmes in support of the PE and School Sport strategy, and other government initiatives relating to young people.

CASE STUDY 3: YOUTH SPORT TRUST

Established in 1994 as an independent charity by Sir John Beckwith, the Youth Sport Trust (www.youthsporttrust.org.uk) has grown to be an influential and important organisation in the delivery system for sport in the UK. The original Chief Executive, Sue Campbell, CBE, is now Chair of the Youth Sport Trust and UK Sport. The Youth Sport Trust is based at Loughborough.

Board/decision making is by a board of executive and non-executive directors, currently led by Sue Campbell, CBE. Chief Executive, Steve Grainger, MBE, leads the Senior Management Team.

Our mission
- Our mission is to build a brighter future for young people by enhancing the quality of their physical education (PE) and sporting opportunities.

CASE STUDY 3: CONTINUED

- We want to increase young people's participation and enjoyment of PE and school sport.
- We want young people to have the chance to experience and enjoy different types of activity at whatever level is right for them.
- We want to ensure youngsters receive the best teaching, coaching and resources possible and have the chance to progress if they show talent.
- We want to help our young people to live healthy and active lives and to be the best they can be.

Our core work
- Raising the standards of PE and school sport.
- Improving educational standards through sport.
- Getting more young people involved in sport.
- Creating opportunities for young leaders and volunteers.
- Supporting sporting talent in young people and a global sporting community.

Commercial sport organisations

The commercial sector in sport is becoming increasingly important, as sectors such as health and fitness continue to grow and commercial sports clubs have increased in their levels of economic activity. Since the 1970s, the number of private operators of sports and leisure facilities has increased, so that now private health and fitness clubs can boast more registered members than the public sector (Business in Sport and Leisure 2008; Leisure Database Company 2007) – 3.38 million members in 2003 compared to 2.46 in the public sector. By 2007, it was estimated that 12 per cent of the British population was a member of a health and fitness club in either the public or private sector. The big growth of health and fitness clubs took place in the 1990s and continues to increase – more clubs and increasing memberships every year. The potential for the future is very positive, with high rates of obesity and low levels of activity providing a lot of potential 'non-participants' still to aim for.

Government targets for increasing participation are also being helped by the commercial sector's desire to tap into new markets and provide attractive and more inclusive activity opportunities. The links between sports such as tennis and fitness clubs have also helped to maintain participation in this sport, despite the costs of such membership. Other commercial sports such as football, rugby and cricket also help to contribute to the economic and social impact of sport. However, they tend not to make huge profits due to the high expenditure on wages and stadia. Much of the income for commercial sport is based on the income from television rights, which is discussed in more detail in Chapter 5. Sport England estimates put the value of the income to the commercial sport sector at over £10.2 billion. The overall value of the sector is extremely difficult to estimate, but £9.8 billion of 'added-value' or 1.5 per cent of England's total comes from sport-related business.

The commercial sector is examined in more detail in Chapter 5 but includes:

* spectator sports
* participant sports
* sports-related manufacturing
* sports-related retailing
* sports-related media (Cambridge Econometrics 2003)

Membership of professional sports clubs and organisations is more likely to involve passive consumption or spectating at sport events, rather than active participation. However, significant numbers (about 17 per cent) of local sport facilities are operated by commercial companies, which is a result of the introduction of CCT in the 1990s. There has also been a growth of partnerships between commercial operators and public or other bodies, such as educational establishments. The main purpose of any organisation in the commercial or private sector is to increase the value of the business, to the benefit of the shareholders or owners. Some privately managed local provision has been praised by the Audit Commission for demonstrating effective management and good value for money, as noted above. However, private operators are sometimes reluctant to invest in long-term capital improvements of facilities they do not own if they have limited contract periods in which to recoup their investments.

The David Lloyd leisure chain, one of the pioneers of the commercial racquet/fitness club, was recently sold for £925 million, to a private holding company. It had previously been owned by the Whitbread company, who also own Costa Coffee and Premier Travel Inn.

Activity

* Investigate one of the organisations or agencies above – how do they influence the sport and activity provision in *your* local area?
* Go along to your nearest public sports facility – has the building been funded by one of the agencies above? When was it built? What sort of activities are provided? How affordable are the services for local people?
* Collect any background material you can about the organisations providing sport facilities in your area, such as their status – are they a private company, charity or public body? How do prices or ease of access vary between providers of different types?

Agencies and non-departmental public bodies

The government funds four separate Sports Councils in the UK, with UK Sport acting as the umbrella organisation for UK-wide issues:

* Sport England
* Sports Council Northern Ireland
* Sport Scotland
* Sports Council for Wales

These agencies are all funded from central government, or their devolved govern-ment in the case of Scotland, Wales and Northern Ireland. Each has specific policies and targets for participation and excellence.

They each support their own Institutes for Sport, for example providing support and specialist facilities for national squads or GB athletes based in their area. Sport England has nine sites that form the English Institute of Sport, including Loughborough, Manchester and Sheffield universities and the National Sport Centres, Bisham Abbey and Lilleshall. Wales has the National Sports Institute at Cardiff, and both Scotland and Northern Ireland also have their own elite institutes.

In 1999/2000, the various sports councils received £70 million in funds based partly on need and population. Current figures, annual reports on progress, current targets and strategies can be found on their respective websites, along with extensive free downloads of relevant documents and publications. In 2005/06, Sport England received £79 million of exchequer funding from the DCMS, not including funding given to specific projects such as 'Step into Sport' delivered by the Youth Sport Trust, or Lottery funding.

UK Sport received a further £30 million (DCMS 2006). Olympic funding is separate and in 2005/06 was approximately £40 million to support the work of preparing for the Games. Overall, there was £265 million invested into elite sport through UK sport, in the lead up to Beijing. With increasing pressure on finance due to global and national economic difficulties, the figure released to UK Sport to support London 2012 was £292 million, some £50 million short of that promised. This meant that some hard decisions had to be made about what sports could benefit and deliver the medal targets in 2012.

Sports Council Northern Ireland is sponsored by the Department for Culture, Arts and Leisure in the Northern Ireland Assembly. It received exchequer funding of about £29 million, with an additional £6 million being allocated via the National Lottery to Northern Ireland in 2008.

In Wales, funding to the Sports Council for Wales comes in the form of 'grant-in-aid' from the National Assembly of Wales of around £10 million per year, and additional funds of around £9 million per year from the National Lottery, for which Sports Council for Wales administers distribution.

Sport Scotland has recently merged with the Scottish Institute of Sport, so covers all levels of sport in Scotland. They received about £46 million from the Scottish government in 2007/08, with an additional £17.5 million in Lottery funding.

Sport England

Following a major review of the work of Sport England in 2004/05, the new priorities were very clearly focused on a more streamlined 'delivery system' of community sport and a greater emphasis on getting greater levels of participation. The vision for sport in England was set out in a framework document that highlighted the need for more and better evidence of the benefits of sport and also more targeted work with the less active segments of the population (Sport England 2004). Sport England is organised regionally, with nine offices, employing over 250 people. Their main role is 'advising, investing in and promoting community sport.'

The current Chief Executive, Jennie Price (as at December 2008), has delivered a new strategic plan for Sport England, with a clear focus on sport rather than physical activity. Due to the often rapid changes in this area, any work on Sport England should include a check on the latest position via the website. The SE board is made up of non-executive directors from the world of sport and business, health and other public bodies. A recent innovation is the establishment of the Active Places database, which enables a postcode or place name search of all local facilities for sport. It is also possible to check the activity level of your local area by searching the Active England resources. This has been informed by the biggest ever survey of activity in England. The Sport England website includes a great many useful publications and reports, research publications and resources to support the promotion of sport and activity, as well as links to governing bodies and other organisations involved in sport.

Legislation impacting on sport organisations

Organisations in sport suffer from the same sort of regulation and control as many other businesses, such as employment legislation, tax, trading standards, health and safety, environmental regulations, disability, sex or age discrimination and so on. If they are charities, trusts or private clubs, there are also additional legal requirements they must fulfil.

Some of the specific laws governing sport provision or impacting on the work of sport organisations have come about as responses to problems such as the Hillsborough Disaster in 1986, which brought about changes in the way football stadia were managed; or changes in policies and procedures by the government, such as the introduction of a National Lottery, with sport as one of the 'good causes'. Though we cannot provide a detailed legal framework here, due to the highly specialised nature of the area, it is useful to have a list of relevant legislation that has implications for the way in which sport is delivered and regulated.

There are particular regulations covering broadcasting, which mean certain sports events (the so-called *crown jewels*) are protected from being broadcast on subscription channels only, for example Wimbledon, some England football matches and the annual Oxford and Cambridge Boat Race. These have implications for the commercial activity around sports events as well as the profile these sports have on 'free to air' channels, as we see in Chapter 5.

Not surprisingly, due to the nature of sport activity, there are a number of relevant safety oriented areas of legislation impacting upon sport organisations, including:

- Various Health and Safety at Work Acts
- Occupiers Liability Act 1957
- Safety of Sports Grounds Act 1975
- Children Act 1989
- Activity Centres (Young Person's Safety) Act 1995
- Football Spectators Bill 1989
- Football (Disorder) Act 2000

Another significant document was the Taylor Report (1990), which stipulated that the top tier of football had to have all-seater stadia, subsidised by public funds. Unfortunately, many of these acts have come about because of accidents or deaths in or around sport; for example, the Hillsborough Disaster, which led to the Taylor Report, and the loss of life of four young people in a canoeing accident in Lyme Bay, which led to greater regulation of outdoor activity centres.

Other legislation:

- Betting, Gaming and Lotteries Act 1963
- Gaming Act 1968
- Lotteries and Amusement Act 1976
- Broadcasting Acts 1990, 1996
- Gambling Act 2005
- National Lottery Act 2006
- Olympic and Paralympic Games Act 2006

This final group covers legislation that regulates the world of gaming and is about how funding can be distributed by the government, the regulation of related taxation and licensing of venues.

Review

In this chapter we have looked at the central and local government structures and policies for sport and how roles and responsibilities are devolved across departments and levels of government. The diverse nature of local sport provision, supported by local government, has also been examined, showing the great variation in approaches and standards across the country. The range of organisational types and their objectives have also been identified, and case studies have examined the particular concerns of different organisational types. Finally, we have identified the various laws and regulations to which sport organisations are subject and which impact upon the sports industry.

The current system of sport organisations in the UK, despite efforts by the government for modernisation and streamlining, remains complex, fragmented and characterised by competition, overlapping responsibilities and conflicting interests. However, the political and economic landscape is subject to change and the London 2012 Games may provide a big impetus for organisational change and greater cooperation. There is evidence that the essential features of public, commercial and voluntary organisations are also changing and the boundaries between them are becoming increasingly blurred. Funding steams and decision-making processes become more complex as many organisations in sport are struggling to modernise and become more efficient and effective. Space has precluded looking closely at grass roots sport and the informal activity that forms the basis of much sport participation in the UK.

It is still difficult to answer the question 'Who runs sport?', as there is not a single, central core of authority in sport – much of it still operates at the grass roots without much help or intervention from government or commercial interests. This lack of cohesion and clarity may yet continue to limit the promotion and development of sport in the UK.

Further study

An excellent, classic text with relevant sections on UK government and sport is:
- Houlihan, B. (1997) *Sport, Policy and Politics: A Comparative Analysis*. London: Routledge – of particular interest is the section on the UK system in Chapters 2 and 3. You should note that the names of some departments may have changed and this book provides more theory on the nature of state involvement and the development of policy.
- Houlihan, B. and White, A. (2002) *The Politics of Sport Development*. London: Routledge – Chapter 4 looks at the Labour Government from 1997–2002 and their 'reinvigoration' of sports development, and provides a good overview of the policies of central government. There is also a chapter on sports development in four local authorities, which provides good examples and details of how sport strategies were put into action.

Online sources:
- The Carter Report (2005) *Review of National Sport Effort and Resources*. www.sportengland.org – provides an excellent summary of key statistics, data on sport and some international comparisons, with sources and links, to enable you to find any more recent updates.
- See the web for current practice and government involvement, as there is a wealth of freely available material about the workings of government and easily searchable resources from the government departments, local government, and various committees. One interesting source is the work of the House of Commons Select Committee of the DCMS, which has investigated swimming, rugby and women's football in recent years, as well as the issues around the Olympics.
- For the government's main site for open access, go to www.open.gov.uk or direct to the DCMS House of Commons Select Committee publications at www.publications.parliament.uk/pa/cm/cmcumeds.htm.
- For a direct link to government advice and links for other searches to find your nearest sports facilities, services and events: www.direct.gov.uk/en/HealthAndWellBeing/HealthyLiving/DG_4018931
- To find your local council: www.direct.gov.uk/en/Dl1/Directories/Localcouncils/index.htm.
- Reports by the Audit Commission are available from www.audit-commission.gov.uk.
- For information about the home country sport policies and sport councils, you should use the excellent resources on each of the respective websites:
  o Sport Scotland: www.sportscotland.org.uk
  o Sports Council for Wales: www.sports-council-wales.org.uk
  o Sports Council Northern Ireland: www.sportni.net

Chapter 5

'Show me the money!' Sport and business in the UK

How important is sport to the UK economy?

This chapter is essentially about the economic and commercial aspects of sport in the UK. We will establish just how important sport and activity is to our economy, and also how this relates to wider global trends and markets. We will link with earlier chapters as we examine some important trends, such as the influence of the media and the social responsibilities of sporting manufacturers and commercial sport organisations. Activities throughout the chapter and Further study are suggested, to help you to explore in more depth current and topical issues. The chapter will conclude by looking at the potential for employment in the sport sector, as a preparation for examining the skills needed for employment and to link with the following and final section of the book.

Learning outcomes

After completing this chapter and the related learning activities, you will be able to:
- identify the important sectors of sport industry in the UK and their contribution to the economy;
- list some of the most valuable sporting brands and identify their influences in global marketplaces;
- discuss the economic arguments around the London 2012 Olympic Games;
- identify the scale and significance of employment in the sport sector.

Sport: economic impacts and activities in the UK

Some essential economics

This section of the chapter will focus on the scale and significance of the sport sector in the UK and the prospects for the future, particularly in the regions. Sport has become of increasing economic significance, and now represents a major contribution to our national Gross Domestic Product (GDP) and employment. The numbers of people taking part in, watching or following sport means that the expenditure involved now equates to many billions of pounds every year – with little sign of this reducing. So, when looking at the economics of sport, we need to look at the broad, national or macro picture, as well as the demand for and supply of sport in the marketplace.

More attention tends to be given to the more glamorous or publicised elite end of the market: professional and international sport. However, much of the value in the sport market is due to the number of players involved in 'mass participation' or more active engagement with sport and recreation, as we will see below.

Gratton and Taylor (2000) categorise sport under these headings for economic analysis:

- Sport is a *non-durable consumption good* – benefits are generated at the time of consumption, rather than being something you can keep to enjoy time and again. A comparison would be to buy a ticket for the cinema, which unlike a record or film, you can only enjoy when you 'consume' it. This form of sport consumption can be applied to both watching and playing sport recreationally, where you are consuming the service – for example, a ticket to a football or other game, or a ticket to enable you to go swimming. The benefits from this sort of consumption can be intangible, or difficult to measure, though it is possible to see how much people spend, if they have a charge to pay.
- Sport can also be a *durable consumption good* – benefits from this sort of good or service can accrue over time, or be deferred till later. Sport activities can be paid for and enjoyed over time, but you will have benefits (in the form of health and fitness) that last past the experience of the activity. For example, purchasing a membership for a health club and improving your fitness through the training provided can give health benefits later. Having bought the membership, you can use this service as frequently as your club (and motivation!) will allow. Other durable consumer goods in sport are equipment and clothing.
- Sport is a *capital good* – it forms part of a *market production process*. By taking part in sport to get fitter, a person may become more productive and thus earn more money. Sport services in the health and fitness market could therefore be seen as this type of capital good, as they involve costs to provide services. Sport facilities also involve capital goods, as they cost significant amounts to build and maintain. A person may also earn money from performing as a result of their hard work in training, i.e. a professional sport performer; in that sense, they are also investing in a form of capital in their own skills and expertise.
- Sport is also a *public good* – it can satisfy the two criteria that economists recognise for public goods. The first is zero marginal cost or non-rivalry – once provided, the costs of additional users are low or zero, or there is no restriction to others who want to purchase or consume. The second criterion is that it is difficult to exclude anyone from enjoying a service, whether or not they pay – they get a 'free ride'. The benefits from public goods come to others, not just those directly taking part or paying. There are many public goods, for example education or health services, which are provided by the government, on the basis that society benefits from well-educated and healthier citizens. In sport and physical activity, the health argument for public provision of services is very strong. By becoming fitter, individuals can help reduce the costs of ill health to the rest of society. This

is one of the arguments that have supported the public subsidy of sporting provision in the public sector. This is also sometimes termed a 'merit good' argument, particularly for public recreation.

Time out

Think about the different ways in which you might take part in or enjoy sport services, activities or goods. You might draw up a household 'balance sheet' to show what services you use and what benefits you gain. How does your participation in sport benefit society? Do you pay fees and charges to play? Do you buy sports equipment and clothing, or watch games?

Macro-economics looks at flows of money in and out of sport and national level impacts, while micro-economics is concerned with the analysis of demand and supply. The sections below will take a brief look at some of the macro and micro aspects of sport.

At a macro-level, Figure 5.1 is an attempt to show the flows in and out of sport, based on Gratton and Taylor (2000). The flows into sport at the elite level include fees from spectators, sponsorships, TV rights and government funding. Flows out go in taxes, wages to players and costs of providing services and support. The Carter Report (2005), based on the Cambridge Econometrics model, showed this complex network of flows into sport, but this was far too complex to represent simply here.

While governments support elite sport, they spend more in supporting the mass level of participation. Mass participation sport also generates large amounts of spending, on clothing, fees and travel, as well as subscriptions.

The flows in and out of the mass participation market for sport are much greater when aggregated together than those relating to professional or elite sport. One significant flow is the taxation that goes back to the government. As we pay taxes such as VAT and other taxes on our purchases in sport, the amount the government receives back from the sport industry is greater than the subsidy it provides. Also significant is the contribution of the voluntary sector in terms of time and resources. It was recently estimated that the volunteers in sport gave the equivalent of £1.5 billion in 'work' to the sector (Sport England 2003).

As shown in Chapter 4, the *supply* of services into sport and their control is a complex 'mixed economy' of public, private and commercial activity. There are also increasing numbers of companies supplying goods and services to the sport sector, and supporting their work through sponsorship.

The *demand* for sport is equally complex and dynamic. The range of goods and services now considered part of this industry is very diverse, appealing to a wide variety of consumers, across recreational and elite levels of sport, active and more passive involvement, and increasingly specialised interests.

Also helping to complicate the picture is the increasingly global nature of sport, sporting goods and practices. The English Premier League is seen on televisions across the world, and helps to sell club merchandise globally. A pair of Nike trainers may be marketed and designed in the US, manufactured in Asia, but sold in a UK-owned sporting

Figure 5.1: Flows of finance in and out of the sport industry

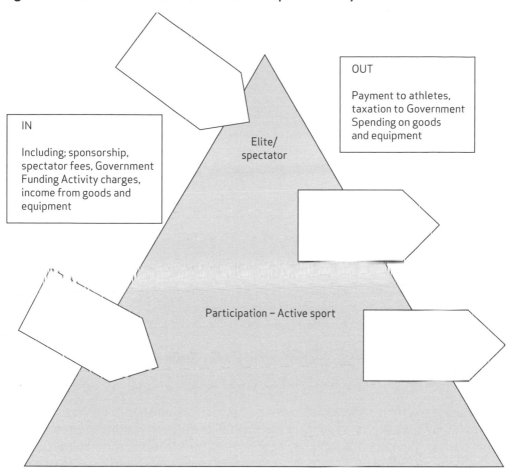

IN

Including; sponsorship, spectator fees, Government Funding Activity charges, income from goods and equipment

OUT

Payment to athletes, taxation to Government Spending on goods and equipment

Elite/ spectator

Participation – Active sport

retail outlet. The sections below consider in more detail the implications of this complex relationship.

Defining the sport industry

Is sport a business? There are many that might suggest sport is a passion and even a lifestyle, but not a business and too difficult to map as an 'industry' because of the complexities of the public, private and voluntary sectors. According to Horne (2006: 3), 'if sport is an industry, it is clearly rather an unorthodox one'. He goes on to point out that, where professional sport is concerned:

> otherwise rational entrepreneurs will invest vast sums of money into commercial teams in pursuit of sport success without serious expectation of financial return. Ego, vanity and self-aggrandisement appear to overrule the rationality of the balance sheet. Sport is clearly much more than simply another industry.

However, we know that the sport industry, despite problems in setting out exactly what belongs in it or not, is valuable, diverse and still growing. More details are provided below of how the sector is mapped out. Statistics sometimes vary because of the base used for measurement, often combining sport with other parts of the leisure industry, because it is too difficult to disentangle some of the more complex companies operating across various sectors, such as catering and hospitality, management operations and the media or even the outdoors, agriculture and land use.

As noted above, it is possible to see sport as part of a production process in the marketplace, where goods and services are provided and consumers purchase them; however, the sport industry has many features that mean that companies and organisations do not always act in ways consistent with businesses in other sectors. Certainly, in sport businesses there is competition but businesses also have to cooperate with each other to form competitions and leagues and there are multi-sport organisations which regulate across sporting organisations. Clearly, not all sport organisations are driven by a profit motive, and so not all sport bodies operate 'commercially' – their services may be provided free or simply to cover the costs of providing them.

Professional sports companies (clubs, teams) make up a significant part of the sector, and the most high profile, but even they have particular problems in operating like a real 'business'. They have been classified as either *profit maximisers* or *benefit maximisers* (Sandy et al. 2004). This means that some may see sport as a means to maximise their assets, while others may look to use their assets to maximise their sporting potential.

Smith and Stewart (1999) set out why professional sport is not like another business:

- *Irrational passions* – fans don't make the decision about what team they support (or will buy tickets to see) on the basis of rational decision making to get the 'best' product, in the way they might buy a car or use a bank. If everyone made such decisions on a purely rational basis, they would change allegiances based on hard data (e.g. league performance) not their emotions. As we probably know from our own experience, passion and emotion play a big role in sporting preferences.
- *Profits versus points* – this deals with the profits versus performance arguments or the choice for profit or benefit maximisers. Some sport bodies would prefer to play well, and/or win tournaments or leagues, than have the highest return on investment. The two are not always mutually compatible – for example, Chelsea is very successful as a football team but has run up significant losses for its owner.
- *Level playing fields* – in most sports, great lengths are taken to ensure a level playing field to equalise competition, whereas in business the opposite is usually the case. It is important to gain advantages over the competition, in order to be successful. Level playing fields are created in technical requirements for cars in Formula 1, or handicapping in racing, weight categories in boxing and similar. Squad sizes, player wage limits or limits to transfers are some of the ways in which some team sports attempt to equalise competition within a league.
- *Variable quality* – this relates to the importance of variation in sport, which is why there is competition. We cannot always predict the quality of performance or the outcome, which is what keeps large numbers of people gripped by sporting competitions. If you knew the outcome of a sporting contest, it would lose its appeal. Similarly, if you could predict the quality of every sporting performance,

an event such as the Olympic Games would be no more than an exhibition, with no chance for the 'plucky underdog' to achieve a medal place. In sporting businesses, keeping the potential fan or consumer interested in the quality of the performance is key – quite different from other businesses, where a standardised approach to quality is associated with reliability and consumer confidence.

- *Collaboration/cartel* – in sports leagues and tournaments, there has to be cooperation in order to have a schedule and rules that everyone can work towards. These leagues act to restrict entry to the market (a fixed number of teams in the RFL Superleague, for example), help regulate prices or salaries and control supply – there is only one set of fixtures. This sort of activity is actually illegal in other forms of business as being 'anti-competitive'. By acting together, the league acts as a cartel in excluding the possibility of competition.
- *Product/brand loyalty* – linked to the point above, the loyalty of fans to their teams or players is almost unique but essential in sport, as the value of the team is based on how much fan loyalty they can maintain. An indicator of brand or fan loyalty is the merchandise sales achieved. Fans of sporting entities (performers or teams) tend to stick to a preferred brand, even if there are 'better' products available.
- *Vicarious identification* – many fans and supporters identify with their heroes in the team, in a way they would not do with other suppliers of services or businesses.
- *Fixed supply schedules* – there is only one FA Cup Final in a year, so despite the demand for tickets, it is impossible to supply more tickets or games to satisfy the demand – hence the supply for professional sport is relatively fixed. Once an event has gone, the opportunity to see it, buy tickets and so on, is lost. Even with the expansion into new competitions or events, for example the development of 20/20 cricket, there is a schedule fixed which remains the only chance to supply.

Activity

How unique is the sport industry?

Using the headings above, you might discuss the 'peculiar economics' of professional sport. There will be plenty of examples in current media, where the apparently irrational passions of both fans and owners seem to take precedence over rational decision making. Are there any other businesses that seem to operate in similar ways? You might compare the music industry to sport, for example.

Deloitte Sport Business Group (2005a) has also identified some of the 'pitfalls' to beset the unwary business in sport:

- The influence of EU directives relating to competition and employment that regulate sport somewhat differently from other businesses.
- The mutual dependence of clubs in leagues – as no single club could be the single supplier, they rely on each other to maintain the value of their market.

- Governing bodies of sport exert the sort of influence on companies and businesses that is unlike other markets or industries.
- Sporting performance (i.e. promotion or relegation) can have immediate impacts on the business – both positive and negative.

The emotive aspects of sport can therefore often cloud the judgement of otherwise hardened business minds. The special nature of the sport business is recognised in the EU, though it is not immune to regulations of employee transfers and rights, which led to the Bosman ruling and other changes with significant implications for professional sport. The Bosman ruling, by the EU in 1995, essentially changed the regulation of player contracts in European sport, and meant that teams could no longer retain control over players once their contract had concluded, by asking for 'transfer fees' or restricting their movement to other clubs. This has had far-reaching implications for the economics of football and other professional sports (Parrish and McArdle 2004).

Sectors, markets and activities

Figure 5.1 above provides some indication of the sort of economic activities and flows involved in the sport industry. However, measuring the levels of participation in sport is actually fraught with difficulty, as so much of it goes on informally and infrequently and may not involve any direct costs. The government's *Taking Part* survey has provided a rolling programme of survey data, on which their progress towards Public Service Agreement (PSA) targets are being measured (see Chapter 4, for details of these targets).

This estimates that, though about 69 per cent of adults (27.5 million) may take part in sport, much of this is recreational activity, of more moderate intensity and could be only once in a 12-month period. Levels of participation have remained difficult to change, and there remains less participation by less advantaged groups in society: those who come from an ethnic background other than white/British, who live in social housing, women, the low paid or unemployed, those with a disability or who left school with few qualifications.

Expenditure on sport

Details of the expenditure in the sector have been compiled from the Sport England commissioned research of the Sports Industry Research Centre (SIRC), who based their reports on the following categories of sport expenditure:

- Sports goods – clothing, footwear, equipment and publications;
- Sports services – entrance charges, subscriptions, fees, subscriptions for TV and video, DVD sales and rental, sport gambling, travel related to sport, and others (this includes food, drink and accommodation associated with sport, both participating and spectating).

In 2006, sports goods represented 36 per cent of the total expenditure and services 63.4 per cent.

Spending on sport

Clothing and footwear accounts for 20.8 per cent of all spending on sport, by far the most important sector. In sport services, the biggest areas are sport gambling and sport-related TV/DVD spending, at 14.4 and 12.6 per cent, respectively. Participation in sport accounts for 11.1 per cent and health and fitness 10.6 per cent. Some more information on selected sectors is given below.

According to the Family Spending report of the ONS, total weekly household spending on 'sporting equipment' in 2003/04 was £23 million, and for 2005/06 had risen to £31 million, an increase of 29 per cent. This included clothing and footwear. It has been suggested that, as participation has tended to remain relatively stable, with only slight increases or decreases in different activities, much of this growth has been stimulated by fashion trends in sportswear, rather than sports participation.

The sport sector: what do we count?

For the purposes of mapping businesses in the sector, Skills Active (2006) has identified that the 'Sport and Active Leisure Sector' includes:

- Sport, recreation and leisure facilities, sports clubs, stadium/arena facilities, sports services, sports administration;
- Sports development, governing bodies of sport, community/youth centres, coaching, activity leadership;
- Health and fitness private fitness clubs, hotel-based clubs, multi-group clubs, workplace clubs, public leisure centres, residential clubs;
- Playwork holiday play scheme, adventure playground, La Play Unit, weekend play scheme, play training organisation;
- School play centre, play association, play bus/mobile unit, after-school club, open access centre;
- Outdoor education, recreation, development and training, sports development, exploration and expeditioning, sport tourism;
- Caravan industry, caravan parks, caravan manufacturers, caravan dealers
- Other sports manufacture, retail, production and associated firms considered to be part of its wider sports cluster.

Business in Sport and Leisure

Business in Sport and Leisure (BISL) is an organisation formed in 1992 to represent businesses in the sport sector. From a small base, there are now around 100 companies as members, including major commercial leisure operators, accountancy and surveying professionals, management consultancies, national governing bodies and media companies. Members include:

- Amateur Swimming Association
- Centre Parcs Limited
- Holmes Place plc

- Sports Aid
- Whitbread plc

They have a growing influence on the sector, due to the value held in these companies and organisations and their importance in employment. One of BISL's key roles is to lobby government to represent the interests of their members, on policies that impact on the businesses in the sector – they are regarded as the 'voice' of the commercial sector in sport and leisure to government. For example, they were in discussion with the government about the impact of the smoking ban on licensed premises. As some indicator of the 'industry sectors' in sport-related business, they have working groups in: employment, gaming, liquor licensing, property and land use planning, as well as sport.

The focus of the sport working group is on 'growing the market'. It is clear therefore that the interests of commercial business and public policy are both involved in getting more people to take part in (and therefore spend more money and/or time) sport and active recreation. The sectors of the industry specifically who benefit from this increased participation are the commercial operators of health and fitness clubs, sport facilities management companies, the governing bodies and public leisure facility operators. This group is also concerned with capital investment in an increasingly aging facility stock, which increasingly involves partnerships between commercial funding and public bodies. Concerns for a lasting legacy of London 2012 has prompted BISL to work with CCPR to lobby for a national participation legacy (see the section below on events and London 2012).

Source: BISL Active Annual 2007/08

The PSAs for local government, noted in Chapter 4, are also very significant to the commercial and voluntary sector, as they can often be delivered in partnership. For example, the commercial health and fitness operators in the sector can help, through their membership services, to achieve a reduction in childhood obesity levels (PSA 12) and increase the proportion of adults taking part in sport (PSA 21). Increased spending by the government on health, school sport and crime reduction also involves more sport-related spending with businesses in this sector, so the forecasts for the sport industry are quite positive. In order to deliver a successful event in 2012, the commercial sport sector will be very important in helping to achieve government objectives, not just in providing sponsorship but also in building facilities and providing services.

The impact of sport on the UK economy

According to sport market forecasts by the Sport Industry Research Centre, (2007a) the value of the market for sport was about £19.5 billion, a slight decrease in volume on the previous year, but representing an increase in value of about 0.4 per cent.

This represents about 2 per cent of GDP and employment, and about 2.5 per cent of consumer spending. As indicated in Figure 5.1 above, much of this is in the spending relevant to participation in sport, rather than in watching on TV or spectating. The expectation is that the sport industry will continue to grow, and could reach a value of £24 billion by 2011. The most dynamic sector is clothing and footwear, which the SIRC expects to rise in value by 34 per cent over the 2007/11 period.

The economic importance of sport may be difficult to quantify, but all estimates appear to indicate that it has increased faster than many other sectors of the economy since the mid to late 1990s. Sport-related economic activity increased from £3358 million in 1985 to £10,373 million in 2000 and £15,471 million in 2005: a 124 per cent rise over the period based on constant prices (SIRC 2007b).

One of the key factors that accounts for the significance of the sector is the growth in employment – now estimated at around 434,000 by SIRC (2007b), or 635,745 by North West Development Agency (cited in Skills Active 2006). These variations come about due to a difference in classifications included in the estimates. All sources seem to agree, however, that growth in the sector has been very significant, and mainly occurring in the commercial sector of the industry.

The health and fitness sector

The Fitness Industry Association's (FIA) *State of the Industry* report indicated 'healthy growth' for the sector (2007). They estimate the value of the UK fitness industry to be £3.6 billion, based on membership fees and subscriptions. This varies somewhat from the Sport Market report above, as the basis of comparison is slightly different.

The FIA (2007) estimated there are:

- 5714 combined public and private sites
- 3117 private clubs
- 2597 gyms in public sport centres

Since 2006, 232 new facilities have been built. There are 7 million members of a private or public health facility. This represents a very significant figure for the government and the sector, given the importance of their PSA targets in participation and obesity. FIA estimates that about 7 per cent of the UK population is a member of a private club and 4 per cent members of a public one. This indicates also that there is great potential for more growth in the sector, as it still represents a small proportion of the UK population. Sport England's *Active Places* research indicates that about 78 per cent of people live within two miles of a private fitness facility and 80 per cent live within two miles of a public one.

One important trend in this sector is the rise of multi-site operators and the fairly constant changes in ownership of brands and sites. Of the 126 new clubs that were opened in the private sector in 2006/07, 58 per cent were independent and 42 per cent owned by multi-site operators. BISL estimate that independent operators now own 55 per cent of clubs. However, they tend to be smaller, with fewer members and so represent less 'value' in the sector. Strong competition in the sector helps to keep membership prices relatively low.

Activity

- Visit your nearest fitness facility – is it private, public or a combination?
- A comparative visit to another club is also useful. How do the two sites differ? What is the same or similar?
- Compare prices and accessibility for different groups (e.g. the elderly, the disabled).
- How far do you have to travel to get the comparison club?

Gambling on sport

Sport and gambling have long been closely related – even back to Ancient Greek and Roman times. More recently, the gaming industry in sport has grown to be worth billions of pounds. Despite previously expressed concerns about so-called 'problem gambling', the British Gambling Prevalence Study in 2007 didn't find any evidence of increased problem gambling in the UK (BISL 2008). Though bingo halls and casinos have arguably little to do with sport, they do represent significant amounts of spending in this sector, if it is included with other betting and gaming activity. Gaming machines are a common sight in many sport venues and can be an important income source for voluntary sports clubs.

Other gambling-based sport includes horse racing, which is regulated by the British Horseracing Authority. There are 59 racecourses in Britain (BISL 2007), who have suffered some decline in attendance at racing. On-course betting is also provided by the Tote, established through an Act of Parliament as an alternative to bookmakers. Profits from the Tote go back into the sport.

Perhaps the most significant contribution of this sector to sport is through the National Lottery. Since 1994, many millions have flowed into sport through this route. As one of the original 'good causes', sport currently receives just under 5p in every pound spent on lottery tickets, and Figures 5.2 and 5.3 show how this compares to the other 'good causes'. Total sales of lottery tickets up to 2008 have been £66 billion, and they have remained over £4.5 billion per year since 2000. But, despite this huge injection of funding into sport, concerns have been expressed by the CCPR and BISL about the

Figure 5.2: The National Lottery Good Causes: proportion of funding allocated – in 2006/07, £1247.9 million went to good causes

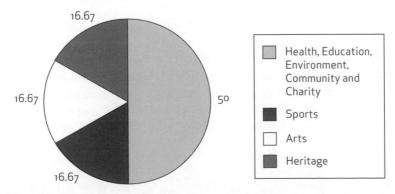

Figure 5.3: National Lottery income over five years
Source: National Lottery Distribution Fund Account, 2006/07

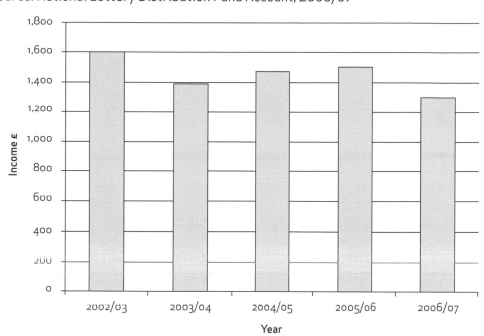

potential diversion of finance from the grass roots of sport due to the costs of the London 2012 Games and the establishment of the new Lottery Game with a specific target to raise £750 million for the Games. We will look again at the link between gambling and sport below, in the section on new media.

Activity

Investigate the sport provision funded by the lottery in your area or sport. What facilities have been built? If you have looked at an area, what are the sports that have benefited? What has been the result of the lottery investment in your selected sport?

Local and regional variations

Both participation and spending on sport have variations at regional level, as well as variations in employment and the significance of particular activities and businesses.

The Northwest region, for example, is relatively rich in professional sport clubs, with seven out of 20 E Premier League clubs, Lancashire County Cricket Club, various rugby union and league teams, and Aintree Racecourse. There are also excellent natural resources for active sport and recreation in the outdoors, for example the Lake District and the coast for water-based sport. The NWDA have begun to develop a regional development strategy for the sector based on these two key factors and the employment needs in the sector have also been reviewed (see the 'Employment in sport' section later in this chapter).

In a recent review of the regional development strategy for sport in the Northwest (KKP Consultants 2008), the following examples were identified:

- Rugby league contributes £55.4 million to the economy and supports 840 jobs;
- English Premier League clubs in the region had a turnover of £542 million in 2006;
- Premier League games alone generated 4.9 million attendances.

In a very different part of the sector, the region has 840 outdoor sport companies, most of which employ 15 people or fewer.

Other regions will clearly have their own blend of suppliers and sporting infrastructure, so care must always be taken with the interpretation of national figures relating to economic activity.

Global markets: sports goods and services

This section considers multinational and global businesses, and some critical perspectives on their influences on consumers. First, the big players in the global market are identified, as we attempt to map the scope and scale of global sport. The amounts of money involved in global sporting events and marketplaces are quite staggering: 30-second commercial slots in the 2007 Super Bowl generated $2.6 million dollars (over £1 million). Tiger Woods' earnings from golf in 2006 reached a cool $25 million, but his earnings of $90 million in endorsements eclipsed even this – by far and away the highest amount by any sports person.

Which are the biggest sporting brands?

Brand value – what it is we think of when we hear the name or see the logo connected with a brand – is essentially measured by how much sponsors are prepared to pay to be associated with or to be endorsed by a particular sporting entity. Sporting brands can be teams, individuals, leagues or events.

A sport brand is essentially all the images, logos and representations we associate with the club, team or individual. They are what we find attractive or distinctive about the performer or team, what makes them recognisable (and ultimately profitable).

Forbes magazine published its list of the top sports brands. They identify Tiger Woods as the most valuable brand amongst athletes, while Manchester United is the highest valued team brand. Nike is the biggest sports business, and the Super Bowl, based on earnings per event day, is the most valuable event (Forbes 2008).

Also in the top ten of the biggest sports businesses were ESPN, the media channel, EA Sports, the electronic game company, and IMG, a sports management company. This shows the range of businesses that contribute to the sports industry globally; however, the value of the US companies means that the US dominates the global marketplace.

Most of the top ten events, or athletes on the *Forbes* list, were based on and produced for the US market, so we could assume that this is the most valuable market for sport, despite the strength of the European football teams in the world sporting economy.

International/global sport organisations

Perhaps the most significant of the global sport organisations is the International Olympic Committee (IOC). The Summer and Winter Olympics are the biggest sporting events, even if, assessed by the *Forbes* method, not necessarily the most valuable on earnings per event day. Its sheer size and scale, along with its planning and development cycle, gives the Olympic movement virtual dominance in international sport.

Other sport bodies include FIFA (football), FIBA (basketball) and the ICC (cricket), which take responsibility for a single sport across the world, uniting the national federations. Sports may have regional federations (Europe, Asia, North America), to which national governing bodies are affiliated.

Other international bodies are responsible for specific aspects of sport; for example, WADA (World Anti-Doping Agency) is responsible for the global regulation of anti-doping across sports.

Sporting goods manufacturers and ethics in the global sport marketplace

One important topical debate surrounding the global sport marketplace is the ethics of sports manufacturers and their social responsibilities in the developing countries where their suppliers are usually based. These debates involve the wider global environment, stockholder versus stakeholder concerns, and wider issues of macro economics and international trade (Wilcox 2002). Concerns have been raised about the exploitation of workers and over-commercialisation of sport, through what might be seen as excessive profit by manufacturers at the expense of poorly paid local workers.

Wilcox (p. 07) has described the emergence of sport as:

> a commodity characterised by commercialisation, privatisation, economic gain and the seemingly abundant challenges of burgeoning bureaucracies and corruption.

He goes on to identify the growth of major players in the marketplace. Through their size and importance, they have come to dominate and effectively compete with each other for ever-greater market share across the globe. The major brands include:

- Nike
- Adidas
- Puma
- Reebok
- Umbro

There has also been an incredible growth in international trade in sports clothing and footwear, some indication of which is shown in the figures above for the UK. This has been fuelled by a huge growth of consumption, resulting in various ethical dilemmas faced by the industry. They have to balance the rights, shared values and responsibilities of employees, shareholders (stockholders) and stakeholders (including fans, participants and suppliers). Consequently, Wilcox (ibid.) identifies various challenges for the sports goods market:

- influence and persuasive practices of global manufacturers;
- economic growth and environmental sustainability;
- labour exploitation and offshore production;
- human dignity and discrimination;
- health, occupational safety, welfare and consumer protection;
- fundamental conflict – stockholders versus stakeholders.

The performance of the manufacturers in meeting these challenges has been assessed by Oxfam International (Connor and Dent 2006: 101) as rather poor:

> while some sports brand owners have made policy commitments to respect trade union rights, implementation falls well short of what is required.

Other ethical questions have been raised by the sponsorships in some sports and events. For example, football, rugby and cricket have in the past been associated with tobacco and alcohol sponsors. More recently, questions are being raised about the ethics of food sponsorships of community football, given the association of sport with health and a growing obesity problem in young people. On the other hand, the football authorities might argue that they are simply accepting the best sponsorship deal, in order to provide services they might not be able to afford otherwise. This is certainly an area worthy of more debate. Similar questions could be raised about the global sport sponsors of the Olympics, for example.

Sport and the media: a match made in heaven?

The analysis of sport and media relations can be seen through various theoretical perspectives, such as sociological or cultural studies, so could happily fit within Chapter 2 to some extent. In Chapter 2 we looked at how the media treats female sport performers; for example, from a socio-economic perspective, we might consider how females are less likely to earn similar amounts in sport, whatever their status, due to the more limited coverage they enjoy in televised sport.

Essentially theories differ in their interpretations of the nature and impact of power relations in sport and media and how this influences and structures individual choice. This section focuses on the influence of the mass media, satellite TV and the internet on the economic and business aspects of sport, as 'without question one of the great passions of the 21st Century has been sport' (Boyle and Haynes 2000: 1) and this passion has helped to fuel the growth of the sport industry to its modern significance. They point to various trends in the twentieth century, including sport and culture, rise of the mass media, sport, media and politics, sport, business and commercialism, which all contribute to ever closer ties between 'two of the great forces of the twentieth century popular culture'.

The relationship between sport and the media has been described as a 'match made in heaven', while others have been concerned about the commodification of sport to fit with the needs of television to provide hours of content for 'entertainment' purposes. Owen Slot, for example, has described modern football as an exercise for providing pictures for the television (2005). There is no doubt that without the riches provided by the pay-to-view satellite TV contracts, the English Premier League (EPL) would not be the richest in Europe. Gratton and Taylor (2000: 12) suggest that:

> the alliance between professional sport and the changing structure of broadcasting (involving terrestrial, cable, satellite and digital) is the largest single influence of the 1990s.

Other sports in the UK also benefit from TV contracts, but we can see the greatest rewards going to football – albeit, it is argued, directly into the pockets of the players and their agents.

Most of the value reported earlier in the global marketplace is due to the media exposure a sports event or athlete can deliver. But sports also benefit from the almost insatiable appetite for sport on TV, as it increases the value that can be raised from the 'rights' to broadcast events, matches or whole leagues. For example, in 2008 it was reported that the US network NBC were to show more hours of coverage of the Beijing Olympics than of all previous summer Olympics combined – an average of 212 hours per day across 12 different platforms; this included live, recorded and streamed via the internet.

The media–sport relationship

The ability of sport to reach and interest so many in the population has been a major feature of the sport–media relationship since the first press reports of village cricket games and other popular activities appeared in the early eighteenth century (Boyle and Haynes 2000). This has led to an ongoing relationship of interdependence between sport, the media and commercial interests.

The appeal of sport to a mass audience meant that it has remained a key part of the printed press ever since. Sport now, however, features in both front and back pages and also often features in the business sections, as increasingly the 'sport' may be of secondary interest from a news perspective. There is also, as indicated above, a significant sport-based publication media in magazines and books. You only need to look at the shelves of a high street bookshop to see the popular appeal of sporting biographies, guides and annual publications. The annual *Wisden*, in cricket, for example, has been published for over 100 years.

After the First World War, with the rise of radio communications, sport became a more global and international concern, with on-site and real-time accounts of events and competitions replacing the reports in newspapers, which often covered events which had taken place days before. The immediacy and atmosphere of such broadcasts meant that 'fans' could follow the events much more closely without attending the games and so mass communication media contributed to the growth of sports across the globe. One of the longest running broadcast media programmes in the UK is 'Sport report', now on Radio 5, which began in the 1940s, giving a round-up of all the day's results on Saturday evening (previously the main day for sport in the media). This particular programme features very highly in my own sporting memories, as it was often playing in the car on the way back from matches.

Time out

What sports media clips would you put into a 'sporting highlights' programme? What are your own memories of 'golden moments of sport' – was it news of a particular event, watching a live event or an interview with a favourite star? What was the impact and significance of this in your own sporting history? It might be interesting to compare your 'top ten' with others of a different age and/or gender.

The BBC had obtained the early rights to broadcast the major sports events in the UK, and their 'Oxbridge' – and usually male – tones were a key feature of popular culture throughout the mid to late twentieth century. This was largely in the early days based on reporting of the facts and results, rather than providing 'entertainment'.

Although commercial TV has emerged to challenge BBC dominance, the public broadcasting of certain events has been protected by the British government, under the remit of the DCMS and the identification of the so-called 'crown jewels' – such as the Wimbledon Finals, Olympic Games and the FA Cup Final, which must all be available on 'free to air' channels. Table 5.1 identifies these in more detail.

While, in the early days of broadcasting, the rights to provide media coverage of sport may have been relatively cheap, the increasing value of the rights has created a very important source of funds for many sporting bodies, and potential outlets for sponsors and other companies who wish to reach the large and valuable audiences attracted to televised sport.

Table 5.1: Listed UK sporting events

Group A

Olympic Games
FIFA World Cup Finals Tournament
FA Cup Final
Scottish Cup Final (in Scotland)
The Grand National
The Derby
Wimbledon Tennis Finals
European Football Championships Finals Tournament
Rugby League Challenge Cup Final
Rugby World Cup Final

Group B

Cricket Test matches played in England
Non-finals played in the Wimbledon tournament
All other matches in the Rugby World Cup Finals tournament
Five Nations rugby tournament matches involving home countries
Commonwealth Games
World Athletics Championships
Cricket World Cup: the final, semi-finals and matches involving home nations' teams
Ryder Cup
Open Golf Championship

Notes:
Group A: no broadcaster has exclusive rights to the live broadcasts of the events listed
Group B: if one category (free to air or pay TV plus) has coverage, there should be adequate and timely secondary coverage by a broadcaster in the other category

Source: Sandy et al. 2004.

From national to global audiences, there is now a very significant media market in sport events and activities, which reaches sometimes billions for all the major events. In 2008, the Olympic Games was expected to reach a worldwide audience of billions. Consequently, the IOC rights for televising the Games were anticipated to raise £1.7 billion for the IOC, along with the sponsorship by corporate 'partners'. Based on the global reach of the event, it is clear that such commercial concerns must exert some influence over the IOC decision making and Games organisation.

The BBC output for Beijing included 300 hours of coverage on BBC1 and BBC2, the main terrestrial channels, but a staggering 2450 hours of coverage was available on BBC online, interactive, radio, news and mobile content. This event also showcased the increasing technical and technological advances in broadcasting, which have increased the availability of sport 'on demand' to fans and meant a greater responsiveness to audience preferences.

Economics of sport broadcasting

This is made up of two key elements:

- Sport broadcasting fits the requirements for a 'public good' – it has a very low marginal cost – whether watched by 50 or 50 million, the cost to the producers is very much the same and it is difficult to exclude people – except through pay per view (PPV) or subscription to satellite or digital. The economic terms, identified above, are *non-rivalry* and *non-excludability*. If an event cannot be shown exclusively by Sky, for example, it is less likely to bid for rights. If, however, they purchase the exclusive rights at great expense, they can recoup more of this cost by charging an increased subscription, selling more subscriptions or a combination of the two. They can exclude those who are not able or willing to pay, unlike the BBC, which transmits on free to air channels.
- Intellectual property laws protect the content of the broadcasting. This is usually held by the league or governing body of the sport, or the event organisers. It is the 'right' to broadcast the sport that creates the economic value of the event or sport (Sandy et al. 2004).

Figure 5.4 shows how the output of one digital broadcaster is clearly dominated by football, comprising 41 per cent of their sporting output; in the 'other' category are athletics, darts, horse racing, water and motor sports, and American football.

We could fill a whole book with debate, theory and data about the economics of sport broadcasting, but it is important here to simply establish the significance of the sport–media relationship. The wealth of the football market in the UK is inextricably linked to the growth of satellite and digital TV.

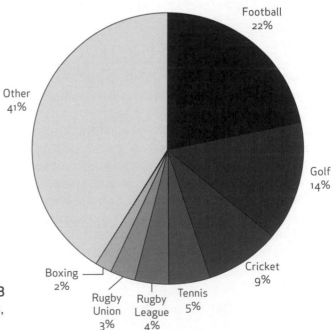

Figure 5.4:
Sky Sports broadcasting 2003
Source: BSkyB Interim results,
February 2004

Issues of access and media: not always a level playing field

How sports use or access the media varies depending on their relative attractiveness to a TV audience and thus potential sponsors. Hence, few female sports performers appear on the main BBC channels, except in the protected events such as Wimbledon or the Olympic Games, or if covering world or major championships, such as World Cup athletics. When England games in the Women's European Football Championships were shown on TV in 2005, they achieved respectable audiences of over 1 million, for live and recorded highlights over 8 million viewers in total for the tournament – an unprecedented response for an event of its type. Since then, other England women's football games have continued to attract viewers – but in nothing like the same numbers as their male counterparts. As noted in Chapter 2, sociologists have also examined the way in which women athletes are reported on in the media – often the reports focus more on how these athletes look than how they perform in their sport.

One recent development to buck this trend has been the introduction of Netball Superleague to Sky TV. Weekly live games and highlights of national Superleague games are now shown, though English Netball have to invest their funds into this; rather than earning a great deal from rights, they hope to gain more interest in watching and playing their sport and make it more appealing to young women in particular.

The mass media can help sport bodies sell tickets to major events, create markets for sponsorship and merchandising, and improve international 'brand' recognition. Perhaps the best example is Manchester United, as noted above, which has for some time been one of the most successful football teams in the world, with a very high media profile. It has extensive markets in the Far East, China and America for merchandise and TV rights, with its own TV channel, MUTV.

The Forbes 'most valuable' list identified above, shows Manchester United as being the most valuable football team, largely due to media earnings, sponsorships and endorsements. Such media coverage has also helped create a 'brand' around some of the top United players – namely Beckham, via Real Madrid, now based in the US, Ronaldo and Rooney.

According to recent reports from Forbes (2008), there is not such a strong relation between sporting success and financial reward as many assume. For example, even though Michelle Wie won only $39,000 in the previous 12 months, her endorsements from Nike, Sony and others netted her $12 million. However, they reported also that 'the gravy train could soon be off the rails' unless her on-course performance improved dramatically; sponsors would be unwilling to re-sign her without some clear top finishes in major events.

As the Forbes lists of top earners in sport show, however, even due to contracts based on their media exposure, soccer players' earnings are far below those of other sportsmen in the US (Forbes 2008). Tiger Woods is exceptional because the amount he earns based on his sport performances is so high ($25 million), along with endorsements ($90 million) that his earnings far outstrip any other sport player. The highest placed soccer player, David Beckham, now has much higher earnings from his endorsements ($36 million) than his football playing ($14 million).

Sport and new media

In more recent years, the growth of satellite and digital channels and web-based media has provided yet another forum for the promotion of sport, and it is now possible to watch your favourite activity virtually – and on demand, rather than by the strict schedules of before. When Sky TV started in the UK, it bought the rights to live football to ensure that it could provide some unique content that many people would want to pay to see. Sport remains one of the key factors in the success of satellite and digital TV sales – by 2003, 43 per cent of homes had access to subscription-based cable or satellite TV, and Sky expect this to rise to 80 per cent by 2010 (BSkyB 2003). The ability to access *freeview* means that some digital output will be accessible to a majority of homes, but the rights to the many events not on the protected list have become increasingly sought after.

The impact of the legislation referred to above has meant that some sports and events remain on terrestrial or free to air channels – but some sports have faced the dilemma of whether to take funds from pay to view channels or maintain lower incomes based on bigger audiences on terrestrial TV (see the activity below on the ECB). While, in the 1990s, the growth of satellite and digital broadcasting prompted significant growth and changes in the profile of the sport media market, the internet and the ability to stream content to mobile phones and laptops will have similar impacts by the end of this decade.

Web-based content has also impacted on printed media and to some extent replaced this form of communication for immediate news updates and longer features. Interactivity, sound and video can be provided to enhance the experience of the reader/fan/consumer.

Such growth and change has certainly not been without criticism, and has prompted much debate amongst sport scholars looking at the influence of sporting manufacturers and others outside of sport to manipulate and change sport to make it more attractive to spectators and TV audiences. Though to a certain extent the government may seek to control sponsor messages seen in the media (for example, tobacco advertising), there is still some debate about the role of alcohol and fast/junk food sponsors in many mainstream sports, such as football.

There is also some concern that an emphasis on watching 'virtual sport' may replace the real thing, either playing or watching, as electronic games and media become ever more sophisticated and attractive – particularly to young people. When the new Wii game was launched, for example, it was seen as attractive for families and groups, offering a more 'active' form of game platform. Wii was even held responsible for several injuries, as games required people to mimic the movements of tennis, golf or boxing in their living rooms.

There is no doubt that the relationship between sport and new media will continue to be crucial in the future, as increasingly new technology will be developed and employed to exploit the potential of the global sport market.

Activity

Look at the changes to a sport of your choice, and consider how the media has influenced them. Does this sport feature on terrestrial TV? How has sporting technology been influenced by the media? What is the value of the TV rights to the sport?

What is the most valuable sport on TV?

Many people would answer football to this question. Indeed, some football events are clearly very valuable – such as the play-off final to decide who will have a place in the English Premier League. However, Deloitte Sports Business group conducted research that found that Formula 1 was the most valuable sport shown on TV globally. They found that each of the motor sport's 17 races produces average revenue (income) of $229 million *per event* – nearly ten times that of its closest competitor, the National Football League, which generates $24 million per game. Their figures show that the NFL and Major League Baseball's overall revenue was $6.5 billion and $5.1 billion in 2006, respectively – substantially higher than Formula 1's total revenue of $3.9 billion, although both the NFL and MLB had significantly more events. The English Premier League clubs' combined revenue was $3 billion in the 2006/07 season (Sport Business 2008).

The $3.9 billion for Formula 1 was comprised of commercial rights revenues (race sponsorship, corporate hospitality and broadcast fees), team revenues (including sponsorship and contributions from partners and owners) and circuit revenues (from ticket sales and sponsorship). Of course, this does not tell us the full story of the sport, as this excludes what is paid out to put these events in place and the costs of running teams. Such costs have recently resulted in the high-spending Honda team to withdraw from Formula 1 altogether. This has prompted concerns that the economics of the sport are becoming unsustainable in the long term.

Dig deeper

Look in depth at the concerns expressed by politicians regarding the funding of cricket by pay TV funds compared to free to air coverage. Using the online sources in the Further study section later in this chapter, investigate how the ECB justified their choice of the more valuable TV deal from BSkyB rather than staying with a free to air channel.

Commercial sponsorship

Commercial companies are using sport to a greater or lesser extent to sell their product, build recognition of their brand or enhance their image to potential consumers. The significance of the media coverage discussed above is clearly crucial to the exposure a company can expect. Hence, as football is so widely televised and attracts a large and fairly well defined audience – often but not exclusively male, aged 18–25, with disposable income to spend on consumer goods and services, it attracts many types of sponsor. These include insurance, alcohol brands and technology manufacturers.

Shirt sponsorship in football contributes huge amounts to the success of clubs at many levels. EPL deals represent the greatest sponsorship value in sport in the UK. Manchester United has recently achieved a contract worth £56.5 million over four years with AIG, a US insurance company. This has dwarfed the £44 million received by Chelsea for their deal with Samsung.

The UK sponsorship business is worth £1 billion a year, with over 70 per cent of this going to sports organisations (Sport Industry Research Centre 2007b). Though recently this has seen a growth in business from mobile phone companies, increasingly online gambling firms are signing large sponsorship deals across various televised sports, such as snooker, football, rugby and cricket.

According to recent data from the World Sponsorship Monitor, iGaming groups are the fastest growing sponsors of sport, with deals worth almost £300 million signed in the first half of 2006 alone (Sport Business International 2006). A selection of recent deals is shown in Tables 5.2 and 5.3. Given the philosophical debates about ethics in Chapter 3 and above, it is interesting to reflect on the relationship between gambling and sport highlighted here and sport's increasing reliance on lottery funding. This prompts the question: why is sport so attractive to the gambling industry?

Table 5.2: Selected iGaming firms and sponsorship deals in sport, 2006

Date	iGaming company	Sport
25/08/06	Coral.co.uk	Rugby
14/08/06	888.com	Football (Sevilla)
03/08/06	888.com	Football (Toulouse)
23/05/06	Mansion	Football (Tottenham Hotspur)
21/04/06	Betandwin	Football (AC Milan)
07/04/06	32Red	Football (Aston Villa)
16/03/06	Sportingbet	Basketball (Euroleague)
01/02/06	BET24	Football (Leeds FC)

Source: various articles on Sport Business.com, 8/9/06.

Table 5.3: Football club revenues, 2003/04

Team	Value (£ million)*
Manchester United	171.5
Real Madrid	147.2
AC Milan	143.7
Chelsea	142.7
Juventus	142.4
Arsenal	115
Barcelona	112
Internationale	110.3
Bayern Munich	110.1
Liverpool	92.3

*Based on day-to-day football operations
Source: Deloitte Sport Business Group 2005b.

Time out

What are the similarities between the audiences and markets for gaming and snooker? How does the role of a 'commercial partner' differ from that of a 'sponsor'? How does their association with a major sporting event or franchise enhance the 'brand' of a gaming company or similar product?

Activity

Print media

Using a selection of broadsheet (*The Times, Independent, Guardian*) and tabloid newspapers (*Sun, Daily Mirror*):

- List the sports covered and estimate the proportion of the papers devoted to sport coverage
- Summarise the nature of the coverage – what are the stories about, what images are used (e.g. action shots)?
- How are features and in-depth articles on sports issues dealt with? Where do they fit in the paper?
- Compare and contrast the two types of paper in their placement and treatment of sport.
- Use highlighter pens to identify particularly interesting stories illustrating contemporary issues in sport in the press in the same week/day.

TV media

Collect a set of TV schedules for various weeks and:

- Highlight in the TV schedules where sport appears – terrestrial TV only or free digital channels
- Count up the hours scheduled for sport coverage
- List the sports covered and count hours per sport if possible
- Compare live action versus recorded highlights
- Identify any sport-based features or documentaries in schedules; what sports or issues are covered?
- Summarise any differences between channels or highlight the differences in the way in which different sport are covered by different media.
- Compare and contrast the schedules of digital sport channels – what sport gets the highest hours in particular weeks? What channels show the most diverse sports?

New media

List the sports sites you can find (internet, gaming, chat groups, discussion boards, etc.) and:

- Highlight the nature of their content and what the site traffic, content or interaction is mainly concerned with.
- How important are these sites for followers of sport?
- Is there a danger that actual participation will be replaced by virtual sport?
- Is it possible to follow sport entirely through the web? Will this replace newspapers and TV eventually?
- How well do sports organisations use this new media? What are the best sports sites?

Sports events and regeneration: more than taking part?

There has been increased attention focused on the value of sport in terms of its impact on regeneration and the economy, particularly in the inner city environment. This will be examined by taking a more detailed look at the Olympics in London in 2012 and the relationship of the Olympics to regeneration and the impact of sport.

The Olympics and business

Though in recent times we associate the Olympic Games with huge potential earnings and spectacular media events, it has not always been the case that the Olympics has been financially viable or commercially successful and thus attractive to cities to host. Only after the 1984 Olympics in Los Angeles was the private sector welcomed as part of the Olympic funding partnership arrangements.

Preuss (2003) looked at the development of the Olympic Games and divided it into four periods, based on the approach to the economic aspects of the games:

- 1896–1968 – many OGOCs had financial problems, but little attention was paid to economic impacts. Cities tended to fund the costs of the games with little net gain.
- 1969–80 – due to the growing scale of the Olympics, there was an urgent need to open up financing. This period saw the growth of TV rights and sponsorship, while public funding (states and cities) increased.
- 1981–2003 – due to extensive losses in earlier Games, the Olympics were awarded to Los Angeles without a competing bid. Increasing commercialism of the Games and the lifting of the amateur regulations opened up the Games to the influences of professional sport and commercial non-sport sponsors.
- 2004–08 – the period of 'future' Olympics involved economic gigantisism and increased risks. More attention was given to the 'ideals' of the Olympics. A new focus on the potential developmental legacy was developed.

Pruess has described the interdependencies between media, industry and Olympic Movement as 'fundamental' to the growth of the Games. More and more companies and hosting cities want to see the rewards of the exposure in this mega event. This has created a competitive approach to investment in the bidding for the Game, which has become almost a 'race within a race' – the winner is the one that is awarded the Games, and can capitalise on the opportunity to be in the shop window of the world. For the 'right' to broadcast the first Games on television in London 1948, the BBC paid 1000 guineas. For the 2008 Games, it clearly paid a great deal more – as the rights were valued to the IOC at over £1 billion!

Planning to host the 2012 Olympics in London has prompted a huge redevelopment plan for East London and the lower Lea Valley. This redevelopment includes physical infrastructure such as roads, rail links and housing, as well as building new major sport venues and the creation of large areas of parkland. But this planned redevelopment is not without its critics and costs have spiralled since the successful bid was published (Kornblatt 2006).

There is some criticism also that the benefits will only be felt in this part of London, and those in the regions or the rest of the UK will see very few of the benefits, either economically or in sporting terms. There has been a great deal of discussion in the media and academic outputs regarding the 'legacy' aspects of the Games. Though this is becoming a rather over-used term, it is clear that the success of the Games depends on what happens afterwards, as much as what happens during the two weeks of competition. The legacy, then, is that which is left behind after the Olympic 'circus' has left town.

The legacy is often split into two broad categories:

- 'Hard' or tangible legacy – physical infrastructure, buildings, sport facilities, or direct employment;
- 'Soft' or intangible legacy – changes in image or perceptions of the city, increased pride, levels of sport participation, health benefits.

It is therefore widely accepted that the 'soft' legacy will be longer term, but very difficult to measure. Some argue this will be even more significant than the 'hard' legacy, as it is more likely to be spread across the UK. It is also clearly not just about economics, but about the inspirational quality of the Games and the potential this has to enthuse a whole generation of young people – a message very carefully played out in the London Bid of 2005. For the games to be a success, therefore, the Games in London will be the start of a longer process of building participation and sporting success in the UK.

Activity

How important is the Olympics 2012 to the UK and London?
Investigate the current projections for the Olympic budget. Does this investment make economic sense? What are the other arguments for spending such large amounts of money in a two-week global sport spectacle? How are the effects of the games going to be spread around the country?

You could organise into three teams – one to look at the positive impacts, the second to consider potential negative impacts and the third to form an audience or 'panel of experts'. Conduct a debate on the issue.

Looking to the future: influences on spending and participation

As noted in the earlier sections on activities and markets, the future for the sector looks very positive. There are some important trends in and external influences on sport participation and spending to consider: demographics and population, technology and sustainability.

The UK population is relatively stable, showing only slight growth; even so, our population is expected to rise to about 65 million by 2026. This will also include some net inward migration. The UK's changing population has some impacts on the potential markets for sport and leisure activities. As life expectancy increases, so the population will include a higher proportion of elderly people and fewer young children. According to the ONS, there were more people of pensionable age than those under 16 in 2007. They expect the gap to reach 4 million by 2031, with obvious implications for pensions, health care, education and employment. For many businesses, future markets will be older, and centred in existing areas of high population density.

There are also significant global economic influences on the sector. Economic forecasts for the UK, rising fuel costs and concerns over global warming will continue to put pressure on businesses to reduce costs and operate in a more sustainable way – that is, to be 'greener'. The costs of borrowing to build new facilities may be more difficult, and existing facilities will need to become more efficient. Consumers, government and thus businesses are increasingly concerned with 'green' issues. While once this was about the corporate social responsibility of companies, increasingly it is also a matter of financial and economic success – that is, a factor in the 'bottom line'.

Many sport activities, particularly those involving travel, have considerable carbon footprints. Swimming in public pools, for example, is a heavy user of energy. Many businesses in the sport sector also contribute to waste and high energy consumption (e.g. floodlit games). Some pitches or sport resources take considerable energy resources in maintenance – water-based hockey pitches, grass football pitches with underground heating, and golf courses with watering systems. In the future, businesses may find costs will drive them to seek alternatives.

On the other hand, some businesses in the sector could be said to be contributing to the mitigating effects of global warming; walking and cycling provision as an alternative to the car, and caravan and camping holiday providers as alternatives to foreign flights.

The London 2012 Games has stated it aims to be the greenest ever, with plans for active travel to venues, and reduced energy consumption, waste and emissions from the venues.

SIRC reports, noted above, project a 29 per cent increase in spending on active sport in the run up to the London 2012 Games. But how much of this will be based on more people playing? Despite the efforts of all sectors, participation rates in sport and active recreation have remained rather stubborn, with consistent and persistent gaps in particular groups.

Employment in sport

The sport sector employs over 6000,000 people in the UK and over 6 million in Europe. Though the employment potential in the sector is very positive, there are regional variations in the level of employment (numbers of people employed) and their roles. As we examine in Chapter 7, there are also significant regional variations in how many are employed, at what level and in which sector of the industry.

In order to fully appreciate the employment potential of the sector, we need to look at all aspects of it, and examine more than the economics, but also the skills profile and type of employment concerned. Not all sport activity requires or stimulates a great deal of paid employment, due to the large amount of voluntary effort that goes into sport. This was estimated to represent over 100,000 jobs.

Activity

- Visit a professional sport event and identify all the various companies involved in the 'delivery' of the event to the consumer.
- Try to estimate the value of the event, based on the spectators there and their likely spending on all activities (including travel).
- What other influences (besides price) may impact on whether a person will attend such an event?
- List as many 'jobs' as possible involved in the event. Compare this to a visit to a participation-based event, for example a local football tournament or hockey game.

Review

This chapter has mapped out the markets and activities involved in sport, mainly commercial, and introduced some of the economic data around sport expenditure and employment. It is clear that sport is becoming a significant contributor to the economy of the UK, and is growing faster than many other sectors. This is partly fuelled by increasing media coverage of sport and a global interest in the major brands in the UK.

Perhaps more significant is the potential for growth, given the UK's relatively low levels of active participation, which nevertheless contribute even more than the professional market back into the UK economy. Various sectors are combining to help 'grow the market' for sport.

Major brands have been identified and some ethical debates highlighted about the sporting goods market. This shows that not all the activity in the sport marketplace can be seen uncritically.

The potential for the Olympics to raise participation in sport is only one of the potential benefits, as East London will be transformed in preparation for the Games. Whether or not the Games can deliver all that has been promised remains to be seen.

Employment in the sector is also rising and has great potential for the future. However, many of the 'jobs' in sport are part time or voluntary, and the sector has some quite specific needs in training and skills to ensure that sport suppliers in the future can meet the needs of a range of consumers and customers, participants and spectators.

Further study

Both of these books provide specialist and more advanced treatments of sport business:

- Beech, J. and Chadwick, S. (eds) (2004) *The Business of Sport Management*. London: Prentice Hall – see particularly the chapters by Bill Gerrard on Sport Finance, and Harry Arne Solberg on Sport Broadcasting.
- Wolsey, C. and Abrams, J. (2001) *Understanding the Sport and Leisure Industry*. London: Longman – has a useful chapter on the commercial sector and sport, by

Irvine and Taylor, and a section on the leisure and sport markets (though some of the data may be slightly out of date, it provides some useful material on consumption and globalisation).

Other resources:

If you are particularly interested in the impacts of a business-based approach on football, the best starting points are these books, which are both accessible and insightful:

- Conn, D. (1997) *The Football Business: Fair Game in the 1990s.* London: Mainstream
- Conn, D. (2004) *The Beautiful Game? Searching for the Soul of Football.* London: Yellow Jersey Press

Deloitte and Touche have several publications providing essential updates on any of the statistics needed for an analysis of football finance, but also include other professional sports:

- Deloitte Sport Business Group (2005) *Annual Review of Football Finance*, London: Deloitte and Touche

Journals:

- *Sport Business International* – a magazine produced monthly, with good case studies, international business features and commercial reports. Your library may stock this if there is a sport management programme or sport business specialism in the university. You can sign up for a free weekly email with news from the sport industry and search archives for topics related to sport business.
- *Forbes* – this has a mainly US focus, with some good international features and football related case studies (www.forbes.com)

Online sources:

- Deloitte Sport Business Group: www.deloitte.com/dtt/section_node/0,1042,sid%253D70402,00.html – this has access to publications and data, with reduced rates for reports to students or academic institutions.
- *Sport Business*: www.sportbusiness.com – searchable archives and up to date news of the sector if you sign up to the site (the publication may be held in the university library).
- National Lottery: www.culture.gov.uk/what_we_do/national_lottery/default.aspx – for more information about the National Lottery good causes and funding.
- House of Commons Culture Media and Sport Committee (2006) *Broadcasting Rights For Cricket: Ashes to Ashes – the death knell for live test match cricket on free to air TV?* London: Stationary office: www.publications.parliament.uk/pa/cm200506/cmselect/cmcumeds/720/72002.htm – for debate on cricket funding and TV rights.

PART 3

Skills, knowledge and careers in sport studies

Chapter 6

Personal development: essential skills in studying sport

Introduction

As noted in Chapter 5, sport is both a diverse and valuable sector of the economy; hence the range of activity and scope gives rise to a range of potential career opportunities that depend upon a similarly broad range of knowledge and skills. This chapter focuses on skills for studying sport and improving your academic performance on sport studies courses. Chapters 7 and 8 deal with issues relating to personal development, careers and employment.

It is important to recognise the growth of sport studies as a subject at university, which has meant that there are probably more students on sport-related courses than ever before. There are many courses under the broader 'sport' banner, which include significant sport studies elements – including sport management, development and marketing. The growth and development of the subject area has mirrored the rise of significance of the cultural, political and economic dimensions of the sport sector in the latter part of the twentieth century and into the new millennium – with no sign of a fall on the horizon. Indeed, since 2005 and the awarding of the Olympic Games to London in 2012, interest in the study of sport in all its forms has continued to grow. With this expansion has come a great diversity in students and variety in the choices of methods and approaches used in teaching, learning and assessment in sport courses. As noted in the introduction to this book, the diversity of curriculum choices within sports studies means that students need to be multi-skilled and adapt to various styles and approaches.

Some of the more common methods and approaches used in sport studies courses are set out below, with a view to improving understanding of how programme teams develop and assess skills, knowledge, application and understanding. The intention of this chapter is to improve understanding of how to become a more successful student of sport, particularly in the social sciences-based approaches we have examined in previous chapters. The chapter is based on over 30 years' experience of studying, teaching, assessing and experiencing sport – and I still consider myself to be learning!

A chapter like this cannot really cover all aspects of studying this subject, but I hope that, armed with the knowledge gained from the chapter, you feel you can make more of the opportunities available to you on your own course. Where possible, I have tried to provide examples drawn from sport studies courses. The main purpose of this chapter is to help you become a more active learner in sport studies.

Learning outcomes

After completing this chapter and the related learning activities, you will be able to:
- identify the main methods of teaching on sport studies programmes and understand your own preferred 'learning style';
- identify and apply useful strategies to improve your personal performance in assessments in social science aspects of sport;
- develop better understanding of the support and guidance available to you through your own institution or programme.

Getting the most from lectures, seminars and practical work

What we need to be able to do is recognise the difference between teaching (something the lecturer or tutor attempts to do) and learning (which is achieved by the student). Learning can come about in many ways and is about many different activities – gathering and organising information, making sense of new ideas, recalling and applying new knowledge. As a student, it is quite useful to be aware of what the teacher or tutor is attempting to do, in order to get the most from the session or learning experience. No matter what teaching strategy or tactic the tutor may choose, learning is really about what the student is able to achieve and interested in doing – it is an *active* process. Hence, tutors use a range of methods to engage and interest students in different ways and to try to achieve different objectives in understanding. They are also well aware that different students learn in different ways and come to the subject with a variety of experiences and expectations.

Most sport programmes, as in any subject, will be based on the same basic approaches to learning: gathering information (research), recording and ordering that information (making notes and keeping records of sessions and data gathered), active learning and making sense of information and ideas, and recalling and being able to apply the knowledge gained.

The teaching strategies include: lectures (in large or small groups), seminars and tutorials (small group or one to one sessions), practical sessions or workshops (based on tasks and practical activities), electronic or web-based or 'blended' approaches, Virtual Learning Environments (VLE), and using webCT, Blackboard or similar online resources.

Within the different types of session tutors will use a range of approaches, from the *didactic*, where the sessions are tutor-led and use a one-way method of communication, with limited opportunities for debate or discussion; to the *interactive*, with more opportunities for two-way communication and a diverse range of methods to get students more engaged with the material.

The emphasis in higher education today is on specified learning outcomes and how best they are to be achieved, rather than a 'one size fits all' approach to teaching. Many sport courses also use some practical or experiential learning – 'learning by doing' – to provide particularly vocational aspects of courses with more relevance and greater emphasis on skills and understanding, as well as applying knowledge in the practical context. Though the large group lecture approach is still found on courses with greater student numbers, such sessions increasingly incorporate a variety of methods to engage and interest students, who often have very different personal preferences for the best way to learn.

In my own experience, the self-assessment of preferred learning style, for which there are numerous online or paper tests available, is very useful. These tests help you to recognise your own preferred approach and can you help adapt your own preferences to suit the approaches used in a course or programme, or by a particular tutor, or with a topic or activity new to you.

Time out

- Think about the learning you have done in the past. At school or college, what sort of session did you enjoy the most?
- When you have to do something new, how do you approach it? Consider cooking something you have never done before, starting to use a new electronic gadget or learning a new sports skill.

Learning styles

Learning styles are essentially preferences for how you prefer to gather and assimilate information and put your new knowledge to work. Various learning styles are recognised:

- visual
- auditory
- reading/writing
- tactile/kinaesthetic/physical

A kinaesthetic learner, for example, will prefer to learn by doing something. Most of us have combinations of styles we learn by, but will have a preference or one particular style we find more effective. In the cooking example above, for instance, we may prefer simply trying out a recipe, rather than reading it first. On the other hand, when we open up the box with a new computer or mobile phone, we may prefer to read the instruction booklet first. Where my previous students have taken a test of their preferred learning styles, many (perhaps not surprisingly for sport students) identified themselves as kinaesthetic learners. They enjoyed practical learning experiences or tasks, demonstrating and carrying out activities. Visual learners, on the other hand, prefer to watch, observe, see or read instructions. Auditory learners will listen, talk about, and enjoy discussing in order to gain their knowledge. Reading and writing is not always the most popular learning style, but is probably the most widely used in formal education, as it is something you are expected to do a lot of in school and university. You will no doubt have heard the expression 'reading for a degree'.

If you are interested in finding out what sort of learner you are, there may be a test you can do as part of the university learning advice and support service. Some sport programmes incorporate such tests into Personal Development Planning (PDP) or academic skills courses.

Looking at learning styles is interesting but, unless you do something with the information, is unlikely to have much of an impact on your performance. For example, if your results suggest you prefer kinaesthetic learning but your course is more geared to writing and reading, then it may be up to you to adapt the learning you do. By providing practical examples, activities and things to do independently, you can make your sports studies course more practical and improve your understanding. You can use books like this, for example, with a range of potential learning experiences in each chapter, including listening to radio programmes, watching films, observing activities, discussing with others, and investigating friends' and family members' experiences of sport and comparing them with your own. These activities are designed to make use of a range of learning styles and preferences. It is up to *you* how effective they are in achieving the outcomes set out.

Activity

Find out if you can complete a learning styles test with the university or go to one of the online or free versions, for example the VARK questionnaire (see the online sources in the Further study section at the end of this chapter). Investigate how useful such questionnaires are.

Not all of the learning involved in sport studies will be in organised, timetabled sessions. Practical sport experiences, either as part of an organised session on a programme, or those enjoyed outside of school or university, whether under your own direction or organised by others, give rise to a whole range of learning experiences – invaluable to a sport student. For that reason, active engagement in sport remains an important tool for any student serious about their studies, and can provide much insight and understanding of the real world of sport in modern society. It is often through their own, or by observing at first hand other's, experiences that students start to understand better what sport is really all about and that it has a depth and range of meaning which is different to many subjects.

The sections below examine some of the most common teaching approaches used and attempt to explain how learning in these sessions can be improved and made more active, even if they may not always match your individual learning preferences.

It also helps to understand the 'protocol' of sessions you might not be familiar with – what is expected from students and what students can expect from their tutors or programme. If students come to courses armed with some understanding of the purpose of sessions and methods used, the more likely they will be able to get on with the job of learning. 'Turn up and take part' is probably the most essential learning style for any student and one I would strongly recommend.

Activity

Go to your programme handbook or department website and read the information available about learning styles, teaching and learning strategies, and methods used in your course. Consider the results of your learning styles questionnaire and set yourself some objectives relating to your own learning on the programme. For example, one objective may be to complete the recommended reading task within one week of a session. What methods or techniques, from the activities above, may be useful to improving *your* learning?

Learning in lectures

Though lectures remain an important aspect of many sport studies course teaching strategies, they are recognised as being fraught with difficulty when it comes to effective learning by students. On the one hand, having all the students listen attentively to your carefully chosen words of wisdom is very appealing to the tutor; on the other the learning the students can achieve by simply sitting in the lecture theatre, hopefully listening to but not necessarily understanding the material is a real concern. However, that is the main 'protocol' to be observed, the lecturer, lectures and the students listen, take notes, and may be called upon to answer questions or provide examples from time to time. Large lecture theatres are often a very alien environment to those straight from school (and can be even worse if there is a longer gap!) or those used to more interactive and engaging classrooms of fewer numbers of students. However, many lecturers include multi-media or PowerPoint presentations, images, discussion points, handouts and other activities designed to maintain interest and engage students in a more active approach to help reinforce their learning. For example, the videos and DVDs noted in earlier chapters have been used within lectures (taking advantage of the projection and sound systems) to help illuminate some of the theory involved in sport studies.

Though lectures are useful for communicating information simultaneously to whole groups – up to 250 in some courses – unfortunately they still provide more opportunity for one-way communication. They are also a very tutor-led form of learning, in that the lecture covers what the tutor thinks is important, not necessarily what the students will find the most interesting or relevant. Nevertheless, as a student this is an important clue to the significance of the material – this is what the tutor expects the student to be aware of and understand, and may form part of what is needed to be able to successfully complete any assessment. Lectures will also use and develop the vocabulary of the subject, to build understanding of important terms, concepts, theories and explanations.

It is possible to get more out of lectures and this doesn't mean simply having a set of notes or a transcript of every word spoken by the tutor. You are very unlikely to ever be asked to reproduce exactly what has been said in a specific lecture, so students are not expected to write down and recall everything verbatim (word for word). Lectures should never be considered 'all there is to know' on a subject. Tutors will expect students to reinforce any lecture session with their own reading on a topic, some reflection or 'thinking' about the subject or other activities. Some tutors may consider the lecture to be broadly mapping out or introducing a topic or area that the student is expected to develop much further through independent reading and research. Others use lectures for more focused sessions to cover in great depth their views or research on a particular topic or issue. It is important for students to recognise the diverse ways in which lectures operate, in order to get the most from them.

> ### Time out
>
> Think about how you currently learn during lecture-based sessions. What do you do to make the most of the experience? What problems do you have with this form of teaching. Is there anything *you* could do to make the sessions more effective?

The following are some of the ways you can make more of lectures.

Prepare

Before you go to any lecture, it is useful to see where it sits in the 'big picture' of the unit involved. Many tutors provide handbooks or guides, which set out the programme of lectures and other activities associated with the unit and expectations in terms of reading and tasks for the student.

If there is some indication of any pre-reading expected, set aside sufficient time to do this, and you will find the lecture should make more sense to you. It can also make taking notes a lot easier, if you have some idea of the more important or significant aspects of the topic. Using structured note-taking also helps, when you need to read your notes for revision or prepare for assessment. The example provided in Figure 6.1 can be developed into a template for your notes and can cut down on the writing you do during any session.

Take part

The best way to benefit from lectures is to make sure you go along to them and take an active role in your own learning. This includes taking notes, any preparatory reading recommended, follow-up activity or reading and some 'thinking' time. Lecturers may provide back-up copies of lecture notes, slides or handouts, but the best way to ensure these are all effective is to be there, taking part. This may seem a bit obvious, but even when lectures are deemed to be 'compulsory' on a programme, some students think they can still achieve the necessary learning by copying someone else's notes or looking at the slides later on the web. For some people, this may be possible to maintain contact for one or two sessions, but is not recommended unless you genuinely cover much more material independently, and are researching the topic in depth outside the lecture – even so, there is a risk that you may misunderstand or miss the 'sense-making' aspect of learning.

Be an active learner

During the lecture don't attempt to write everything down, but concentrate on key phrases and bullet points. Make note of any authors you may be expected to follow up on

Figure 6.1: Example of format for structured notes from sport studies lecture

Template for your own notes

Unit/Module title:

Date/week of session:

Tutor:

Lecture/session title or subject:

Links to: (note any previous lectures or week numbers or related assessments), e.g. *follow on from Lecture 4 – historical perspective*

Aim

Note aim set out by the tutor, in your own words – what is the purpose of the session?
Or refer to slides if attached (as you won't have time to write everything down, don't copy anything out you will already have available as text)

Learning objectives/outcomes/themes to be explored
Your tutor may set out what they expect to cover or achieve within the session; that is, what, by the end of this session, you will be expected to achieve in your learning – knowledge, understanding or even skills. They might identify what this session will include, or what you should be able to do as a result of the session and associated reading.

Note these if given at the start of the session, e.g.

List the main historical methods available
Identify key reading on methods in sport history
Provide examples of different approaches

Introduction: note any key points raised in first few minutes – this is usually where the tutor will set out the main purpose and key concepts to be addressed.

Section 1 – these relate to first objective

Section 2 – second objective or area

Section 3 – these sections could continue if the lecture covers more areas

Follow-up activity (What do you need to do as a result of the lecture today?)

Recommended reading
Author, date (if book, just note name and date and title; if necessary, you should be able to look up on the unit reading list or in library catalogue).
Journal articles (note the author, journal and year; you can then find via electronic search engines, such as Ingenta or Sport Discus).

Other reading of interest on this topic: note down any authors referred to that you want to do more follow-up reading on.

Evaluation of session:
Think about the earlier sections – fill this in after the lecture. Were the objectives met? Are there any objectives you need to go back to and do more work on? Any questions for next session or seminar/tutorial? Note any follow-up questions or notes for later revision.

– more detailed references should be in the recommended reading or handbook. Make a note of questions or reflections as you go through; if there is any opportunity for discussion or questions, you will have something ready to contribute.

Follow up and reinforce the lecture

The best way to achieve a 'deeper' learning experience is to have opportunities to write or talk about the material, ask questions and apply the knowledge as soon as possible afterwards. You should continue to reflect as you go through more reading on the subject. If such opportunities are provided in face-to-face or virtual environments, take them! They will have been designed with your learning in mind. Attending seminars or contributing to discussion boards will help to review the material and help your understanding, even if you may not always agree with fellow students or your tutor – that might well be the point, to show a range of views is possible on a particular issue.

Always review your notes shortly after the lecture – if you have a busy schedule, this may be a day or two afterwards, but ideally should be within 24 hours. This is to ensure:

- that the material is complete, sensible and provides a good summary of the lecture content;
- you understand and have achieved the learning outcomes for the session.

Activity

- Write down three things you could do to improve the effectiveness of your learning in lectures.
- Design your own lecture note template, using Figure 6.1 as a guide.
- Look at alternative ways to organise your notes – for example, mind maps.

Health warnings in lectures

Based on experience, many students do not always follow what might be the best advice on lectures, but may still manage to pass at the end of the year. On some courses, lectures are recommended but not necessarily compulsory, so students decide they can learn better without them, or they have more interesting things to do. Unfortunately, only when they have ruined their summer with re-sits or referrals, or spent hours cramming for an exam, do they appreciate the significance of the sessions they missed.

There are a few things that seem to guarantee reduced performance:

- not going to lectures;
- sitting at the back, where you cannot see or be seen, and taking no active part in the session;
- not taking a pen or paper (because the slides are on the internet!);
- when actually in lectures:
  o catching up with your texting
  o reading the newspaper

o organising a trip to the student union bar or discussing the previous night out
o taking no notes.

Perhaps surprisingly, what seems to irritate many students the most about lectures is the behaviour of other students. For many students, lectures provide a welcome framework for their studies, plenty of new and interesting material to consider and a chance to be enthusiastic about their subject. Hopefully that describes you!

Seminars and discussion-based groups

The term seminar is used to describe group sessions, which are discussion based. These are usually combined with lecture sessions, or possibly labs or practical sessions, to cover a specific topic or issue in more depth, to stimulate reading or examine a particular question. Very few courses operate the 'Oxbridge' approach of intensive one to one teaching, or 'supervisions'. However, seminar or discussion groups can be as small as six to ten students or as large as 25 to 30 students. For discussions, larger groups may be further subdivided into more manageable and fruitful group sizes. Too large and it is unlikely that everyone will get the chance to contribute, and too small and they may provide a more limited or less stimulating discussion, though this depends on the inter-activity of the session and the individuals concerned. Seminars provide more space for students to develop their own 'thinking about' the subject. Seminars might provide some answers, or promote more questions but they will rarely arrive at 'the answer', as in sport studies, these are often complex and contested, with different viewpoints to consider.

Sport studies seminar topics might include:

• Why do female sports performers get such poor media coverage?
• What are the barriers to participation faced by those from ethnic minorities?

In the early stages of the course, seminars are often more tutor-led but, as the programme develops, students will increasingly be asked to lead seminars and present their own ideas and investigations. Well-designed courses and sessions offer the chance for students to interact, reinforce the learning through lectures and/or independent study, question and debate. The number of seminars, their formats and arrangements vary a great deal. Preferences of the tutor, practical issues of timetabling and the objectives of the session or unit, mean that seminars may happen weekly for some units, but only every three or four weeks for others. For the student, it is important to check the frequency of seminars and follow again the principles of preparation, active engagement and reflection established above for lectures. As these opportunities have been designed with student learning in mind, assessment of learning will often be made on the assumption you have taken advantage of them – over and above any attendance regulations you may be expected to fulfil.

Seminar titles and discussion points or tasks may be provided in lectures or in the unit handbook. Students may be allocated specific sessions at which they will be expected to take the lead in setting up a discussion or outlining the key points from some directed reading, either individually or in groups. Therefore, students are expected to prepare for their specific role. In the previous chapters, some of the discussion points provided are based on seminar sessions I've used previously. Common approaches include: the selection of possible seminar topics to reflect potential examination areas; debates on topics that involve teams 'for' a motion and those opposing; or a critique or analysis of a specific paper or chapter on a topic. Alternatively, on the selected topic, students may be asked in turn to lead the discussion on a particular paper or article they have been asked to read and prepare in advance.

During seminars the discussion will address the issue or topic (for example, the problem of female representation in the sport media) and all students should expect to contribute in some way. This might be through pre-prepared questions to group members on their experiences or opinions, reviewing examples of media representations of different types, or providing observations on a film or TV clip. In Chapter 5, for example, there is a range of media-related tasks that might lead onto or be incorporated into seminar-type discussions.

The most interesting and useful sessions are when students take a more active role and are prepared, so they are able to make more meaningful and thoughtful contributions. Students can share their ideas and interpretations to help check on understanding and to consider different viewpoints. This may require some 'refereeing' from the tutor, so that everyone gets their chance and to maintain some structure and control in the session – but approaches to this will vary. Some sessions may be designed with less advance notice and preparation, to see how students deal with more novel ideas or thoughts and also how they control their own discussions, with only limited input from tutors.

There are some practical issues to consider with seminars. For example, if you are asked to prepare a presentation for a seminar, check if you are expected to use any audio-visual aids, such as PowerPoint, and if the computer and projector are available (see advice on oral presentations below). Students may be asked to comment on the contributions of others, so the tutor may set out some 'ground rules' regarding acceptable comments and behaviour, or formats for feedback. A useful principle to follow here is based on the 'golden rule' referred to in Chapter 3: respond to others, as you would like to be responded to!

Reflecting back on seminars and integrating this with other learning is an important part of the experience. Keeping a note of the main points from a seminar or your reflections from it can be a very useful way of maintaining good resources for future reference, in the preparation of assessments or in revision for examinations. This needn't be an onerous task, but the sooner you do it after the seminar, the better. The information will still be fresh and you may get a really good idea that can provide an interesting link later or idea for more reading you can do to help improve your own understanding.

Increasingly, tutors are using electronic discussion boards for supporting or conducting seminars (in webCT, for example). Such contributions are often expected from each student and can therefore be tracked or monitored. For some issues, a chance to reflect on the various points raised allows students to take more time and space to provide a more in-depth response than might occur within the session. Also, some students prefer the 'virtual' discussion, as they have less confidence in speaking out with other students, or more time to think about what they want to say. It is also interesting to be able to read other's contributions at your own pace and compare these to your own as your own understanding develops.

Practical and workshop sessions

In sport courses, not surprisingly, practical sessions can often feature as part of an overall teaching and learning strategy. These are more likely to be integral to physical education, coaching, sport science or sport therapy programmes. However, they are also found in some sport studies degrees or broad 'sport'-based courses. Such sessions may be compulsory on some courses, with some assessments of personal competence or performance, depending on the nature of the programme and the requirements for any professional body. The general assumption is that if you have opted for a course relating to the study of sport, not only would you enjoy this type of experience, it would be an essential part of developing your understanding of the area, as it would involve the practical application of the theory involved.

It is perhaps more of a challenge to make practical sessions more relevant to the application of the more abstract or theoretical aspects of sport studies, but it can be achieved. For example, in understanding about the development of 'fair play' ideals, or the importance of 'rules', a practical session might explore the different forms of games and activities, examine the impact of rule changes, demonstrate examples of rule breaking or how to deal with problems occurring in sport competitions. This can be through role play, simulation, scenarios or improvisation – students could be asked to develop a game using a selected set of equipment, or adapt an existing one, to accommodate those with a particular disability or disadvantage.

Individual competence in specific sporting activities is usually only a relatively minor part of any sport studies programme, but would be helpful to enhance and broaden personal experience of sport and perhaps enable the student to demonstrate appropriate and safe practice, if relevant. Engaging in a practical session is a great way to experience, and thus better understand, how various practical sport-based skills can be developed.

As students on non-sport programmes also enjoy sport at university, accessibility of facilities and the range of activities is usually very high. The expectation is that students on sport courses are active in their personal sporting careers, and most programmes are designed to facilitate this. Personal fitness is also encouraged in sport students, in preparation for potential sport-related careers, where active engagement and demonstration of skills is expected – such as physical education teaching or coaching. Of course, many sport studies students also prefer a more 'passive' approach to sport – they enjoy the watching/observing/analysis of sport to the practise of it!

However where practical or task-oriented workshops are provided, they are used to provide the 'learning by doing' opportunities students often find very rewarding. To get the most from them, again an active approach is recommended. Preparation, engagement and reflection can relate the session to other learning experiences, such as reading about a theory, putting it into practice and then reflecting on the learning achieved. Skills of observation, listening and demonstrating or reproducing actions may be different but similar to those employed in other forms of learning, but the physical actions involved and the interactions with other students and the tutor can be quite different. Sometimes, as part of discussion-based sessions, students are asked to reflect on their experiences in practical contexts of sport – even if the session is not a practical one, it nevertheless draws upon students' real-life experiences and practices.

Writing up notes and reflections on the practical is also useful to keep a record on the activities and practices involved, and for your own observations and feelings about how the session went, and whether or not you developed your skills and/or knowledge. Some programmes may require such records to be developed as part of a portfolio approach (see below) or to aid the development of reflective practice.

Visits and field work

An element of practical work could include a field trip or visit to a sporting venue, event or organisation. This may involve engaging in sport, listening to presentations or observing an activity or event. To assist in the value of the visit, tutors may prepare worksheets or provide tasks, where the objective is to gather some specific evidence or information, which may be needed for later sessions or contribute towards assessment. Such visits should provide interesting and worthwhile learning experiences and a welcome break from routine sessions. Some of the topics in the earlier chapters suggest some potential study visits or field trips, for example a visit to the National Football Museum or to the site of the Manchester Commonwealth Games venues. Sometimes such field work is also to develop teams or groups, or to enhance the interpersonal skills of students (see Chapter 7). An example of an assignment based on such a visit is provided in Figure 6.2, in the section on assessment.

Directed and self-directed study

Most university programmes are based on a mixture of what is often called 'contact time' and directed or self-directed study. A standard ten credits of university learning at undergraduate level, for example, represents 100 hours of learning by the student. Only about ten hours of this will be 'contact time' in lectures, seminars or practical sessions, as described above. The remainder is expected to be spent on directed reading or self-directed study, in order to achieve the learning outcomes, which are developed and assessed through *formative* and *summative* assessments (see below).

Some students find that the balance between self- and tutor-directed learning is not always easy to achieve, when the contact time for each subject is much lower than they were used to at school or college. Chapter 7 includes some practical advice on how to organise time to make sure all the bases get covered and there is still time to play sport, socialise or even gain work experience.

Time out

- Think about your approach to studying. For example, look at your weekly timetable: how much of your time is spent in lectures, seminars or other sessions? (You could compile a table and work out time and proportions of the week.)
- Identify how many learning styles you currently use. What is the most commonly used style? What style do you prefer?
- Identify three ways to increase the range of styles you use.
- Think about the amount of self-directed and directed study you do. Are you setting aside enough time to achieve the expected hours of learning?

Assessments in sport studies

The first thing many students do as soon as they start a unit is to turn to the assessment page of the unit handbook in order to find out how they will be assessed. I suspect sport studies students are no different in this respect to students of other subjects. The following sections consider the different types of assessment commonly used in sport studies programmes, and how grades can be improved by following some basic advice and guidance. Most sport studies courses use a range of assessments, both coursework and examination. Examinations can also vary in the style of submission expected: from short answer to longer short essay type responses, or seen or unseen topics or questions, with notes allowed, or even 'open book', where students can bring in their own resources or set texts to assist them in formulating the answer.

Types of assessment

Formative assessment is not part of the final module grade. This may include assessed or non-assessed tasks set out as follow-up activities, preparation for seminars or lectures, recommended reading or self-directed, additional reading on topics of interest, and preparatory assessments where feedback is provided in order to develop skills as well as knowledge.

Summative assessment covers achievement in the unit. Summative marks can be accumulated over a number of pieces of work, to arrive at the final unit grade. Summative assessment covers the learning outcomes. Your grade may be based on skills as well as content.

How to tackle a task for assessment

Students should ask some essential questions when first presented with an assessment:

- First things first – what is the task?
- What do I already know about this topic or question?
- Where can I get more information on the topic or question?
- How do I need to present my findings or research (format)?
- When do I need to complete this by?

Once you have a clear picture of what is required, look carefully at the assessment criteria (see below) and the format of the submission.

The following is a checklist for assessments:

- Draft a plan of the tasks needing to be done, leading to the submission date.
- Identify relevant reading.
- Gather the relevant research together (library, desktop or other).
- Read and assess the material (allow sufficient time for this).
- Check your material against the criteria again – have you included all the relevant points/sections?
- Check how the assessment needs to be presented or submitted.

- Write out or complete in appropriate sections (or complete PowerPoints or other formats as necessary).
- Write out full assessment and proofread carefully (use the spell check facility on your computer).
- Check for correct English – use the facility on Word to highlight any potential problems with sentence construction or words used (see Chapter 7 for how to do this).
- Check all references and sources.
- Check against the learning outcomes for the unit.
- Check all relevant details are provided (student number, unit number, etc, cover sheet if necessary).
- Complete relevant submission sheet.
- Print and collate the day before the 'submit by' day.
- Keep a back-up copy.
- Submit before the final deadline (relax and treat yourself to a break!).

Techniques like mind-mapping have been developed to help visualise and draft out ideas, knowledge or concepts (Buzan and Buzan 2006). Students can use this approach to map out what they know and use it to help organise and develop a plan for their assessments, or summarise notes on a topic or issue, or brainstorm ideas in groups. Other methods of creative thinking, pioneered by Edward de Bono, are also widely used.

Getting better grades: writing styles, formats and approaches

Not all forms of writing for assessment in a sport studies course will necessarily be the same. Students may be expected to complete a short essay (750–1500 words) or something lengthier and more detailed (1500–2000 words up to 5000 words, to replicate the length of an academic journal article). Many degree courses involve the completion of a major extended piece of writing based on personal research, in the form of a dissertation or project report. Foundation degree students may not have A-level qualifications involving essays, but have a great deal of valuable work experience. Foundation degree writing tasks tend to be more work-based, such as reports. Students come from a range of backgrounds and have a great diversity of qualifications (A-levels, BTEC qualifications, foundation degrees or vocational qualifications) when studying sport at university. As a result, many courses adopt a developmental approach to writing, building up from initial attempts and essays in early stages, to more advanced and complex writing tasks later. Students can also receive some advice and guidance in their writing from university learning support services, particularly if they are inexperienced in extended writing tasks.

Writing essays

The first task for essays is to ensure the topic, title, question or focus are clearly identified. Common errors or causes of lost marks include a failure to answer the specific question, essays with no central point or argument, or missing out an important element of the question. This is particularly crucial when writing an essay under time-constrained conditions or in examinations. Having a clear structure and organisation to the essay is crucial in forming ideas in a clear and logical way, and ensuring all relevant aspects are included. Essentially, the essay should make the clear the student's knowledge and understanding and demonstrate appropriate application, analysis or interpretation, using appropriate and clearly expressed language.

It may seem obvious, but the essay should use correct English grammar, with no spelling or typographical errors. For academic submissions, the essay will include reference to other's ideas and cite a variety of sources in support of arguments and observations. There are important conventions to follow for references, which are looked at in more detail below.

The best way to ensure a good grade in essays is to have a clear plan, developed from a good overview of relevant research on the topic, with careful attention to presentation. It may be possible to check a plan with the tutor before submission, through seminars or tutorial sessions – if these opportunities are provided, this can be very helpful in developing confidence that a particular interpretation or approach is appropriate, acceptable or suitable.

Start at the beginning – have a clear introduction, addressing what the essay is about and what it covers. The main body of the essay should address, in a logical order, the key concepts, issues or arguments. These should be developed along a logical thread or discussion, and, depending on the purpose of the essay, showing evidence of good research and an analytical approach. Most essays have a conclusion, which summarises or draws together the key points made in the proceeding sections. An example of a suggested structure or plan for a first-year essay is provided below.

Essay title: An examination of gender and sport – female representation in the media

The introduction should include brief opening remarks about the work on gender and media. Explain the relevance of the issue of representation, how it is defined, and how you have structured the work below.

The main body of the essay should examine in more depth the main concepts and arguments presented (one or two paragraphs on each) on the topic of female representation, gender and sport, in the reading you have completed. You should relate the key findings or conclusions of the authors. These can be backed up with reference to wider reading. Summarise how the authors deal with the issue of representation differently. You should be basing this on reading published articles in journals or chapters of the books from the recommended reading. At the very least this will be the material you were asked to read for the topic in the relevant lecture. Part of the assessment will no doubt be about how you select and utilise the sources.

Essentially, you should highlight what the literature you have looked at has to say about this topic and analyse the conclusions drawn. For an introductory essay, there may be more description of the concepts and findings, but with some attempt to analyse what you have read on these issues.

Always finish the essay with some brief concluding remarks. Describe your main conclusions from this short review on the subject, referring back to the question or title

Report writing

Reports may be used as an alternative to essays, which means adopting a slightly different writing style and format. If asked to produce a report, for example based on individual or group investigations of sport organisations or programmes, students should check the format expected by their tutor or department. There might be a standard format, for example using the subheadings or sections provided below.

A standard report would normally include:

- Executive summary
- Introduction, including terms of reference, background to the problem or issue
- Procedures/methods of investigation
- Findings (subdivided as necessary)
- Conclusions
- Recommendations
- References/notes
- Appendices

Reports will usually have a contents page, and may have numbered sections as well as numbered pages.

A good way to prepare reports is to consult examples of relevant reports to provide a model or style for the structure and language to be used. Paragraphs tend to be shorter, with numbered references or notes to reduce the breaks in the text for references. Subheadings are used to break up the various sections. There may be appendices attached, though these are often limited for submissions for assessment. These may be technical descriptions, lists or tables, not all of which are necessary in the text. If appendices are attached to a report, they should be referred to in the text and have a clear purpose, not be simply a collection of material added to bulk up an otherwise thin report.

Other formats

Tutors are often looking to innovate in methods of assessment and to keep students enthusiastic about their studies. New technology has also allowed for more methods: submitting work on CD-ROM, online or using other methods of presentation, including audio-visual aids. For example, a colleague teaching a unit on the History of Physical Education asked students to use MS Publisher to produce a leaflet as a topic guide suitable for A-level students on a particular period of the history of PE, rather than submitting an essay. Students were encouraged to search for images, use different fonts and colours to emphasise their key points and provide sources for further study. Presenting assessed work in other formats means that different skills may be needed and this can often provide an opportunity for more vocational or work-related scenarios or information technology to be incorporated into programme assessment strategies.

Oral presentations

Presentations, either in groups or individually, are a very common form of assessment in sport studies. The criteria below provide the elements usually found in oral presentations. Though many students prefer them, nevertheless oral presentations can provide a challenge to students who find it difficult to speak to large groups or under pressure of being assessed. Having a clear plan and structure – i.e. knowing what you are going to say and how you are going to say it – is an important prerequisite for a successful presentation. It is important to get the skills of presenting right, as well as making sure the content: (a) is appropriate for the question, title or task; (b) is detailed and well supported by research; and (c) shows the appropriate level of analysis and understanding.

Advice for effective presentations

Bear the following in mind:

- Prepare well and rehearse before you present for assessment.
- Use notes or cue cards and have a back-up in case your PowerPoint demonstration or computer fails.
- Do not read directly from the notes, but have them to hand to refer to.
- Keep to the time limit.
- Maintain eye contact with the audience and never turn your back to them.
- Think about possible questions from the audience and have additional information you might need to hand

Examples of presentation topics include: barriers to sport participation in ethnic minorities; investigations of child protection policies in various sports; the potential impacts of London 2012 on sport participation.

Posters

Posters – up to A0 size (1m²) – are often used in academic sport conferences, and so are increasingly utilised as an alternative form of submission. MS PowerPoint slides or other software can be used to generate the required size of sheet. They usually involve a blend of text and illustration, with charts, tables or pictures. By necessity, the amount of text is limited to essential content, limited description, explanation, findings or arguments. References for cited sources are also required and correct captioning of any illustrations, just as in a written report. Most tutors will provide specific format requirements, or refer to the guidelines for professional or academic conferences, such as BASES, which usually have poster presentation sessions.

University media departments can also provide information about how to send the posters to them, if you want to print off a large colour poster onto an A0 paper sheet. This isn't something to attempt on a home printer!

Some posters may be acceptable in the form of a series of A4 PowerPoint slides pasted together – this is dependent upon how important the presentation of the final version is. Posters can be a very interesting way for all the students to see the results of fellow group member assessments and they can incorporate some discussion or explanation of the poster in a mini-conference session. For example, if each group produces a poster on their investigation into a particular social group or historical sporting event, it can be a very interesting session for everyone to compare their findings by looking at and talking about each other's posters. This is a more active form of learning than simply writing an essay about the topic, and can incorporate other skills, such as creativity, working as a team and IT.

It is helpful to produce an A4 version in black and white, before going to print with the full-sized, full-colour version, which is often expensive to produce, even through university reprographic departments. Posters are usually assessed on both content and presentation, with marks available for the impact, depth and clarity of the work. By printing off a draft copy, simple spacing or typographical errors can be checked for and corrected.

Portfolios

Portfolios may provide the opportunity to complete a range of varied tasks, over an extended period, to help illustrate the achievement of learning outcomes. They may include short writing tasks, completed tables, searches, examples of material gathered from different sources, copies of certificates, plans, diagrams, copies of completed worksheets or tasks completed within seminars or practical sessions, or logbooks of activities completed. Essentially, they are a collection of evidence required to demonstrate learning has been achieved against some set of criteria.

There may be some choice in terms of what the portfolio contains – or a very specific list of required elements. Portfolios are usually assessed on both completeness and the standard of achievement shown. The basic advice about all these formats is to check very carefully how to present work for assessments and to allow time in preparation to produce the finished piece. This includes printing or copying the relevant work, and organising the folder and contents pages for easy navigation and assessment. Some folders may be submitted online or on CD-ROM to save on printing and bulky folders, so students need to have the IT skills to scan or convert to suitable formats and use appropriate software for writing to a CD-ROM or uploading content. Portfolios are increasingly being used in more vocationally oriented assessments, or for PDPs.

Assessment and grading

Whatever the task for assessment, there will usually be a set of published *assessment criteria*. These are the things the tutor expects to find in the assignment, the criteria upon which your grade will be based. Students achieve the best grade by fulfilling all the criteria at the highest level. The most important advice is to read all guidance given carefully and ensure the work presented fulfils those criteria. The relative weighting or marks available for any particular aspect of the assignment can also provide clues as to how important they are. A final mark is made up by aggregating (adding and/or weighting) marks for the various elements, which assesses content or knowledge, analysis and presentation or organisation. All assignments are designed to provide evidence of the student achievement of the unit learning outcomes.

In general, numerical grades (expressed as a percentage) are provided for assessments or units, though individual elements may have letter (A, B, C) or band (acceptable, good, excellent) grading.

An example of the assessment criteria for an essay based on a study trip to Manchester is shown in Figure 6.2.

Figure 6.2: Assessment criteria for an essay based on a study trip to Manchester

Title: An analysis of the development of sport opportunities in East Manchester since the Commonwealth Games In 2002 (1500 word essay)

Specific assessment criteria (with marks available indicated)

Content (60 marks)
- Identification of issues and concepts relevant to sport and leisure provision by the relevant organisations (city council, governing bodies, professional sport) and their roles in the development of sporting opportunities
- Identification of leisure and sport opportunities at Sport City and in the local area (informed by worksheets attached)
- Use of social and other relevant theory to explain and analyse impacts of sport opportunities since the Games (supported by sources)

Research (30 marks)
- Evidence of research using a range of sources
- Interpretation and evaluation of material, with some description of factual data
- Completion of the study visit observations worksheet (attached as appendix to the assignment), which should be referred to in the main body of the essay

Presentation (10 marks)
An essay format with correct grammar and appropriate style of writing is required.

Honours degree grading bands are usually as follows:

Degree classification

First class	70% or above
Upper second	60–69
Second	50–59
Third	40–49

A *Pass* degree is sometimes awarded for honours work graded at 35–39%, but work given this grade is normally classed a 'fail' for individual assessments.

The standard pass rate at undergraduate level is 40%.

You should look at the descriptors for work at various levels of your degree to provide some indication of the characteristics of work awarded marks at different classifications. Most universities publish their standard criteria in the student hand-books. For specific assignments, you should be able to identify what the characteristics of a good piece of work are.

Activity

- Consult your programme handbook and identify the range of assessments used in each unit you need to complete. Identify which units are coursework only, exam only or a mixture of the two. How do these proportions change as you move through the degree?

- Think about whether or not you may need to develop more skills to be able to submit work in different formats (in IT, for example), based on the advice in the sections above. Identify any potential sources of help or advice for the university examinations.

A brief word about examinations

Examinations are used in many sport studies courses, but they often involve a range of approaches, as noted above, as the limits of the time-constrained essay format are recognised. Some examinations will be more about the application of knowledge to particular scenarios or cases, or using and applying theory, than simply reproducing it.

The important thing is to understand what constitutes the 'success' factor in the examination, and to be an active learner in the approach: be prepared, practise the technique or method, and use that approach regularly in the 'revision' phase of the programme. To find this 'success factor', look at the outcomes being assessed by the exam; find out the format for the paper – the choice of topics or questions; and work out the format expected in answers – detailed, short answers based on objective knowledge, multiple-choice or more in-depth essays.

The clue to what is expected in this phase is in the word 'revision' – this implies that the student will be looking again; so, where the assessment for a unit involves an examination, it is important not to leave all the work for the night before. If tutors offer revision or advice sessions about examinations, it goes without saying that students are expected to take full advantage of these – though I have often been surprised to see students at such sessions turning up without pen or paper! Indeed, some do not turn up at all.

One of the best methods to use for revision and preparation is to set or find questions (in the style of the proposed examination) and practise answering them. If there are previous papers available, get hold of them and use them to produce answers under the same conditions as you will experience in the examination. It might be possible to form small groups where students can 'test' each other. Some tutors will use the same type of questions in the seminar programmes for example, so seminars might provide a useful guide to what might be expected in an examination answer.

Feedback and how to use it to improve your grades

In my own experience of sport psychology lectures, I was taught that knowledge of results (feedback) was essential for the development of learning and improved sport performance. As I moved into teaching in higher education, I found this lesson was very important, as I found students rarely improved their work or learning without some feedback.

Feedback can occur during sessions, including lectures and seminars, when students can check their understanding by responses to questions, through quick verbal feedback. It is through the feedback on assessed work, either formative or summative, that you are provided with the most useful information about your progress and results. Such feedback indicates what you have done well, and perhaps not well enough, and may provide some advice on how to improve future submissions. Reading and reflecting on feedback on assessed work is very important to a more active approach to learning.

However, it is often the case that students focus on the numerical grade awarded, rather than on the written feedback provided by tutors on the assessment criteria. Even if the work received a very positive grade, this feedback can provide important clues as to how to get even better grades in future. Of course, if the grade awarded was less than expected, you also need to be aware of how and why your work was not so favourably assessed by your tutor. Students who have a similar grade awarded can have very different pieces of work, as they may have different strengths and weaknesses. If tutors use highly structured feedback sheets, it might be possible to see the breakdown on particular parts of an assessment. By taking an active approach to reading and reflecting on feedback, you can improve your grades.

Some universities provide a space for student reflection on mark feedback forms so that you can note your response to particular points of feedback, on either the content of the assignment or how you approached the work. For example, a poor grade might be a fair reflection of a lack of research or denote a problem with your understanding of a key aspect of the assessment.

If you find feedback confusing or unclear, you should seek some help from either personal or academic tutors, depending on the arrangements at your university. Consistent feedback, for example, that your work lacks depth or is poorly expressed or organised, should immediately alert you to the fact that you need to improve your research and use of sources, or writing style, essay planning or depth of reading. The following section on finding and using sources more effectively may be helpful to those who find this a problem when tackling assessments in sport studies.

Finding and using sources effectively

Learning resources: more than books

To make more effective use of the academic sources available to support learning in sport studies, you need to become more effective at finding relevant material using the resources available, i.e. human – the subject librarian, and technological – electronic and media. The following section provides some help and guidance on short cuts, improving skills and working smarter, not necessarily harder, in sport studies.

In modern campuses, libraries are being replaced with 'learning resource centres', 'learning hubs' or other such developments. The building may still be the same, but what is on offer inside is very different to the libraries of the past. Students may actually have to visit libraries less often, as many of the resources can be researched from the comfort of the laptop. Learning resources are all those materials that students are expected to draw upon to aid their learning.

Many libraries provide *subject guides* on where and how to locate the resource you need, as well as access to an online catalogue of all resources held. This catalogue may also provide details of what is provided as an electronic resource, such as online databases, eBooks or electronic journals. If the university does not already do so, it is useful to create a shortcut to the University Library catalogue on your desktop. The library is much more than a place that houses books; it is often the source of invaluable help in searching and obtaining a wide range of resources and learning support.

Many programmes or courses have a subject-specific learning resource guide, and each unit will identify those most relevant, or recommended by the tutor. The resources and services useful to students of sport may be included within other disciplines – physical education within education, sociology of sport within the sociology section, sport management within management or business school resources, for example.

The learning resources of interest in sport studies may include:

- books
- journals
- CDROM/DVD/video or sound recordings
- pamphlets and reports
- government publications
- periodicals or newspapers
- short loan or reference material
- theses or other university publications

In each of the preceding chapters, a range of relevant resources has been identified and referred to. The range of relevant material in this subject is very diverse, as sport is an aspect of popular culture that can have both academic interest and entertainment value. As noted in Chapter 1, for example, popular films and television documentaries can also be useful resources for sport studies.

Make friends with your subject librarian

Many large university libraries will have a subject specialist, a professional librarian who maintains the collection and services for a particular subject. They usually process the book orders from tutors and monitor learning resources requested and listed in unit guides. Their help in tracking down a book or article can save many fruitless hours browsing the shelves or catalogues.

The desktop sources at your fingertips

I remember the hours spent searching through index cards or micro-fiche records in order to locate some material relating to assignments at university. Even as a tutor, I have waited to get hold of an article or book from inter-library loan. When I studied for my Masters degree, I had a two-hour train journey to visit the library, with another 30-minute walk to a specialist library for some journals needed for my study. This meant I had to be organised about my time and how I used the library once I got there.

Now it is possible to search through catalogues from my own and other libraries, millions of pages of web content or through online databases, with only a few clicks of the mouse, from my home or the office desk. I can reserve books to be collected at my convenience and access the articles over the internet as 'full text' without having to print them, or even walk across to the library to take them from the shelf. Students today have almost limitless sources available at their fingertips.

As an academic I can discuss issues with colleagues in my discipline across the world, via dedicated online discussion groups. Such developments have opened up access to academic resources in ways we could not have imagined in the days of card indexes and computers that filled whole floors of the university computing centre. The computer I accessed as an undergraduate was located in another university, and I could only communicate with it via cards, delivered weekly to the IT services – imagine having to wait a week to find out a wrong instruction had made the request invalid (the computer regularly said 'no')! Hence, when students say, 'I couldn't find anything on it. . ', many tutors would be rather unsympathetic, knowing that vast resources are available from the average laptop, let alone the shelves heaving under the weight of the printed texts.

Searching for material on a specific topic is now much quicker and more open – but more resources can sometimes mean we have to be more selective in what we look at. Disciplined and systematic searches will produce more relevant and appropriate material – the skill this involves will gradually develop with time and experience but there are some pointers that can save time – time that can be better used in reading and analysis of what you do find.

- Use key word searches on books and for journal titles in the library catalogue (not as vague as 'sport' – you simply get too many to look at).
- Follow first the references suggested in the unit handbook or lecture notes.
- Search via online databases for specific articles on a concept or topic – but try to be aware of the various terms that could indicate similar things; for example, if investigating 'drugs' in sport, also use 'anti-doping' and 'sport' or 'athletics', as some authors may use variations on these terms.
- Limit searches by date, author or format to narrow your search to those resources that are more relevant or recent, or available as full-text resources.
- If you find a particularly relevant article, look at the references provided in it to see other or similar material on the topic.

Health warnings on web sources

Though there is much interesting material available on the web, not everything could be described as appropriate for academic purposes – hence some 'health warnings' are needed. Some university tutors will ban the use of certain sites, such as Wikipedia or self-published blogs – though conversely others would encourage the democratic approach to knowledge and ideas. Students are often expected to verify and justify for themselves the appropriateness and credibility of the site content they use. A good way to ensure the site is credible is to use a subject gateway such as Intute, the recommended gateway for sport web-based resources. Sites listed will often be pre-vetted for content, reliability and validity and the gateway may indicate the potential value of material on the site in the short introduction they provide.

Some things to remember when conducting a web-based search:

- Not everything on the web is appropriate (verifiable, accurate, up to date research or evidence based); even if looking for 'opinion', it is important to remember the origin of the information.
- To reduce the irrelevant and unsuitable, confine your search to academic sources, through 'google scholar' or online database such as Sport Discus or similar – the details of which should be available via your university electronic resources catalogue.

Making the most of sources

Be a more active reader of the material you find; simply skimming a chapter or article will not provide the depth you need for undergraduate work. Using a more active approach to reading, as indicated below, you should be reading more deeply, and thereby gaining more understanding. This approach often involves asking questions such as, 'how does this fit with what I've read before? or 'how does this compare with another point of view on the same issue?' You then need to ensure you refer to this work when constructing your essay or assignment, to show to the reader that your essay is developed from a range of sources and is not simply based on your own opinion or anonymous views or generalisations.

For example, your essay may refer to 'some authors', without giving specific examples of who these authors are; it is better to provide brief citations that select out the authors, usually by name and date. In order to refer to these sources, we must also be aware of and use the correct conventions in citing authors and providing the references. In this way, the time spent finding, reading and analysing your materials will be evidenced in the depth and critical analysis of essays and written work produced. Such reading and analysis forms the basis of evidence, debate and argument within social science-based work in sport.

References and citations

As noted above, the expectation for any academic assessment is that it should draw upon a range of relevant sources or evidence. When ideas, arguments or evidence are used, they should be correctly cited in order to demonstrate this wider reading but also to avoid the academic misconduct of *plagiarism*. This is where another's work or ideas are presented as if they were your own, or the source is not provided. A major problem is the direct copying of sections of lecture notes or set texts, for example, and the increasing use of essays for sale via the internet.

References are provided in order to show the source in full at the end of the work, rather than in the body of the text. The full details should enable someone to find and retrieve this material – either to check whether your interpretation is correct or accurate, or to read more on this issue. Most departments or universities provide their own detailed guide to referencing and on how to avoid plagiarism. There are policies and procedures in university regulations that lay down the various forms of academic malpractice or misconduct.

Some important conventions:

- If any direct *quotation* is used, the page number should be provided in the citation.
- Only the main details – usually author and date – are used in the text, with details provided later. For example, the full reference for Burns and Sinfield (2003) is found in the references section at the end of the book.
- Various referencing styles are in use, but the main ones in this area are the Harvard (author/date) or the American Psychological Association (APA) styles. The detailed guidance on these styles fills books on its own, so you need to check the formatting and style requirements in use in your own department or institution.

Common problems in referencing:

- Not listing all the sources used in the text.
- Adding a list of books or articles because others have listed them – only list references for the sources you have read and referred to in your work.
- Providing references for work referred to by someone else – beware of secondary citations.
- Not providing full URL and date of access for your web sources – get in the habit of copying this information directly into references at the end of the assignment, not in the text.

Analysis and critical writing in sport

What makes the difference?

Most students find that adapting to a more critical and analytical style of writing is quite difficult, particularly if they come to sport studies from courses where writing was not a major part of the assessment. Clues come from the terms used in higher-level assessment criteria and learning outcomes such as: critically analyse, synthesise, argue, evaluate and apply. This involves students showing:

- synthesis and re-ordering of knowledge;
- evidence of a range of and depth to reading;
- well-structured and evidenced argument;
- clearly articulated and/or expressed views on a range of issues relevant to their subject.

An important way to improve analysis and writing is to become a more active reader and to try to model or shape your style in similar ways to those used in the subject material – that is not to say simply copy what you read, but to look at how sentences are structured, the vocabulary, development of ideas, the use of sources or evidence and how it is examined.

Active reading and analysis

Burns and Sinfield (2003) provide a useful guide to a more active approach to reading. Their technique is about becoming a more active and questioning reader, taking a deep approach to learning. Taking notes and summarising key points is part of the approach, as is marking up copies of articles or sections of books (not directly onto the books unless they are your own copies!). They also advise dividing reading tasks into smaller sections and taking practical steps to organise all the relevant tools and materials to hand (highlighter pens, sticky notes, pencils, paper clips), to make more efficient use of your time.

By having a clearer picture of why a particular text is (potentially) relevant, you are much better placed to think about and understand its significance. Hence, start by thinking about the significance of the material and where it fits in the topic/issue or question. A brief look at the main headings or skim reading might give a quick indication of the relevance of this text, but you need to ask more questions as you read again. Burns and Sinfield also advocate taking notes or making annotations on the text as you go – underlining, highlighting or making longer notes as you read or after each section.

While actively reading chapters or articles in this process, things to note include:

- key ideas or arguments
- concepts or explanations
- theoretical perspectives or approaches
- links to other material
- similar arguments
- evidence or justifications

Main conclusions

Active reading is really about becoming more engaged and involved with the material, thinking about and processing the ideas and information, rather than attempting to remember it in order to simply reproduce it later.

Assignments or examinations will never say 'write down anything you can remember about what X said about the problem of doping in sport'. They might, however, ask you to analyse a particular viewpoint or theory about doping, or examine why doping in sport is considered so important an issue, or develop an argument as to why doping should be allowed. To synthesise the views of many authors or perspectives on a topic, students are expected to have read quite widely. To simply reproduce what has been said might indicate a certain level of knowledge, but for better grades and at higher levels, more active reading can produce more depth and substance to your work.

Most universities will have some guides or sources available to assist in identifying the writing approach expected. Active reading of any assignment information is therefore also very important, and any relevant advice provided, such as the word length, range or type of sources, format and style of response, should be carefully noted and checked. For academic work at higher levels, you would be expected to demonstrate more complex writing skills, an appropriate and wide vocabulary, and the ability to structure your response to suit the demands of the task.

Seeking help and support

Sometimes, however carefully they have read the texts, or spent hours drafting out assignments, students find they can reach a dead end in their studies, or have problems in understanding whether they are on the right track with their work. Most departments will have some form of student support and guidance, through personal or academic tutors, online support or specialist tutors in essential study skills. Unfortunately some students do not ask for help until quite late in the process, when they find their grades are not as good as they expected. My advice would always be to take full advantage of all the assistance available – and for students to take an active role in the process from the start. Chapter 7 has more ideas about development and planning techniques you might use. It is possible to find a student guide on every topic in this chapter but which is best for any particular student is a very individual choice. If there are issues that arise as you move through the sport studies programme, you should be able to identify who might be in a position to help you. Your first port of call would probably be the student handbook for your course, department or programme, in order to identify whom to speak to.

Planning your personal academic development

After reading this chapter you should better understand some of the demands of studying sport from a social science perspective. It should be possible to enhance your studies through developing more personal skills, which we cover in Chapter 7. By completing this chapter and the activities, you should have identified:

- your preferred learning style;
- methods of teaching and assessment strategies;
- how your learning is assessed;
- standards and formats required in your written work or other forms of assessment;
- the balance of directed and self-directed study expected;
- sources of help and support in the department or university.

Armed with this knowledge, it should be possible to set yourself targets or objectives to be completed as you progress. This should also help you to complete the personal development plan that most universities now have running alongside their academic programme. Further information about this can be found in Chapter 7.

Review

This chapter has emphasised that, in learning about sport, the onus is on you to become an active learner, which involves using a range of methods and approaches to better understand complex social phenomenon. In this case the study of the processes and practice of sport. Sport studies draws upon a great range of sources, theories and ideas. This means that you need skills to find and use these sources effectively. Where possible, these should be developed through the context of sport and include practical and interactive approaches to teaching and learning. You are encouraged to take an active interest in taking part in, watching and enjoying all aspects of sport, but to balance this with studying and thinking about the subject!

The essential requirements for success in this subject are similar to any other. They rely also on an underpinning of enthusiasm for sport (in all its forms), and an active engagement in the learning process.

Getting the most from your studies is all about *you* – what you want to achieve and what you do to achieve your goals.

Sport studies courses are very diverse, so it is important to find out all you can about your own sport studies course and the choices you have available, in order to get the most from it.

It may be necessary to adapt and work out the best way for you to achieve your objectives, as not everything will be geared to your own interests and skills. You might have to change and adapt some things to better suit your own preferences and strengths, for example completing the activities in this book, to help bring the subject to life and make the subject more relevant to your own interests and enthusiasms.

It is also important to take a planned approach to your personal academic development, to plan and develop the skills you need to achieve your own objectives. Using a personal development plan may be a useful tool to help you.

Further study

For more advice on coping with student life and university level work, see:
- McIlroy, D. (2003) *Studying at University: How to be a Successful Student.* London: Sage

For an excellent and detailed guide to how to write the type of essay commonly found in sport studies, using a social science-based approach, see:
- Redman, P. (2006) *Good Essay Writing.* Milton Keynes: Open University Press

Online sources:
- VARK – a guide to learning styles on line: www.vark-learn.com/english/page.asp?p=questionnaire – this site also has help sheets to give you some specific study strategies for each of the preferences.
- Qualification and Curriculum Authority: www.qca.org.uk; Quality Assurance Agency: www.qaa.ac.uk – both of these sites offer information about university credits, levels and qualifications.
- Intute (formerly ALTIS): www.intute.ac.uk/socialsciences/sport – an academic gateway for recognised and evaluated resources on sport, offering approved and organised web searches.

Chapter 7

Balancing work and play: enhancing personal skills through sport studies

Introduction

This chapter develops further the development of personal skills, with particular emphasis on the links between your sport studies course and employability. It aims to provide advice in helping to balance the potentially competing demands of work (study) and play (sport). As noted above, many students enter sport-related programmes with a clear view of entering the sport sector for a career. On the other hand, sport studies students often go on to enjoy a very diverse range of careers. This chapter is therefore about maximising the potential of the sport studies programme for enhancing your personal and work-related skills and to make you more aware of the potential for building on sport studies for your future career – what ever that may eventually be.

Learning outcomes

By completing this chapter and the related learning activities, you will be able to:
- identify the personal skills relevant for future employment and better self management whilst studying;
- devise personal planners and other aids to improve time management and personal effectiveness;
- implement personal development planning skills and goal setting to support your course of studies and future career planning;
- investigate the employment potential in the sport sector.

Personal skills for work and study

Personal skills are those practical abilities which we may have or need to acquire in order to perform effectively in our day to day life, in the work place or whilst studying. In Chapter 6 we looked at skills for studying, here, we focus on those relating to your personal or time management, and skills that are transferable to the world of work.

- *Communication* – written, oral, 'one to one', or 'one to many' communications.
- *Organisational skills* – time management, goal setting, prioritising and problem solving.
- *Working with others* – teamwork, management and leadership, negotiation.
- *Information technology (IT)* – word processing, spreadsheets, databases, internet information retrieval.

The skills identified above are selected for their relevance to sport studies programmes and courses and sport-based or other careers. The sections below deal with how you can use your sport studies programme to enhance your personal and transferable skills. You are also advised to use the relevant resources of your own university in order to maximise the benefits you gain from the course and to ensure you are fully supported in the development of your skills.

Personal development planning

What is personal development planning?

Personal development planning (PDP) is:

A structured and supported process undertaken by an individual to reflect upon their own learning and performance and/or achievement and to plan for their personal, educational and career development. The primary objective for PDP is to improve the capacity of individuals to understand what and how they are learning and to review, plan and take responsibility for their own learning, helping students:

- Become more effective, independent and confident self-directed learners;
- Understand how they are learning and relate their learning to a wider context;
- Improve their general skills for study and career management;
- Articulate personal goals and evaluate progress towards their achievement;
- Encourage a positive attitude to learning throughout life.

(QAA 2001: 1)

Since the initial adoption of personal progress files in higher education, PDP has been developed to include a range of approaches and techniques in use across the sector. I first started to use PDP around 2001, when we wanted to enhance the employability and academic skills of sport studies students. This process was introduced by universities after various high level reports had indicated that expansion in higher education had meant that some students were entering universities lacking skills previously taken for granted, and that on leaving, they were still inadequately prepared to compete for graduate level posts due to a lack of work-related skills. However, according to Monks et al. (2006), partly due to the diverse ways in which PDP is applied, there remains lack of evidence that it is being effective.

Though personal development planning has its critics amongst academics, the assumption is that, with increasing numbers of graduates entering the job market, students need to prepare for their future whilst studying rather than leaving it until graduation. Employers have also criticised the university sector for not preparing graduates for the world of work sufficiently.

The notion of producing a formal plan has been adopted because this process relies on an approach to self-development that not everyone finds easy or natural. In order to develop particular skills in an individualised way, you are expected to be proactive, self-directed and self-aware. For some people, this is very natural and something they do without much direction or support. But a formal PDP system is a way of clarifying and setting out the process in a logical and ordered way, which may be particularly useful for those who might otherwise possibly drift along and be at a disadvantage later, when it comes to applying for jobs and being successful in the workplace.

I have often find the most resistance to PDP comes from the most able or least able – for the former, because they cannot see how spending time on such planning will help them do what they can already do, and the latter, because they cannot always appreciate the need for planning ahead or lack awareness of their own limitations. For most students, there is some real benefit in addressing the PDP process, even if it might not be apparent until quite late in the course, or even until you start to apply for jobs.

For any student, following the guidance provided through PDP can be helpful in being more systematic and helping to clarify personal objectives. This can be quite motivating when at times the course is not going particularly well, or if you identify a particular need for help. PDP is basically about working out what your development needs are and addressing them, in a planned and systematic way. Many effective and successful people would find the principles behind PDP quite natural – they might not have completed a PDP, but they nevertheless carried out many similar processes. The theory of PDP is based on that of Kolb (1984) regarding reflection, and the concept of the learning cycle, and also Zimmerman (1992) and his ideas on self-regulated learning (as cited in Monks et al. (2006). PDP also applies Bandura's (1997) theories of self-efficacy and motivation, in goal setting.

The elements of PDP are:

- self-appraisal or audit of skills, strengths and weaknesses;
- objective or goal setting;
- action planning (actions to achieve objectives);
- reflection and review of progress, or profiling.

Many sport courses have developed PDP alongside academic and personal skills or employability units, which can be credit bearing or represent the equivalent of a module. These might include some form of assessment, often in the form of a reflective log or portfolio. Others will embed PDP in the personal tutor, pastoral and careers support system, and keep it quite separate from course assessment, though it would be expected to contribute to improved academic performance overall.

Research by Monks et al. (2006) has found that, as a result of PDP, students' perceptions of their skills improved, as did motivation toward studying for their degree. But they also found that PDP had to be combined with 'learning to learn' support, as outlined in Chapter 6, for skills like time management and organisation to improve. Simply by completing the plan, students did not necessarily improve their skills. Therefore, they found that self-efficacy (belief in one's competence), self-awareness and resourcefulness are at the core of a model of self-regulated learning, which PDP can influence in a positive way.

In practical terms, PDP requires coordination between various aspects of the university systems for student support, for example:

- library (learning resources)
- careers
- academic tutors
- pastoral tutors
- ITC

There are many diverse ways for universities to implement PDP and student progress files, but these are found to have potential benefits to retention (due to improved motivation to study) and graduate outcomes, in finding appropriate posts after graduation.

Skills audit and self-assessment

Many universities now provide the opportunity of a skills audit, which can be completed online or through approved materials linked to the PDP. Essential skills will be identified, and should be assessed. Some audits are more complex than others, but should identify:

- those skills that you feel comfortable with;
- those skills that you need to improve;
- those skills that you do not have, or lack confidence in.

You should complete a skills audit in order to go on to complete a SWOT analysis, as described below.

Activity

- Complete a skills audit – if there is one provided by your course or university, complete this, or use one of the many available over the internet.
- Complete a SWOT analysis of your personal strengths, weaknesses, opportunities and threats. Your strengths and weaknesses relate to your personal qualities and skills, whilst opportunities and threats relate to external factors that can be a help (opportunity) or hindrance (threat) to your personal development and achievement. We will use this analysis later in coming up with potential objectives or gaols, strategies or targets. Your SWOT should fit into the grid in Figure 7.1.

Figure: 7.1: SWOT grid for personal skills

Internal – *based on skills audit and self-assessment/feedback/reflection*	External – *based on reviewing the external environment, e.g. sport sector, current trends in employment and technology, politics and policies*
Strengths What am I good at?	**Opportunities** What are the things that will help me achieve in the future?
Weaknesses What do I need to improve?	**Threats** What are the things that may hinder my chances in the future?

Action planning: target setting and defining your goals

As befits a book in the *Active Learning in Sport* series, this chapter outlines an action-oriented approach to objective setting and planning. Based on the activities set out above, you should be more aware of your personal skills and what might impact on your future career plans. Once you have identified where you currently stand in relation to your skills development, and identified the potential external factors you need to take into account in your study and career plans, the next stage is to set yourself some objectives or targets. You need to think carefully about what you want to achieve and what motivates you to do so. You may have shorter-term goals – for this term or for this time next year or by the end of the course. Longer-term goals might be to identify where you want to be after five years.

If, at this stage, you don't have a clear plan for that far ahead, you might want to express more general goals – to have a job or be studying for a higher degree or have the choice of either possibility. If you want to have the freedom and flexibility of choice at a later stage (and why not), you need to think about what sort of goals and achievements would help you have the choices you want.

Specific targets and goals depend on your own interests, skills and enthusiasms. You should make sure, however, that you are as aware as possible of the potential directions you might follow. Your careers service, tutors, course information and other students can be helpful. You should also investigate areas you have an interest in working in, to find out what sort of skills, qualifications or abilities are valued. Looking at the advertisements for current jobs would help identify the sort of things employers are looking for. You might need to send off for more details of posts that interest you, even if you are not in a position to apply formally. Look at the 'essential' and 'desirable' characteristics for posts in the job descriptions or person specifications. This can help identify what you must have gained or what would be useful to have gained, from your time at university. Skills Active provides some interesting careers resources, as does

ISPAL. These may be limited to sport, but could identify the common factors that employers are looking for. Developing your employability skills is looked at in more detail later, however some preliminary investigations should be undertaken early on in your studies to give some initial pointers for PDP.

Once you have identified what you might need, or skills you need to develop, the next stage is to set out a plan of how you will get there. In PDPs, this is usually set out as an action plan that sets out:

- What you need to *do* (action).
- *When* you intend to do it (plan).

This should be set out with particular time-related milestones identified, so you can identify the various steps that might be needed to achieve your longer-term goals.

An example action plan might identify that you need to learn to use spreadsheets in Excel(tm) for use in management modules or to go into business careers later. An action plan approach would set out some actions you need to follow, and when, in order to achieve this. In your PDP, this may be incorporated into some form of table or chart – as shown in Table 7.1.

Table 7.1: Example of action plan for IT skills

Goal: Improve Information Technology skills by becoming proficient at using spreadsheets and charts	
Year 1 Enrol on Excel training course through study skills unit by the end of summer term, ready for the research skills module in year 2.	Deadline: June
Year 2 Make use of study guide from IT services to incorporate charts and tables in assessments by end of year assessments. Take course in SPSS for use in surveys for year 3.	Access materials and training by December
Year 3 Enhance spreadsheet and statistical analysis skills through taking advanced course in final year, for using in dissertation analysing usage of sport facility by different social groups.	Course date: November

Converting SWOT to TOWS

You might be able to do little about external factors, but you can devise strategies or actions to minimise the threats and maximise opportunities. For example, recent 'credit crunch' concerns may reduce the number of graduate posts available, so your strategy would be to enhance one of your strengths to make this an asset that employers are looking for in a competitive marketplace for jobs.

Complete the grid in Figure 7.1 again, this time with actions you might take in line with your PDP.

Table 7.2: Strengths and weaknesses grid

Enter strategies or actions at the intersections

Copy your earlier analysis into the relevant boxes	Strengths e.g. good at analysis of texts and reports	Weaknesses e.g. some lack of confidence in speaking to groups
Opportunities e.g. local authorities looking to develop sport and physical activity	What will make the most of your strengths and take advantage of your opportunities?	What do you need to do about weaknesses that might prevent you from taking advantage of opportunities?
Threats e.g. competitive job market in sport administration	What strengths do you need to develop or build on or emphasise to minimise the impact of threats?	What weakness can you improve on to minimise the threats?

Skills for work and study

Teamwork and leadership

One of the things that the participation in sport is thought to enhance is the ability to work as part of a team. Many employers value teamworking skills, as much of the work in many different careers is carried out in teams or groups. Many courses incorporate group work as an important teaching and learning strategy for just this reason. Not only is group work in sport studies contributing to your skills development, it is also a good way to learn and improve your understanding and work on more complex projects than you could achieve individually. Experience of good teamwork can be very positive – on the other hand, poor teamwork can result in a very unsatisfactory experience for everyone involved. It is useful therefore to reflect on what role you play in a team, and how your personal contribution can be more effective.

A commonly used approach is to look at Belbin's Team Roles Inventory(tm), which works out people's preferred roles in teams. Belbin (1981, 1996) identified eight, then later nine, team roles that individuals fulfil when working in a team:

- Company worker (implementer)
- Chair (co-ordinator)
- Shaper
- Innovator (plant)
- Resource investigator
- Monitor-evaluator
- Teamworker
- Completer/finisher
- Expert (specialist)

Belbin used a series of questions to arrive at scores for individuals to indicate the sort of role they most often fulfilled in teams. This team role inventory is sometimes helpful when analysing personal contributions and to check on the balance of roles in work situations, hence it is still quite widely used in industry as a tool in teambuilding or organisational development (see the online sources at the end of the chapter).

Each of these roles has a particular part to play in a successful team, and any individual may find that, at different times or in different circumstances, they take on more than one. For example, a Company worker is the 'do-er' of the team – they complete the specific tasks identified, while the Shaper tends to undertake more of the direction and leadership to ensure the task gets done. We can all probably recall a situation where perhaps we had too many Shapers and too few Company workers – lots of talk about what needs to be done, but ultimately not many getting on and doing it. Belbin devised this tool to apply to work situations, so, though it is an interesting exercise to try to complete the inventory, you should treat any 'results' with caution.

Another management-related theory found useful in team and group development is the Action Centred Leadership theory of Adair (1996). According to this widely used approach in leadership development, it is possible to become better or more skilled at management of teams and individuals by focusing more on the actions a good leader might take (hence action-centred). An effective leader will do things to manage the team – as well as develop the individuals in the team – and ultimately get the task done. The model is usually represented as a set of interlocking circles, each representing one of Task, Team and Individual, as shown in Figure 7.2.

These leadership actions are based on having a shared understanding of the task, listening to contributions from each team member and recognising the strengths of individuals, in order to be successful in achieving the task. Again, this is a business technique that might have some interest for you as a student of sport, but it is really about leadership for a work situation.

Working in groups

A lot of work at university is organised around groups, sometimes in order to reinforce and develop the important teamworking skills referred to above, or to help achieve more demanding or complex projects than might be expected from individual students. Not everyone is positive about group work, but because it forms an integral part of the teaching and learning approaches on many sport courses, as with other subjects,

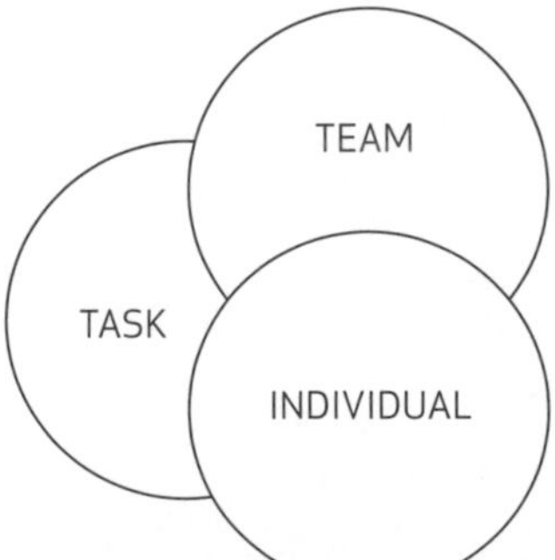

Figure 7.2:
Action Centred
Leadership model
(based on Adair 1996)

students need to consider how best to use groups to their advantage and how to make themselves a good group member.

When groups are randomly allocated, the group needs to quickly become productive or the work deadline will place greater pressure on everyone. Once involved in self-selecting groups, a previous history of poor contributions to groups will potentially give you a bad reputation, making it hard to find others who are prepared to work with you. It makes sense therefore to be a positive, active contributor to any group work you are involved in.

Becoming a more effective team or group member

Bear these points in mind:

- Plan work carefully at the outset and agree individual roles and contributions.
- Complete your tasks and contributions on time.
- Be reliable about attending meetings arranged to discuss progress.
- Be honest about your own strengths and weaknesses (i.e. don't suggest you look after specific areas in which you have a known weakness and don't pretend to be an expert on something you are not).
- Be active in suggesting how to tackle a problem or issue – don't sit back and let everyone else decide.
- Set realistic deadlines and stick to them.
- Allow time for revising drafts on the feedback from group members.
- Be positive about other's contributions and give constructive feedback when needed.

Time management

This section is about how you can use your time effectively and get the most out of the experiences on offer in sport programmes. Students sometimes underestimate the lecturers' understanding of the balance needed to learn, work, rest and play. After all, many of us went through very similar programmes and faced similar problems while studying. One thing we are fairly certain of is that time is a finite resource – and there are only 24 hours in any one day. Whilst at times the demands of any particular course might be heavy, they have been planned to be 'do-able' within the time available. Where tutors and students sometimes disagree is over the amount of this time and where and when it falls.

Using the rule of thumb that for each ten-credit unit there are 100 learning hours, programmes are designed to be completed through a mixture of contact with tutors and independent learning.

Achieving the learning for a six-module, year-long programme of 120 credits involves 6 x 200 hours = 1200 learning hours. Over 30 weeks, which includes the exam or assessment period, this is about 40 hours a week – the equivalent of a full-time job for many people. Some students perhaps do more hours – and others less.

An important point to make is about the quality of the time – and the distribution of this time in the normal week in term. So the expected amount of work can be fitted into a regular working week – though if you take out sport matches on Wednesdays, or prefer a late start in the morning, you may have to be working in the evenings and at weekends to keep up. Indeed, in some courses, the demands of some reading and other work regularly involve evening and weekend working, as the course is completed in fewer weeks. At different times, for example when assignments are due, the balance may show a great many more hours in some days than others.

What happens when we add part-time work, volunteering and or playing sport into the equation? This places more pressure on our learning time and so a greater need to prioritise and organise time, in order to fit in what we need to do and devote the quality of time our course demands.

Having a PDP approach can help in identifying where working, volunteering or playing sport can help with your skills development, and also where they may have to take a back seat to actually complete your course requirements.

Activity

Complete Table 7.3 to work out how you currently spend your time. Then use the planner in Table 7.4 to show your programme timetable in a typical week.

Table 7.3: Activity in your regular week

Activity	Time	Weekly total
Essential activities Sleeping	_ hours per night	_ x 7 =
Meals (including cooking if not catered for)	Per day: Week Weekend	
Travel	Daily	
Other sport related	Daily training x days Match Travel (minimum)	
Part-time work Basic hours	_ per day x _ days	
Committed hours		Total weekly hours committed to essentials = (total the hours above)
Available hours = 168	Total available hours = 168 minus committed hours	Total available =
Study related Class attendance	Total normal weekly timetable = _ hours	Total for study =
Independent study	Planned in normal week =	

Do all my study related hours add up to between 35–40 or above?
Do I need to look again at other commitments?
How can I make the most of the time available to me for study?

Table 7.4: Weekly work planner

Draw up a weekly timetable that shows how the contact and independent study fit into a regular week. The times in the example below can be amended to show weekend days if necessary. One you have filled in timetabled lectures and seminars, etc., identify time slots to complete library searches, group meetings or project work to cut down on travelling and make full use of your time at university. Enter your sporting, family or work commitments, to see how this balances out. Some examples are shown below to illustrate – assuming six slots of lectures/seminars in a week.

For a typical term week	Study time	Morning (9–12 am)	Afternoon (1–4 pm)	Evening
Monday		Lectures/seminars	Library	
Tuesday		Lectures/seminars	Lectures/seminars	Training
Wednesday		Library	Sport	Social
Thursday		Lectures/seminars	Lectures/seminars	
Friday		Lectures/seminars		
Weekend?				
Total		Notes for other weeks/commitments to add?		

Information technology: skills for sport courses

A range of IT software is usually available for students. As a sport studies student, you will need to develop your skills in word processing and other packages in order to produce more impressive and professional looking work. By doing so you will also cut down some time in managing your studies and sources for example, but these are also the IT skills needed when entering the workplace. Basic competence in all the main 'Office' programs or their equivalent is expected in many types of career. More specific vocational areas, such as sports coaching, may have other programs you may be expected to be familiar with, for example for notational analysis or digital video editing.

For all of the software you will be expected to use within your programme, there should be guides and resources made available by the university ITC services. If not, advice is usually available from the websites of the software or popular texts. Depending on your learning style, you may prefer to work through things yourself by trials and error, go along to training sessions or read guides. However you do it, using and improving your IT skills will be important whatever career you eventually choose.

Enhancing employability

The skills covered earlier are all considered transferable to the world of work. While such skills can be enhanced through your academic studies, there are other ways to make you a more attractive candidate in the increasingly competitive job market. There has been some criticism of graduates entering the job market seemingly unprepared to deal with real-life issues and practical problems. Actually, sport students can often do well because they understand and often prefer to be 'hands on' and active in their approach to work. Balancing the demands of part-time work or volunteering in sport, active roles in student sport clubs, or different demands if competing at a high level – working in a team or being highly motivated and hard working – are all qualities demanded of sport studies students that employers may value.

Volunteering, part-time work and placements

There are numerous opportunities provided for part-time employment in sport-related projects and even more for voluntary involvement, which also provide invaluable experience for developing employability. Placements, either informal or formal, can also contribute to enhancing employability, through providing work-like or realistic experiences of sport-related careers.

Table 7.5 shows volunteering opportunities at local, regional and national levels, and who would be responsible for them. The important thing is to be proactive and seek out those opportunities that interest you. These can be in a club or after-school club, for a youth or community group. The national scheme to encourage volunteering in sport is managed by the Youth Sport Trust – 'Step into Sport' – but may be coordinated more locally by your County Sport Partnership.

Through volunteering it is possible to develop the experience that future employers want, as well as providing additional confidence, new skills and potential networks of contacts for other opportunities. Volunteering can also be very rewarding at a personal level, as it brings great satisfaction to see others enjoying their sport, particularly if you have played a role in contributing to their enjoyment.

After volunteering, you should take some time out to think about the specific skills you have gained. For example, dealing with problems, working as part of a team and delivering sport programmes to young people with behavioural problems can develop communication and listening skills, the ability to get your ideas across, and negotiation or mediating skills in conflict situations. Some volunteering opportunities will provide and/or expect you to gain qualifications or additional training, for example in child protection and welfare, first aid, or in working with people with a disability.

Some sport studies programmes may offer the possibility for a formal or informal work placement. This places students in a work-based learning environment or gives them full-time experience, which may be part of a credit-bearing module. If this opportunity is offered, it will provide invaluable experience and the chance to identify and develop those work-related skills that graduates are often lacking. This may eventually give an edge over similar candidates in an application situation.

Placements may include time with a sports organisation, a project managing an intervention or programme, conducting some research on behalf of the organisation, or simply working alongside the usual team of staff on specific projects, or delivering their day-to-day services. In the past I have been responsible for students working in exotic or faraway locations (lifeguarding on Waikiki beach, summer camp counsellor in the US) to the more close to home (working in the ticket office of a county cricket club, outreach sport development worker, teaching assistant in a PE department). However, these placements have also enabled students to appreciate and understand their sport

Table 7.5: Volunteering in sport: support and opportunities

Level and organisations		Role	Programme and support
Local: Local authority sport department Local clubs School Sport Partnerships Universities and colleges		Local providers of sport development opportunities, coaching, leadership, courses, qualifications and support	Training for coaching, first aid, club development, volunteer coach deployment Ask for details in your local sport development unit
County/regional: County Sport Partnership Regional sport organisations Governing body may have regional role in development and sport volunteering		Coordinate programmes across the county Organise annual or other events, coach and club development across districts or governing bodies	Annual Youth Games County level coordination of courses above Register with your own county partnership or regional development officer with a particular governing body
National	Sport England	National volunteering programmes, strategic lead, information and resources to support clubs and national governing body schemes, grant aid	Volunteer Investment Programme Running sport resources Links to governing body sites – see the SE website for more resources and information about volunteering
	CCPR	Support and coordination of national governing bodies	Advice and support for sport leaders and coaches in clubs
	British Sport Trust	Provider of national qualification and training programme	Provider of qualifications, e.g. CSLA, JSLA
	YST	Lead agency dealing with School Sport Partnerships	e.g. Step into Sport, Top Link festivals and similar activities engaging young volunteers
	Governing Bodies	Providers of sport coaching or other qualifications	Leadership, officiating courses, see the relevant website for details of how to get involved in a particular sport

studies courses more fully. Being able to work in a sport environment gave them the additional insight and understanding needed for their final year work in particular – it enabled them to appreciate how theory can be applied in the 'real world' and how the experience of sport can be very diverse and engage people in quite different ways. They were also in a stronger position when it came to thinking about careers – even if their experience convinced them they were not headed for a job in sport.

Cheshire Youth Games

I was one of the first volunteers for the inaugural Youth Games held in Cheshire in 1999, and in 2008 I was involved in my tenth Youth Games, once again as a volunteer. My children have also been involved, as either participants or volunteers– so I have had various perspectives on this event over the years.

Like many events of its type across the country, the Youth Games are organised by the County Sport Partnership. Similar events in Greater Manchester, Merseyside and London had previously been operating very successfully for a number of years. The model developed in those games was extended to other counties, with the establishment of County Sport Partnerships in the late 1990s. In 2000, the events culminated in a national Millennium Youth Games, funded partly from the National Lottery, where teams from across the country qualified through their county games in a range of sports – the main provision was that those taking part were not already competing at county level or similar in their sport. Up till recently, the Games were an integral part of the development work with young people in many areas, but funding and organisational changes have meant the Youth Games no longer operate in quite the same way. Some counties have discontinued the Youth Games or altered their format – as has happened in Cheshire.

The Youth Games is a multi-sport event, with each local authority represented by a team of young people drawn from schools across the district. The sports involved have been those identified as benefiting from district-based development – with participants who may not already be part of a club or have been involved in county-level sport before. The sports in Cheshire have included hockey, girls' football, girls' rugby, swimming, tennis, table tennis, badminton, basketball and boccia. In many districts children go through some form of trial and a training programme in order to compete at the Games.

In 2007, after significant changes in the county sport partnership, a change in approach meant fewer sports as competitions and more as 'tasters' – introducing new sports into the event, such as cheerleading, and changing the recruitment to those children who may not usually take part in activities at school. The taster sports on offer in 2007 included futsal, handball and archery, as well as urban sport, skateboarding and climbing, with approximately 750 children from across Cheshire taking part.

Despite the changes described above, the Youth Games are a great example of partnerships working in action and the significant value of volunteers, schools, clubs, governing bodies and sport development agencies working together to provide an enjoyable and fun day for young people. Over the years I have been involved in the Youth Games, I have seen students progress from helping a local borough team to being a team manager or running one of the sport competitions on the day. Many then return once they are qualified, as sport development officers or working for governing bodies at the event, or simply as volunteers.

Other young people have also been gaining sport volunteering experience, as schools often encourage junior sport leaders to help with teams in the younger age groups. Volunteers help with setting up and maintaining the site, act as 'runners' between event and competition organisers, officiate, distribute programmes or information, or help with team management. The event organisers can offer placements in the pre-event organisation, which is where many HE students can gain useful experience of multi-sport or multi-agency working.

Activity

Find out about the county Sport Partnership Games or their equivalent by contacting your local authority Sport Development Unit. Enquire about volunteering or placement opportunities locally or with the County Partnership.

What skills do employers value?

You can find clues to valued skills in job advertisements. The university careers service will provide guides and information, and research into the sort of career you might be looking for. Armed with this information, it should be possible to look at the results of your skills audit and consider if there is anything you might need to do in order to prepare yourself for the world of work later. This might mean simply ensuring you present yourself in the best possible light, and highlighting the skills you have and the experience you have gained whilst studying, volunteering, working part time or through work placement.

Employers value:

- adaptability
- problem-solving skills
- leadership
- interpersonal communication skills

Finding out about potential careers in sport can be relatively simple, as many of the major employers advertise in outlets like *Leisure Opportunities* (see the online sources at the end of this chapter). Or go to the excellent resources offered by Skills Active, the industry training body, or ISPAL, the professional body for those managing in the sport sector. Unfortunately, many of the lower level jobs in sport are advertised locally – so it is not always easy to see entry-level or graduate opportunities without registering with the careers service.

A selection of sport jobs and salaries advertised in *Leisure Opportunities* in October 2008 included:

- Sports Facilities Manager, City Academy (£25,000 + bonus)
- Football Project Officer, City Council in the North (£27,000–31,370)
- Leisure Club Manager, four-star hotel (£20,000)
- Senior Sport Officer, university (£21,072–25,135)
- Sports Development Officer, City Council in London (£23,742–28,311)

Most of these posts required extensive experience and some additional vocational or technical qualifications, though sport studies graduates could expect to have the necessary academic requirements. For the sport development officer post, the following skills and qualities were highlighted in the advertisement:

- being motivated, focused and reliable
- being able to work on own initiative and as part of a team
- possessing organisational skills, including personal time management
- having budget management skills
- being proficient in IT, such as Excel, PowerPoint and Access
- being a confident communicator
- having an ability to influence others

This sort of specification is not untypical in a sport-based job, and shows the relevance of the earlier points about employability in the sector and more widely. Many of the employers in the sector will also expect prospective candidates who will be working with children to undergo a CRB check, as noted in Chapter 3.

Writing and enhancing your curriculum vitae (CV)

Curriculum vitae (CV) are widely used as a form of application for posts. As employers look for evidence of the skills noted above, a well-written CV can be invaluable when trying to highlight your knowledge and skills ahead of the many others with often similar qualifications. Having gained additional skills and experience through volunteering, paid work or placement, the important thing is to make sure this is reflected in the CV because employers will often them use to shortlist potential applicants.

A CV is essentially a short summary of your life and experiences to date. There are a range of potential layouts and templates available, so there is usually no shortage of examples of how to set one out – the difficulty comes in deciding what to put into it. The CV has to be informative, but also unique to you. It will create the first impression – along with the covering letter it usually goes with, to any future employer, and so has to be clear, well presented and point out to them what makes you a potential candidate for the job.

One problem encountered by students is their lack of work experience – as they have concentrated upon gaining qualifications, many students lack all but summer or part-time employment. Or they may be sport performers, who have spent time on training rather than work-related experience. The CV needs, therefore, to make the most of the experiences gained and highlight why these would be relevant to the post in question.

Construct a basic CV for 'all purpose use' and adapt it for particular posts, emphasising relevant past experience or knowledge, expertise or interest. The covering letter can also be important in making sure your application is tailored to a particular vacancy.

Your CV should show your employability through academic knowledge and skills gained during your studies – don't expect an employer to know what you have knowledge of in a sport studies degree. You should also highlight vocationally relevant knowledge and skills. For example, if going for a post in sport, state what particular sporting qualifications you have gained and what experience you have in sport environments or organisations. You may also have other relevant skills such as language skills or IT skills; and having a driving licence may be necessary. Through coaching with young people, for example, you might have gained greater confidence in speaking to larger groups or working with teams, or improved your time management.

When putting together your CV have all the relevant information to hand, but also spend some time thinking about and reflecting on what you have gained from your experiences. This is where the PDP process should help, as you should have all the relevant material together to help you put together a complete and comprehensive CV.

Contacts you have acquired through part-time work, volunteering or placements can also provide the necessary references to add to a CV. These should be your employer, club official or mentor/supervisor in a placement, who should be in a position to advise on your suitability for the post or report on your (no doubt excellent) performance. Never add 'available on request' – this infers you do not have anyone already committed to providing a supportive reference. If you have not had prior agreement from them, you should always contact prospective referees personally in advance of adding their details to the CV. This is both a courtesy and to check they are still at the address you have for them.

Your CV can be enhanced by making sure that you have fully exploited the potential of all your skills and knowledge, and have gained as much as you can from the additional experiences you have taken advantage of whilst studying.

If posts stipulate the use of an application form rather than a CV, the same principles apply and all the relevant information and reflection is still needed. You can often cut and paste the relevant information, or if necessary use handwritten forms. Online applications are increasingly popular, so having all the information gathered together in an electronic form of CV is also very useful.

Studying and sport performance

TASS and similar schemes for sport performers

The government and higher education establishments have supported the development of a number of schemes to help young sport performers get the most from higher education. These include sport scholarships, bursaries and specific support programmes, such as the Talented Athlete Support Scheme (TASS). Of course, these programmes are not just for sport studies students, but it is highly likely that those interested in studying sport may include some high level performers. Even if this does not apply, it is useful for sport students to understand, as part of the overall system for sport in the UK, how such schemes work and why they are put in place.

Sport performers may get assistance through formal systems like TASS, described in more detail below, or through programme or departmental mechanisms, such as personal tutors, student support offices or a sport directorate.

TASS and sport scholarships

The Talented Athlete Scholarship Scheme (TASS) is a government-funded programme aimed at potential medal winners in further and higher education. Devised as a partnership between education and sport organisations, the scheme caters for athletes from a range of sports, who want to combine high-level sport performance with their education. Those eligible are between 16 and 25 (35 for disability sports), in 40 identified sports. Fifteen of the sports are disability sports. Additional TASS 2012 scholarships have been made available for selected ten to 20 year olds, who are working towards likely representation at the London 2012 Olympic Games.

The support available is to cover services to the value of £3,000, though individual athletes do not receive the money directly. The money is provided to the governing body, which designs customised support programmes for the athletes. These might include specialist coaching, sports medicine, physiotherapy or lifestyle management. The aim of TASS support is to allow athletes to combine high-level sport and to remain at their university or college. Universities also put in place additional support and guidance for their TASS-nominated athletes.

Customising your programme to match career aspirations

Many courses under the banner of Sport or Sport Studies look very different from each other. In some programmes there is considerable choice in the modules you might study, in others the choice is more limited. However, by taking a holistic view of the programme and using the PDP process, you should be in a position to optimise the choices available to you when choosing units or modules or even modes of study. By choosing wisely, you can ensure your career aspirations are supported, as well as meeting the academic requirements for your programme of study.

If you identify what skills and knowledge a particular career might favour, you can find out whether or not these can be achieved through your module choices, or the choice of subject or topic for projects, assignments or placements. There may be more vocationally relevant assessments or practical work in some units that may be more geared to potential careers in sport or to developing transferable skills. For example, a sport studies programme may include units organised into pathways or routes, e.g. related modules in sport development, sport management or physical education. Whatever the choice available, you should look at all the potential opportunities to enhance your enjoyment and the relevance of the course to your own enthusiasms and interests – but at the same time, make this helpful when you come to considering potential careers.

Coaching awards, for example, can be completed alongside academic programmes without necessarily following a degree in coaching. While you enjoy coaching, you may not consider this to be your ultimate career. Nevertheless, by completing the course, and being in a position to earn from your coaching, you will be gaining very useful and relevant experience of sport, and learn many useful skills for other careers later – not least how to work with others and get the most from them.

For those interested in a career in teaching, acquiring several coaching awards and experience in working in schools is becoming essential even before gaining a post-graduate teaching place, such is the competition for places.

Individual students at whatever standard of performance can therefore create their own unique profile in a sport studies course – made up of academic, sporting, work-based and social experiences.

Review

In this chapter we have considered a range of methods, techniques and approaches to help you identify, develop and enhance your personal development and employability. By using an active approach to learning, managing your time more effectively and having clear goals to work towards, you should be in a better position to make the most of your sport programme. Key to this approach is the use of the PDP process, and taking positive steps to achieve your goals. Most universities have excellent support available to combine work for a sport degree, sport performance or participation and career development. You need to ensure you know what is available to you, and how to take full advantage of this support.

Further study

- Cotterell, S. (2003) *Skills for Success*. Basingstoke: Palgrave Macmillan – this book is highly recommended by the tutors involved in teaching study skills and employability. Once you have identified your areas for improvement, you might follow up that particular topic using the activities in this book. It is about developing general and transferable skills rather than skills for a particular career or subject, but it does embrace an 'active' approach, based on the PDP process outlined above.

Dig deeper

Find out about the professional bodies for those working in sport: ISPAL, ISRM, SportscoachUK and so on. Look at the criteria for membership and the resources available for students.

Online sources:
- Belbin team roles inventory and related resources: www.belbin.com
- ISPAL: www.ispal.org.uk – the professional body for the sport sector
- Skills Active: www.skillsactive.org.uk – for details of skills needed in the sport sector
- Leisure Opportunities: www.leisureopportunities.co.uk – sign up to receive free weekly job updates and news
- Institute of Sport and Recreation Management: www.isrm.co.uk
- SportsCoach UK (SCUK): www.sportscoachuk.org

Chapter 8

Where to now? After graduation in Sport Studies

Introduction

This chapter sets out some important signposts towards a range of career opportunities that can seem quite bewildering in its diversity and scope. Though some students have a clear picture of where they want to be after their degree, many are also unaware of the potential a sport studies programme has in providing an advantage in employment. In this chapter an action planning approach is applied to preparing for a career, whether in or out of sport, as it is also important to work out how to achieve career aspirations whilst studying. An appreciation of the potential applications of your knowledge and skills can help make your studies seem more relevant and may help motivate you while you work towards your academic goals.

Learning outcomes

After completing this chapter and the related learning activities, you will be able to:
- identify possible careers in and out of sport, for which a sport studies degree will have relevance and value;
- understand the current frameworks for skills in the sector, and the links between vocational qualifications, National Occupational Standards and Continuing Professional Development;
- identify the role of Skills Active, Prospects and professional bodies in supporting career progression;
- evaluate the employment prospects of the sport sector;
- apply learning from previous chapters into a more active and holistic approach to career development planning

---

From sport studies to the world of work

Many careers do not specify a particular subject for a degree, so students who want to move from sport studies into other careers need to consider what it is about their programme and their own individual qualities, skills or performance that would be attractive to potential employers – those qualities that would help them stand out in a very crowded and competitive field: graduate entry to work and careers.

Academic qualifications can be built upon with more specific technical or specialised vocational qualifications in developing a sport-related career.

Potential careers in sport for a sport studies graduate

Some careers would directly draw upon the knowledge and skills within a sport studies course. These include:

- Sports coaching – elite/performance or community sports coaching, youth or other specialist coach
- Health and fitness – instructors, trainers, managers
- Sport facility management or event management
- Commercial sport management
- Public sector management or administration – community sport, sport development
- Sport business management – retail, manufacturing, marketing, finance
- Teaching – physical education, secondary or primary, further or higher education
- Research and consultancy, academic institution, public (civil service) or private
- Social project or similar, outreach or youth work in sport
- Sport media, journalism, production
- Specialist operations roles, including technical, hospitality, merchandising, promotional, media/public relations

Amongst the reason for the relevance of the sport studies degree to such a diverse range of careers is the 'customer' focus of many of the study units, the development of a good understanding of the needs and demands of sport participants or consumers and of the relationships between sport organisations, state and individuals, in sport policy.

Many sport degrees, as we have noted in earlier chapters, also include work in practical and problem-solving situations, and extended individual research work, which draws upon analytical skills, creativity and communication skills. For example, sport studies, through the practical elements referred to in Chapter 6, can provide knowledge of how to plan, design, implement and evaluate practical sporting activities, projects and programmes. The demands of any professional career mean that graduates also need to have a clear grasp of ethical practice, as discussed in Chapter 3, particularly related to non-discriminatory and inclusive approaches, integrity and personal ethics. Given the welfare orientation of many of the organisations concerned in sport, sport studies graduates can therefore have much useful knowledge and understanding for a range of professions.

Other careers where a sport studies degree and the relevant skills and knowledge may be useful, but not a requirement include:

- General management, business or finance
- Legal or professional services, e.g. accountancy

- Retail management
- Local government
- Civil Service
- Journalism, media

Employers in the sport sector include professional sports clubs, sporting good manufacturers, retail operations, event management companies or venues in the commercial sector and public bodies such as local government departments, or agencies, projects or facility operators. There is a great range of types and sizes of organisation involved in sport, as was identified in Chapters 4, 5 and 7.

A paradox of the sport-based job, like many in the broader leisure industry, is that you are working to help others play. This is not always an easy thing to get used to – and will not suit everyone. So, if you prefer to keep sport as an interest or enthusiasm, you may want a career that allows you to continue to play alongside your career, rather than making the sport industry your career goal.

What do graduate employers look for?

According to some recent research, the most highly ranked skill for employers was communication skills, followed by team working and integrity (Archer and Davidson 2008). You could interpret that as a work ethic and honesty, which are obvious qualities an employer would value. Perhaps more surprisingly, analysis and decision-making skills were only ranked tenth. Numeracy and literacy were ranked only slightly higher, as employers might consider these are a 'given' for graduates, though in fact they were often disappointed in these basic skills. Employers value the 'deep' intellectual skills of graduates, but particularly when they can be applied to practical issues and skills – to be more 'work ready'. This is where sport students can often be at an advantage – their practical application of the skills can be demonstrated both through their studies and their experience in sport.

How to find out about potential careers

Beginning a search about sport careers should usually start with graduate careers advice services available through your own university or the Prospects website (see the online sources at the end of this chapter). This site has a great deal of very helpful information about the opportunities available, including what particular careers entail and how to access the relevant vacancy information. Skills Active also have useful careers information, though would not necessarily have vacancy details. The service provided by publications like *Leisure Opportunities* or professional bodies like ISPAL can provide information about careers, current developments in the industry and current vacancies. If you have the opportunity to have a formal or informal work placement, this is another method of finding out about careers – talk to those you work alongside, and find out as much as you can about their work and, if you are interested in that type of career, how you might progress. Building a good network of personal contacts is also a good way to find out about potential opportunities you may not have considered before.

Visit your local sport centre or a sporting venue and identify all the different jobs that are involved in running the service. See whether jobs are advertised at the venue. How many of them require or expect a sport studies degree? Try to get to speak to the manager of the centre, or an officer in the local sport department and find out how they got into their role. Have they followed a vocational or academic route or combined the two?

Taking your degree further

Not everyone is clear about a possible career; others find that they would be better placed for their chosen career with additional academic qualifications. Following a general or broad-based study of sport may inspire you to continue your studies with a view to specialism later, for example in sport sociology or sport development. This could lead to either an academic career or gaining a strategic level post – again, in or out of sport. Some students re-enter academic life after one or two years of postgraduate experience, as they only find an area in which they want to develop greater knowledge or expertise once they get out into the world of work. Some of the careers noted above will need a specific postgraduate qualification, for example accountancy.

Today, there are many very interesting and quite specific academic courses at Masters level in sport. Less than 20 years ago, a PGCE in Physical Education attracted many students interested in sport as a career, as PE was one of the main sport-related careers available, with only a limited number of Masters courses in Sport Science or Recreation Management as an alternative. On a recent search on the Prospects website there were 213 potential postgraduate courses for 'Sport' listed for England (with additional possibilities in Scotland, Wales and Northern Ireland). These included both science and studies-based courses, for example:

- Child Welfare and Protection in Sport
- Professional Development – Sport
- Coach Education and Sport Development
- Sport Development or Coaching Studies
- International Sport Policy
- Sport and Christian Outreach
- MSc in Sociology of Sport and Exercise
- MSc in Sport and Recreation Management

If you are interested in a research career in sport, then you may consider an MPhil or PhD, for which universities may offer bursaries or funded places. A high level of achievement, usually a 2:1 or above, would be expected, and many posts are hotly contested. A good service for information about research careers or academic posts in sport is www.jobs.ac.uk, where you can browse for places or bursaries, or register for weekly vacancy updates.

Vocational qualifications and training in sport

Part of the process of working out where you might want to go, and how you might get there, involves learning about the potential for additional vocational training and qualifications to complement or build upon your degree.

For those entering the sport sector, there are a range of National Occupational Standards (NOS) that underpin different levels of qualifications. These qualifications may be required or just recommended by potential employers.

The following section outlines the key features of NOS and the role of Skills Active, the industry body responsible for vocational training in this sector of employment. The NOS set out what a potential coach, sport development officer or manager would need to know, and what tasks they would be expected to be able to carry out.

The emphasis on skills in sport is part of a wider trend towards vocational qualifications, skills and workforce development in industry, particularly since the government published the Leitch report in 2006.

In building a career in any particular sector, a process of professional updating, or Continuing Professional Development (CPD) is usually required. Sport as a sector has arguably been slow to adapt to this approach, as degrees in sport studies are a more recent phenomenon, but the development of vocational qualifications at graduate level in sport is evidence of the recognition of the increasing professionalism expected in many sport organisations.

This professionalisation process has been going on across Europe, in order to try to facilitate mobility between the different states. For example, to enable you to qualify as a physical education teacher, coach, instructor or sports administrator and then be able to work in other countries in Europe would clearly be easier if the same essential standards are applied, in knowledge and competences. So far this is not applicable across all sport careers, though a process of harmonisation is going on across Europe. Individual countries still have specific arrangements for the recognition and status of vocational qualifications in sport. For example, if you were to go to France, you would need to take the appropriate qualification in ski-instruction locally, before you could be employed. However, if you wanted to study in France for a postgraduate qualification, the only problem might be that, though your degree qualification would be recognised, there are few courses that involve instruction in English. Many sport-related qualifications in Europe are expected to be added to an appropriate degree or diploma, so are expected to be underpinned with good levels of academic knowledge and skills.

National Occupational Standards and Skills Active

National Occupational Standards (NOS) represent the benchmarks of competence, i.e. what someone should be able to do in a particular job, whether in sport or any other occupational area. National Vocational Qualifications (NVQs) bring together particular occupational standards at the appropriate levels, so individuals can be assessed and have their competence recognised and verified. Various organisations act as awarding bodies, as shown in Table 8.1.

Skills Active is the government-backed Sector Skills Council for the active leisure and learning sector who have set out the NOS. They are one of 25 bodies covering all sectors of UK business. In Active Leisure, there are five sub-sectors, one of which is Sport and Recreation. The other sub-sectors are:

- Health and Fitness
- Playwork
- The Outdoors
- Caravans

Skills Active is strongly employer-led, which means that the standards and qualifications are based on what employers have indicated they need from their workforce. These employers come from commercial, public and community-based organisations, as well as trusts and other not-for-profit bodies.

As well as maintaining the register of qualifications and training, they are a valuable source of information, help and guidance on careers, skill development and workforce development for the sport sector. Table 8.1 is based upon the information provided by Skills Active.

Table 8.1: Occupations, qualifications and organisations in sport

Occupation	Qualifications examples at levels 3, 4, vocational or Masters level	Awarding body
Coaching	NVQs	National Governing Body with First4sport
	UKCC	
	MA/Msc in Sports Coaching	Sports coach UK, via UCAS
Physical activity, health and exercise	Levels 1, 2, 3 NVQ	Skills Active
	Personal trainer Exercise to music Gym/weights	Register of Exercise Professionals (REP), Fitness Industry Association
	MSc Sport science, exercise, health promotion	UCAS
Physical education	PGCE	GTTR – to apply through UCAS
Sport development	NVQ Level 4 Sport Development	Skills Active
	MA/Msc	UCAS
Sport management or administration	NVQ MA/MSc Specialist marketing, finance, human resource or other management qualifications	Skills Active UCAS
Facilities operations	NVQ MA/MSc	

Source: Skills Active – spreadsheet of qualifications (October 2008), *Prospects*.

Table 8.2: Levels and competences of vocational qualifications

Levels of vocational qualifications

Level 1	Competence, which involves the application of knowledge and skills in the performance of a range of varied work activities, most of which may be routine or predictable.
Level 2	Competence, which involves the application of knowledge and skills in a significant range of varied work activities, performed in a variety of contexts. Some of the activities are complex or non-routine, and there is some individual responsibility and autonomy. Collaboration with others, perhaps through membership of a work group or team, may often be a requirement.
Level 3	Competence, which involves the application of knowledge and skills in a broad range of varied work activities performed in a wide variety of contexts, most of which are complex and non-routine. There is considerable responsibility and autonomy, and control or guidance of others is often required.
Level 4	Competence, which involves the application of knowledge and skills in a broad range of complex, technical or professional work activities performed in a wide variety of contexts and with a substantial degree of personal responsibility and autonomy. Responsibility for the work of others and the allocation of resources is often present.
Level 5	Competence, which involves the application of skills and a significant range of fundamental principles across a wide and often unpredictable variety of contexts. Very substantial personal autonomy and often significant responsibility for the work of others and for the allocation of substantial resources feature strongly, as do personal accountabilities for analysis and diagnosis, design, planning, execution and evaluation.

Source: QCA 2008.

There are NOS related to sport management and administration, sport development, coaching, playwork, outdoor education, for which Skills Active is responsible. PE teaching has its own requirements via the Post-Graduate Teaching Certificate (PGCE), regulated by the QAA.

NOS can be used to develop the content for training programmes and, sometimes, academic courses, as they help outline the expected knowledge and understanding in a particular area. The more vocationally oriented your programme, the more likely it is that the content will be linked to specific NOS in sport.

NOS define the main roles and responsibilities of a job or job type and set out what needs to be done to be able to successfully perform that role. NOS provide a detailed and systematic breakdown of the task, knowledge and skills and are organised around the levels of qualifications that make up the NVQs, as shown in Table 8.2.

The NVQ levels demonstrate a progression, where the undergraduate entering into sport may be working at Level 3 or 4, in terms of vocational competence, depending on the extent of personal autonomy or responsibility for the work of others. However, the knowledge and understanding they have would be expected to be at Level 6 in the National Qualifications framework (honours degree level).

Example of a National Occupational Standard in Sport

The following example is taken from the Level 4 qualification in Sport and Physical Activity, Administration and Governance.

Unit A15: Contribute to developing and maintaining ethics, regulations and requirements for sport
This unit is divided into two parts. The first part has three things you have to be able to do:

- A15.1 Help to develop ethics, regulations and requirements for sport.
- A15.2 Investigate possible infringements of ethics, regulations and requirements for sport.
- A15.3 Make decisions on the evidence of possible infringements of ethics, regulations and requirements for sport (Skills Active 2008)

An example of how A15.1 could be demonstrated is devising a Code of Conduct for coaches employed by a sport project, or setting up the rules for a tournament. The second and third may be shown when having to deal with a complaint of a possible infringement of the Code of Conduct, and acting upon any dispute, for example, sitting on a disciplinary panel for a club or organisation.

The unit also sets out specific knowledge that would be required, for example keeping up to date with developments in ethics or rules for the sport.

As this is a Level 4 qualification, the expectation is that a relatively senior role in the organisation would involve considerable autonomy and a key role in developing appropriate systems and procedures in the organisation, for example a senior Sport Development Officer, or a national programme manager in a governing body. If you look further at this particular unit, it is clear that the knowledge expected of someone carrying out this role is heavily dependent upon material we have covered in Chapter 3.

If you look carefully at your own studies it should be possible to link the knowledge you've gained in historical, sociological and philosophical aspects of sport, and the organisation, economics and governance of sport, to other units involved in the NOS. There may be other vocational qualifications and occupational standards that might be useful to look at further, for example in Management and Leadership, based on the NOS from the Chartered Institute of Management. Depending on your potential career route, therefore, NOS are worth investigating further to identify what sort of tasks, skills and knowledge expectations there are in a specific occupation.

Though these qualifications are available, in different situations it may not be a requirement that you have them before taking up a post, but rather that employers may expect you to obtain (and so fund/support) training while you work. Perhaps the only exception to this is PE teaching, as this is the only example where you need to qualify before embarking on your teaching post. However it is possible to train while working in a school. If you were contemplating a PE career after your Sport Studies degree you should be gaining some of the lower level coaching qualifications in specific national curriculum sports, and experience of working with young people, before you apply for a PGCE. So fierce is the competition for PE places, you may have to complete a year's experience as a technician, classroom assistant or after-school club coach, before being accepted onto a programme for PGCE or school-based training. Places are limited and it is a very popular qualification.

Employment in sport

As indicated in the section on markets and activities in Chapter 5, the employment potential in the sector is both diverse and dynamic. While over 600,000 are employed in sport, not all of these jobs are at graduate level or require a degree in sport. Within the sport sector, there are gaps and differences. For example, *Sport Coach UK* (September 2004) identified that three-quarters of all sports coaches are male; and, of female coaches, only 30 per cent hold a formal qualification. A very high proportion of jobs (47 per cent) in the sector are part time. There are also regional differences in the number and range of jobs available in the sport industry. Graduates in sport studies therefore need to carefully consider where they enter the sector and if they need to gain any additional vocational qualifications in order to progress along a particular career path.

> ### Skills and regional plans for workforce development
>
> - There are 60,200 paid staff in the sector in the Northwest, including 6100 self-employed people (approximately 1.7 per cent of the regional workforce).
> - There are 3,800 sport and active leisure businesses in the region.
> - Volunteer estimates vary immensely for the sector, from 26,000 up to 680,000 volunteers.
> - There are almost 2600 businesses employing ten people or less.
>
> The sport and recreation sub-sector employs the largest number of paid workers (36,300 people in 2004), accounting for 60 per cent of the paid workforce, followed by the playwork sub-sector, which employs 15,100 people (25 per cent of the paid workforce). However, a relatively low proportion of employment is in larger organisations – 43 per cent of people work in the 230 businesses employing 50+ people. This compares to 55 per cent of the workforce in the economy as a whole who work in large businesses (SALSPA 2006).

> **Activity**
>
> Investigate whether or not your region has published their skills action plan for sport (see the Skills Active website). Discuss within your group, your own interests in employment in the sector – how many people are employed in your chosen area nationally? Identify the main challenges you might have to overcome to achieve employment in your chosen field.

Sporting futures: 2012 and beyond

Developments in the industry mean that graduates need to project some time into the future to consider how the industry will look for their potential career – technology, politics and economics can all change at a rapid pace. As we move ever closer to the Olympics, for example, we will inevitably be concerned with the immediate impacts of this huge event in the sector. However, the sector is also gearing up for life after 2012, and the projected increases in participation, performance and commercial activity will provide the impetus for continued growth in employment. A lot of this growth is expected to be in non-graduate or support work in venues, services and events, but the increased emphasis on professionalism and effectiveness of management, administration and policies to improve sport organisations' performance means that the future is particularly bright for well-qualified and proactive sport graduates.

In coaching, for example, concerns about the level of competence and professionalism are driving up the demands for more coaches to have a broad sport education, as well as specific technical skills, so they can better cope with this diverse and demanding role. Coaches may need to work with people of differing abilities, ages and backgrounds, in a range of contexts. This can include community coaching, working with difficult and demanding client groups, or performance-oriented coaching, where the coach is expected to be sport scientist, counsellor and manager. This has led to the development of the UK Coaching Certificate (UKCC), which will influence the future potential for employment and qualifications in this area.

> ### SportscoachUK and the UK Action Plan for Coaching
>
> The National Coaching Foundation was established in 1983 as a result of the amalgamation of the British Association of Sports Coaches and the National Coaches Association. The NCF became SportscoachUK in 2001, as a result of a reorganisation of UK Sport and Sport England and the publication of the *Vision for Coaching*. SportscoachUK is the government-recognised body supporting coaches and coaching in the UK, which receives funding direct from Sport England and UK Sport.
>
> SCUK are charged with 'building a world class coaching system in the UK that delivers the right coach to the right place at the right time'. They do not employ coaches directly but support the development and recognition of

coaches and coaching qualifications, working closely with Skills Active and the governing bodies of sport.

Brief timeline for SCUK and Coaching Policy since 1991

1991   *Coaching Matters* published, calling for greater recognition and professionalism of coaches, prior to NVQs in coaching being adopted

1991   Initial pilots for Champion Coaching Scheme (eventually to run till 2000)

1999   *UK Vision for Coaching* set targets for 2012, which would see coaching recognised as a profession

2000   Coaching Task Force set up to take a comparative approach to the funding for coaching, coach education and development

2002   Report of CTF led to increased funding (£28 million over three years) from the DCMS, and appointing of community sports coaches and coaching development officers. UK Action Plan devised, covering to 2012

2006   UKCC is launched, with five levels of coaching, against agreed criteria to eventually work across all sports (phased introduction)

Whether or not you intend to work in sport, the Olympics and their legacy will be driving a lot of the work for sport students up to 2012 and beyond, so we are entering a very exciting time for the industry and for sport studies. Undoubtedly, as under-graduates, students will be well placed to get involved in many volunteering programmes and projects. Despite the concerns that have been expressed about the cost of the Games, there is no doubt this event will have the most significant impact on this sector ever experienced in the UK.

Another area of potential growth is in different forms of sport – with the growth of 'social enterprises', for example. These are 'not for profit' organisations, often smaller and more community oriented in their scope and focus. There are also larger organisations; for example, a very large social enterprise is Greenwich Leisure, which operates many leisure facilities in London. In these enterprises, there are likely to be fewer highly paid jobs, but as they operate with a clear social objective, working for them can provide other rewards and satisfactions to a sport graduate. These organisations rely heavily on community support and engagement so will draw in those who like to work with others, with less emphasis on business forms of profit and more on social profit and inclusion. I think this sort of sporting career will become even more important in the future, given the economic and political climate for sport.

In the future, I expect sporting careers to be very diverse and dynamic, much like the industry. It will be unusual for someone to remain with the same organisation or work in the same area for his or her whole career. For this reason, students working towards a sport-based career need to consider as many options as possible and retain a flexible and adaptable approach to learning and development well into their career.

Being prepared to change and adapt will mean that you would be well placed to cope with a fast-moving and dynamic industry. You might, for example, start work as a community coach, go on to lead a successful inclusion project for the local authority, then set up as a trainer of others working in the voluntary sector, be self-employed or work for a national agency. I've met many people who have followed very similar paths, some of whom started as students on sport studies degrees. On the other hand, I have known other students who began by working as marketing and promotion assistants in their summer break, were offered a permanent job on graduation, then worked through the same company, to reach very senior management roles in business (earning well in excess of my salary) within only a few years of graduation. What my experiences have taught me is that there is no such thing as a typical career for a sport graduate. This is not that likely to change in the future, as the industry becomes even more professional and sophisticated in potential routes and specialisms.

Professional bodies

These organisations fulfil an important role in supporting those who work in the sport industry, across a range of possible careers. The relevant membership-based bodies in sport include:

- ISPAL – Institute for Sport, Parks and Leisure (formerly ILAM and NASD)
- ISRM – Institute for Sport and Recreation Management
- BASES – British Association of Sport and Exercise Scientists
- REPS – Register of Exercise Professionals

ISPAL (Institute for Sport, Parks and Leisure)

ISPAL is the professional membership body for a fast-growing, vibrant industry, representing sport, parks and leisure industry professionals. The institute was formed in January 2007 by the amalgamation of two previous bodies, ILAM (Institute of Leisure and Amenity Management) and NASD (National Association of Sports Development). The key aim of the institute is to provide support, advocacy and professional development for those involved in the sport, parks and leisure industries.

Education and training
ISPAL provides continuing professional development (CPD) for its members, by providing training courses. The aim is to launch a new professional qualification scheme for the industry by March 2009.

Conferences and events
ISPAL organise major conferences, for example:

- Outdoor Activities Conference
- National Leisure Conference
- National Sports Development Seminar

As well as these events, which have a national profile, ISPAL also has regional meetings for members.

Information

ISPAL offers all members access to an information hub, with full-time service support. This can be useful for students looking for information on practical or professional projects or issues. ISPAL also sends out a weekly e-zine to keep members up to date with the latest industry news and jobs. ISPAL produce *INFORM*, a full-colour quarterly members' magazine.

Advocacy

ISPAL works to influence government policy in the areas that affect their members. As the recognised body for the sector professionals, ISPAL is consulted by government on relevant issues.

Membership

ISPAL offers student memberships and some universities, such as Manchester Metropolitan University, have entered into partnership arrangements whereby students can join for free or at reduced cost. This partnership also means the students can gain more insight into the industry and possible careers.

Source: ISPAL (2008)

For those thinking of entering the fitness and health sector, an organisation to think about is the Register of Exercise Professionals (REPS). REPs membership is now embedded as the 'licence' required by all of the major employers in the industry to practise as a fitness instructor in their centres, according to Skills Active (2006). Even if you have not followed a BSc Sport and Exercise Science route, if your course has included the right sort of content, knowledge and skills you may be able to access REPS through your degree qualification, or you may need to take additional vocational qualifications after graduating. You would be expected to have knowledge relating to basic sport science, training methods and the needs of different client groups for exercise.

Review

This book has set out to provide an introduction to sport studies, as well as to reinforce how the study of sport can provide a platform for longer-term skill and professional development. In this final chapter we have considered a range of possible careers inside and outside of sport, for which a sport studies degree will be relevant or useful. The framework for vocational qualifications in sport has also been identified, along with the important organisations and bodies responsible for skills and qualifications in the sport sector. Advice about career and professional development and sources of further information and support has also been provided.

Along with the sources listed in the Further study section, you should now be in a position to evaluate more clearly the employment potential of the sport sector, as well as relate your sport studies degree knowledge and skills to your personal career objectives and goals. By completing the additional activities and reading you should able to map out a longer-term development plan to prepare you for entering the world of work once you have completed your sport studies degree. You should look carefully at the potential of the PDP approach outlined in the earlier chapters and ensure this takes your longer-term career goals into account.

Further study

For careers advice:
- Skills Active Careers: www.skillsactive.com/careers
- Register of Exercise Professionals: www.exerciseregister.org
- Jobswithballs: www.jobswithballs.com
- Leisure Opportunities: www.leisureopportunities.co.uk
- UK Sport: www.uksport.gov.uk/jobs.asp
- Skills Active (nd) Active advice for active careers, in *Skills Active Careers*, 4(16), available online or in print from Skills Active, www.skillsactive.com

Professional bodies:
- Institute of Sport and Recreation Management: www.isrm.co.uk
- Institute of Sport, Parks and Leisure: www.ispal.org.uk
- British Association of Sport and Exercise Sciences: www.bases.org.uk

Others sites with relevant advice or careers related materials:
- Prospects – the graduate careers service: www.prospects.ac.uk
- Learndirect Advice: www.learndirect-advice.co.uk
- Learning and Skills Council: www.lsc.gov.uk
- Institute for Outdoor Learning: www.outdoor-learning.org
- London Community Sports Network: www.communitysports.org.uk
- Sports Leaders UK Awards: www.bst.org.uk

> ### Dig deeper
>
> Using the vacancy details provided by Leisure Opportunities or a similar service, identify a particular job that appeals to you, and for which your sport studies degree could be acceptable. Send off for the full person specification and job description in order to identify how well you currently match the requirements of the job. Set yourself some clear objectives in order to be in a position to apply for a similar post when you graduate.

The final word

The book has set out to provide an active learning approach to sport studies. I hope in each part that you have found some useful and relevant advice, knowledge and sources of further information.

Part 1 identified essential theoretical perspectives and approaches in sport studies. This knowledge should provide a useful basis for further study in sport at degree level, and help underpin various vocationally relevant programmes in sport, such as sport development or physical education.

Part 2 emphasised the governance of sport in the UK: the politics and economic aspects of sport, the diversity of organisations and agencies involved, and their roles and significance. You should be able to look more deeply at the role of government and business in shaping and regulating sport activities and choices.

Part 3 focused on the development of the skills necessary to study and work in sport, and on the approaches to career and personal development a sport studies degree should equip you with.

Each of these parts has included additional reading and sources for more advanced study, to enable you to take this approach further as you progress through your studies in sport. In this final section, I would like to encourage you to consider the links and applications between chapters and parts of the book, in order to apply a multi-disciplinary approach to a complex and dynamic phenomenon – sport. We have had quite a specific focus on the social, historical and philosophical, in the 'studies' approach, which I hope you have found interesting, and you are now motivated and interested to take further, by looking at the recommended Further study.

I have found that in sport studies, there is a continual process of updating and change, which I have found to be one of the most interesting aspects of working in this area – studying sport involves many different disciplines and perspectives, for which you should now be well equipped!

References

Adair, J. (1996) *Effective Team Building*. London: Pan

Archer, W. and Davidson, J. (2008) *Graduate Employability: What Do Employers Think and Want?* London: Council for Industry and Higher Education

Atherton, M. (2008) ECB relieved after government takes moral lead. *The Times*, 26 June, p. 73

Audit Commission (2006) Public sports and recreation services: making them fit for the future, www.audit-commission.gov.uk/reports, accessed 10/1/07

Bandura, A. (1997) *Self-efficacy: The Exercise of Control*. New York: W. H. Freeman

Belbin, R.M. (1981) *Management Teams: Why They Succeed or Fail*. London: Heinemann

Belbin, R.M. (1996) *Management Teams*. Oxford: Butterworth Heinemann

Bernstein A. (2002) Is it time for a victory lap? Changes in the media coverage of women in sport. *International Review for the Sociology of Sport*, 37(4): 415–428

Boyle, R. and Haynes, R. (2000) *Power Play: Sport, the Media and Popular Culture*. London: Pearson Education

Brante, T. (2001) Consequences of realism for sociological theory-building. *Journal for the Theory of Social Behaviour*, 31(2): 167–195

BskyB (2004) Interim Annual Report. www.bskyb.com, accessed 3/3/05

Burns, T. and Sinfield, S. (2003) *Essential Study Skills. The Complete Guide to Success at University*. London: Sage

Business in Sport and Leisure (2007) *Active Annual, 2006–07*. London: BISL

Business in Sport and Leisure (2008) *Active Annual, 2007–08*. London: BISL

Butcher, R. and Schneider, A. (2007) Fair play as respect for the game, in W. J. Morgan. (ed.), *Ethics in Sport* (2nd edition). Champaign, IL: Human Kinetics, pp. 119–140

Buzan, T. and Buzan, B. (2006) *The Mind Map Book*. Harlow: BBC Active

Cambridge Econometrics (2003) *The Value of the Sport Economy to England: Final Report*. Cambridge: Cambridge Econometrics

Carter, P. (2005) *Review of National Sport Effort and Resources*. London: Sport England

Chappelet, J.-L. and Bayle, E. (2005) *Strategic and Performance Management of Olympic Sport Organisations*. Champaign IL: Human Kinetics

Clarke, J. and Critcher, C. (1985) *The Devil Makes Work: Leisure in Capitalist Britain*. Basingstoke: Macmillan

Coakley, J. and Dunning, E. (eds) (2000) *Handbook of Sport Studies*. London: Sage

Coakley, J. and White, A. (1992) Making decisions: gender and sport participation among British adolescents. *Sociology of Sport Journal*, 9: 20–35

Collins, M.F. (2003) Sticking to the plan, *Recreation*, May, pp. 32–34

Collins, T. (1998) *Rugby's Great Split: Class Culture and the Origins of Rugby League Football*. London: Frank Cass

Connor, T. and Dent, K. (2006) *Offside: Labour Rights and Sportswear Production in Asia*. Oxfam International. www.oxfam.orgau/campaigns/labour/06report, accessed 22/03/07

Cunningham, H. (1980) *Leisure in the Industrial Revolution, c. 1780–1880*. London: Croom Helm

DCMS (2006) Annual report, part 4. www.dcms.gov.uk/images/publications/DCMS_AR06pt4, accessed 12/12/07

DCMS/Strategy Unit (2002) *Game Plan: A Strategy For Delivering Government's Sport and Physical Activity Objectives*. London: Cabinet Office/DCMS

Deloitte Sport Business Group (2005a) *Annual Review of Football Finance*, London: Deloitte and Touche

Deloitte Sport Business Group (2005b) *Annual Review of Football Finance*, London: Deloitte and Touche

Donnelly, P. (2000) Interpretive approaches to the sociology of sport, in J. Coakley and E. Dunning (eds), *Handbook of Sport Studies*. London: Sage, pp. 77–91

Dunning, E., Malcolm, D. and Waddington, I. (2004) *Sport Histories: Figurational Studies of the Development of Modern Sports*. London: Routledge

Eitzen, S.D. (1999, 2003) *Fair and Foul: Beyond the Myths and Paradoxes of Sport*. Oxford: Rowman & Littlefield

Elias, N. and Dunning, E. (1986) *Quest for Excitement: Sport and Leisure in the Civilising Process*. Oxford: Blackwell

Fitness Industry Association (2007) Healthy growth in the UK fitness sector, www.fia.org.uk, accessed 5/6/08

Forbes (2007) The world's top sports brands. www.forbes.com/2007/09/26/sports-brands-teams-biz-sports_cz_mo_0927sportsbrands.html, accessed 5/7/08

Forbes (2008) Where the money is. www.forbes.com/forbes/2008/0630/114.html, accessed 5/7/08

Gaffney P. (2007) The meaning of sport: competition as a form of language, in W. J. Morgan (ed.), *Ethics in Sport* (2nd edition). Champaign, IL: Human Kinetics, pp. 109–118

Gensler, H. (1998) *Ethics: A Contemporary Introduction*. London: Routledge

Giddens, A. (2006) *Sociology* (5th edition). Cambridge: Policy Press

Gratton, C. and Taylor, P (2000) *Economics of Sport and Recreation*. London: E&FN Spon

Hargreaves J. and MacDonald, I. (2000) Cultural studies and the sociology of sport, in J. Coakley and E. Dunning (eds), *Handbook of Sport Studies*. London: Sage, pp. 48–60

Hargreaves, J. (1994) *Sporting Females: Critical Issues in the History and Sociology of Women's Sports*. London: Routledge

Hobson, R. (2008) Collingwood is victim of his own misguided judgment call. *The Times*, 26 June, p. 73–74

Hoch, P. (1973) *Rip Off the Big Game*. New York: Doubleday

Holt, R. (1989) *Sport and the British*. Oxford: Clarendon Press

Horne, J. (2006) *Spirit in Consumer Culture*. Basingstoke, Palgrave Macmillan

Horne, J., Tomlinson, A. and Whannel, G. (eds) (1999) *Understanding Sport: An Introduction to the Sociological and Cultural analysis of Sport*. London: E & FN Spon/Routledge

Houlihan, B. (1991) *The Government and Politics of Sport*. London: Routledge

Houlihan, B. (1997) *Sport, Policy and Politics: A Comparative Analysis*. London: Routledge

Jarvie, G. (2006) *Sport, Culture and Society* London: Routledge

Johnes, M. (2003) *LTSN Resource Guide for Sport History*. www.heacademy. ac.uk/assets/hlst/documents/resource_guides/sports_history.pdf

Kay, T. (2003) Sport and gender, in B. Houlihan (ed.), *Sport in Society: An Introduction*. London: Sage, pp. 89–104

KKP Consultants (2008) *Presentation on NWDA Sport Strategy*, Manchester: KKP Consultants

Kolb, D.A. (1984) *Experiential Learning: Experience as the Source of Learningand Development*. London: Prentice Hall

Kornblatt, T. (2006) Setting the bar: preparing for London's Olympic legacy, IPPR discussion paper No. 0 December, www.ippr.org/centreforcities/publications andreports/publication.asp?id=514, accessed 12/12/08

Lee, M. (1998) *Young People, Sport and Ethics*. London: Sports Council

Leisure Database Company (2007) Healthy growth in the UK fitness market. www. theleisuredatabase.com/news-archive/healthy-growth-in-the-uk-fitness-market, accessed 5/6/08

Leitch Report (2006) *Prosperity for All in the Global Economy: World Class Skills*. London: HMSO

Loy, J. and Booth, D. (2000) Functionalism, sport and society, in J. Coakley and E. Dunning (eds), *Handbook of Sport Studies* London: Sage, pp. 8–27

Malcomson, R.W. (1973) *Popular Recreation in English Society, 1700–1850*. Cambridge: Cambridge University Press

Mangan, J.A. (2006) A personal perspective: twenty five years, IJHS. *International Journal of the History of Sport*, 23(1): 1–2

Mason, A. (1980) *Association Football and English Society, 1863–1915*. Brighton: Harvester

McFee, G. (2004) *Sport, Rules and Values: Philosophical Investigations into the Nature of Sport*. London: Routledge

McNamee, M. (2005) *Resource Guide to the Philosophy of Sport*, hlst.ltsn.ac.uk/ resources/philosophy.html

Mills, C.W. (1970) *The Sociological Imagination*. Harmondsworth: Penguin

Monks, K. Conway, E. and Ni Dhuigneain, M. (2006) Integrating personal development and career planning: the outcomes for first-year undergraduate learning, *Active Learning in Higher Education*, 7(1): 73–86

Morgan, W.J. (2000) The Philosophy of Sport: a historical and conceptual overview and conjecture regarding its future, in J. Coakley and E. Dunning (eds), *Handbook of Sport Studies*. London: Sage, pp. 204–212

Morgan, W.J. (2006) *Why Sports Morally Matter*. London: Routledge

Morgan, W.J. (2007) Caring, final ends and sports, *Sport, Ethics and Philosophy*, 1(1): 7–21

Parrish, R. and McArdle, D. (2004) Beyond Bosman: the EU's influence on professional athletes' freedom of movement, *Sport in Society*, 7(3): 403–419

Polley, M. (1998) *Moving the Goalposts: A History of Sport and Society since 1945*. London: Routledge

Polley, M. (2007). *Sports History: A Practical Guide*. London: Palgrave Macmillan

Preuss, H. (2003) The economics of the Olympic Games: winners and losers, in B. Houlihan (ed.), *Sport and Society: A Student Introduction*. London: Sage, pp. 252–271

Quality Assurance Agency (2001) *Guidelines for HE Progress Files*. London: QAA, www.qaa.ac.uk/academicinfrastructure/progressFiles/guidelines/progfile2001.pdf, accessed 10/7/08

Quality Assurance Agency for Higher Education (2008) *Benchmark Statements for Hospitality, Sport, Leisure and Tourism*, www.qaa.ac.uk/academicinfrastructure/benchmark/statements/HLST08.pdf, accessed 10/9/08

Qualification and Curriculum Authority (2008) *Levels and Competences of Vocational qualifications*, www.qca.org.uk/qca_7134.aspx, accessed 10/9/08

Rigauer, B. (2000) Marxist theories, in J. Coakley and E. Dunning (eds), *Handbook of Sport Studies*. London: Sage, pp. 28–47

Rugby Football History (2007) The great schism. www.rugbyfootballhistory.com/Schism.html, accessed 7/11/08

Rugby Football League (2008) History of the sport. www.therfl.co.ik/about/page.php?areaid=46, accessed 7/11/08

SALSPA (2006) *Regional Action Plan, 2006–12 for the Northwest Region*. Warrington: NWDA/Skills Active

Sandy, R., Sloane, P.J. and Rosentraub, M.S. (2004) *The Economics of Sport: An International Perspective*. London: Palgrave Macmillan

Schindler, C. (1998) *Manchester United Ruined My Life*. London: Routledge

Scraton, S. and Flintoff, A. (eds) (2002) *Gender and Sport: A Reader*. London: Routledge

Skills Active (2006) *Engaging Employers In Foundation Degrees: A Guide for Universities and Colleges Developing and Delivering Foundation Degrees in the Active Leisure and Learning Sector*. London: Skills Active

Skills Active (2006) *SALSPA Action Plan 2006–12 for the Northwest Region*. Warrington: NWDA/Skills Active

Skills Active (2008) National Occupational Standards, Level 4, A15. www.skillsactive.com/training/standards/level-4/Sport-and-Physical-Activity-Administration-and-Governance/A15%20Contribute%20to%20developing%20and%20maintaining%20ethics%2C%20regulation.pdf, accessed 10/9/08

Slot, O (2005) Empty San Siro creates a sporting nightmare, *The Times*, 29 September

Smith, A. and Stewart, B. (1999) *Sports Management*. St Leonards: Allen & Unwin

Sport Business Group (2008) F1 generates more money per event than any other sport online, www.sportbusiness.com/news/166985/f1-generates-more-money-per-event-than-any-other-sport, accessed 17/9/08

Sport Business International (2006) Selected iGaming firms and sponsorship deals in sport. www.sportbusiness.com, accessed 8/9/06

Sport England (2003) *Young People and Sport in England: Trends in Participation 1994–2002*. London: Sport England

Sport England (2004) *The Framework for Sport in England*. London: Sport England

Sport Industry Research Centre (2007a) *Sport Market Forecasts 2007–2011*. Sheffield: SIRC

Sport Industry Research Centre (2007b) *The Economic Importance of Sport in England, 1985–2005: Summary Report*. Sheffield: SIRC/Sport England

Struna, N. (2000) Social history and sport, in J. Coakley and E. Dunning (eds), *Handbook of Sport Studies*. London: Sage, pp. 187–203

Suits, B. (2007) The elements of sport, in W. J. Morgan (ed.), *Ethics and Sport* (2nd edition). Champaign, IL: Human Kinetics, pp. 9–20

Times, The (2008) Olympics good for a having a party and not much else, 2 December, p. 3

Tomlinson, A. (2007) *The Sports Studies Reader*. London: Routledge

Walvin, J. A. (1975) *The People's Game*. London: Mainstream Publishing

Whannel, G. (1992) *Fields in Vision: Television Sport and Cultural Transformation*. London: Routledge

Wilcox, R.C. (2002) From microfirms to multinationals – survival and ethics in the global sport marketplace. *12th Commonwealth Sport Conference, July 2002. Book of Proceedings*, pp. 86–102

Index